THE CENTRAL ASIAN STATES

Westview Series on the Post-Soviet Republics

Alexander J. Motyl, Series Editor

The Central Asian States: Discovering Independence, Gregory Gleason

Lithuania: The Rebel Nation, V. Stanley Vardys and Judith B. Sedaitis

Belarus: At a Crossroads in History, Jan Zaprudnik

Estonia: Return to Independence, Rein Taagepera

Published in cooperation with
The Harriman Institute, Columbia University

THE CENTRAL ASIAN STATES

Discovering Independence

GREGORY GLEASON

WestviewPress

A Division of HarperCollins*Publishers*

Westview Series on the Post-Soviet Republics

Copyright © 1997 by Westview Press, A Division of HarperCollins Publishers, Inc.

Published in 1997 in the United States of America by Westview Press, 5500 Central Avenue, Boulder, Colorado 80301-2877, and in the United Kingdom by Westview Press, 12 Hid's Copse Road, Cumnor Hill, Oxford OX2 9JJ

Library of Congress Cataloging-in-Publication Data
Gleason, Gregory.
    The Central Asian states : discovering independence / Gregory Gleason.
        p.   cm. — (Westview series on the post-Soviet republics)
Includes bibliographical references (p.) and index.
ISBN 0-8133-1594-8 (hard). — ISBN 0-8133-1835-1 (pbk.)
    1. Asia, Central—Politics and government—1991–   2. Asia,
Central—Economic conditions.   3. Post-communism—Asia, Central.
I. Title.   II. Series.
JQ1070.G54   1997
958´.04—dc21
                                                                        96-46419
                                                                           CIP

The paper used in this publication meets the requirements of the American National Standard for Permanence of Paper for Printed Library Materials Z39.48-1984.

10   9   8   7   6   5   4   3   2   1

▪ Contents ▪

• Tables and Illustrations •

▪ Preface ▪

Early in 1991, as the Soviet Union began careening toward its demise, Alexander Motyl of Columbia University and Susan McEachern of Westview Press conceived the idea of assembling a series of studies on the separate "post-Soviet states." The series envisaged chronicling and analyzing developments in each of the newly independent countries. The intent was to describe and analyze these new countries in terms of their unique historical traditions and of the lingering effects of the common legacy of the Soviet period. The series sought to treat each of the new countries independently in a compact yet reasonably comprehensive way.

From the outset of this undertaking, treatment of the five former Soviet republics of Central Asia presented special problems. Geography, history, language, and culture had closely linked the societies of Central Asia. Present-day Kazakstan, Kyrgyzstan, Tojikiston, Turkmenistan, and Uzbekiston shared common languages, historical traditions, and values in a way that bound them together as inheritors of common cultural traditions. None of these states had ever existed as an independent country. They were linked by their common traditions much more closely than were, for instance, the countries of Western Europe, Latin America, Africa, or even colonial America. In light of these considerations the series editors, as both a practical and theoretical matter, posed the following question: "Are the present states of Central Asia one or many?" This book should be read as a detailed answer to that question.

The Central Asian states are nominally independent, but they are not islands. They are passing through a process of independence and decolonization that will continue to strongly influence their national traditions and aspirations. The lessons of other cases of decolonization should be borne in mind from the onset. Comparisons between the current Central Asian situation and the "decade of decolonization" (1957–1967) in Africa, for instance, offer many suggestions regarding the pitfalls and promises of the process of decolonization. Another lesson that should be drawn from the experience of other decolonizing countries is the importance of international organizations. The CPSU—the Communist Party of the Soviet Union—was previously referred to as the "leading and guiding force" in Soviet society. The IBRD—the International Bank for Reconstruction and Development—may replace the CPSU as the most important guiding force in Central Asia's future.

Although these great "geopolitical" and institutional forces will continue to exert a strong influence on the outcome of the transition to independence, the outcome of this drama will probably be determined not by outside forces but by the inner qualities, the intelligence, and the resourcefulness of Central Asian societies. How are these societies adjusting to the cultural and psychological changes of the collapse of communism and the entrance into a new, often foreign, and sometimes hostile international community? How will individuals confront the personal challenges posed by such dramatic and sweeping political changes? How do the political and economic leaders of these new societies see the road ahead? How will unique Central Asian traditions, languages, cultures, and habits of thought and practice influence the choices ahead?

Field research for this book was made possible with support and encouragement from the International Research and Exchanges Board (IREX) and the cooperation of the Academies of Sciences of the republics of Kazakstan, Turkmenistan, and Uzbekiston as well as that of the Russian Federation. I am particularly grateful to Kimberly Kotov and Lisa LeMair of IREX. Rick Curtiss supplied the maps.

For help and encouragement I am grateful to D. Balgamis, J. Chavin, T. Daves, L. Donaghey, D. Fane, C. Kedzie, J. Levison, S. Marcum, and M. Olgun. Much of the interpretation recorded here relies upon the perspectives of my Central Asian colleagues, particularly M. Abdusaliamov, L. Anoshkina, B. Atabaev, S. Ataev, S. Borbieva, S. Dzhusupov, A. Esentugelov, A. Faizullaev, A. Ilkhamov, U. Ishankhozhaev, B. Islamov, K. Kekenbaeva, B. Khudaiberdyev, T. Kochumanov, A. Mannonov, M. Mukhitdinova, K. Ovezov, S. Saliev, M. Tazhin, A. Ukubaev, and A. Zholdasov. Responsibility for statements of fact and judgment is mine alone.

Gregory Gleason

A Note on Languages in
· Central Asia ·

One of the most persistent issues in books about Central Asia is how the names of the countries are actually spelled. Is it Tadzhikistan, Tojikistan, or Tojikiston? Is it Uzbekistan, Uzbekiston, or Özbekiston? The answer to these and other questions regarding the writing systems of Central Asian languages is a simple one: It all depends.

Most of Central Asia's indigenous societies are Turkic-speaking. The Turkic languages as a group consist of Turkish (as spoken in Turkey) as well as Uzbek, Turkmens, Kyrgyz, Kazak, and several other languages. All of the Turkic languages are closely related—but they are not all mutually intelligible. Printed material regarding Central Asian countries appears in a number of different languages written in a number of different alphabets. The alphabet common today in Central Asia is Cyrillic, the alphabet in which Russian is written. Some material, particularly in Tojikiston, appears in Arabic script. The amount of material written in Arabic script is growing, but this alphabet does not constitute a major medium of communication.

In recent years an increasing amount of material originally published in the Central Asian indigenous languages has appeared in the Latin alphabet. Moreover, governments in the Central Asian countries have announced plans to switch officially from the Cyrillic alphabet to the Latin alphabet, using an alphabet similar to that of modern-day Turkish. Turkish is written using a variant of the Latin alphabet widely known and used throughout Europe and the Americas. This transition from the Cyrillic to the Latin is expected to require about a decade to complete.

Transliteration is the process of moving from one orthography into another. Transliterating simply means that words are spelled in a different orthography; they are not translated. Until the transition to new writing systems has been accomplished in the Central Asian countries, it will be necessary to transliterate references. Moreover, it will continue to be necessary to transliterate historical references.

All systems of transliteration are based upon certain conventions. There are better and worse ways of doing this, but the goal in transliteration is not so much to attain a perfect system as to maintain a common standard. The standard system for transliterating from the Cyrillic alphabet into the Latin alphabet is the ALA-LC system. This system is endorsed by the American Language Association (ALA) and is used by the U.S. Library of Congress. An alternative system may be found in Edward Allworth, *Nationalities of the Soviet East: Publications and Writing Systems* (New York: Columbia University Press, 1971). The Allworth system is more technically exact. The ALA-LC system, however, is simpler and more widely used. In this book I have used the ALA-LC system but have further simplified it by omitting diacritical marks.

A third standard is the system officially introduced in Uzbekiston during the summer of 1995. The official Uzbek version uses the Latin alphabet but excludes the letters *c* and *w* and eliminates all diacritical marks. All Uzbek words are written with some combination of the following letters: *a, b, d, e, f, g, h, i, j, k, l, m, n, o, p, q, r, s, t, u, v, x, y, z*. Some sounds common to Uzbek but not to Russian are rendered by letter combinations, in particular: *o', g', sh, ch,* and *ng*.

Even if one of these transliteration systems is faithfully followed, however, there are still many points of ambiguity. Regarding proper nouns, for instance, should one use the indigenous forms of the names of historical figures or the Russianized ones? Using the Russianized version may seem a slight to the indigenous languages. Yet using the indigenous forms would make many historical references unrecognizable. To take some examples, if we follow the Allworth system, the name for Uzbekiston, for instance, is Özbekistan. And should the name of the first president of Uzbekiston be "Karimov"—the Russianized version that is known generally to the outside world—or should it be transliterated from the native Uzbek as "Kärimav"? If we use the ALA-LC system, should the name "Ulugbek" be transliterated from the Russianized version or should it be transliterated from the native Uzbek form, which would be "Ulughbek"? One looks in vain through any encyclopedia for "Al-Qarezm" but may find "Al Khwarezm," a form that was transliterated at one point into Russian or German and adopted as a standard spelling.

As the language reforms unfold over the next decade, many of these issues will find some resolution. And these are not merely linguistic questions: They are issues highly charged with symbolic meaning. Some enthusiasts of Central Asian political independence insist that scholars and analysts switch over immediately to terminology that eliminates any vestige of Russian colonialism. There are advantages to such a move, but there are also disadvantages.

I spell the name of Uzbekiston with an initial *U* and with a final *o*. There are other ways of doing this. However, spelling it with an initial *U* keeps it in the same place in alphabetical order, yet spelling it with a final *o* defers to the native Uzbek pronunciation of the word.

Some people, particularly nonnative Kazak nationalists, consider it important that Kazakstan be identified as "Qazaqistan." For the outside world to insist on using "Qazaqistan" rather than the Russianized "Kazakhstan"—which is the international spelling for the country that virtually all Kazaks use—would be to place some indistinct psychological gains ahead of the practical confusion that this would create. Until a short time ago, after all, many Kazaks (Qazaqs?) had never even seen a language with a *q* in it. They did not recognize this as the first letter of their country's name. Of course, if Europeans and Americans repeat it often enough, the Kazaks soon will recognize "Qazaqistan" as the name of their country. But would this be any less of an external imposition than a Russianized form?

Most computer keyboards do not accommodate diacritical marks (even if the software is capable of producing them). For this reason, many highly educated Central Asians today insist on shifting as quickly as possible to a simplified, Latin-based alphabet. They insist that since English has become the language of the international computer community, such a transition is unavoidable. Some Central Asians go further and claim that English should be used as the "international language," that is, English rather than Russian should be used as the medium for communication among Central Asian groups.

In this book I have tried to take a pragmatic approach to these language problems. I have avoided the use of diacritical marks. As a basis for transliterating, in some cases I have used the indigenous forms, and in some cases I have used the Russianized versions. For instance, I have used the modern spelling "Tojikiston" except in citations to written works, where I have tended to use the Russianized spelling "Tadzhikistan."

Names of countries are symbolically important. It is not an exaggeration to state that lives have been lost over this symbolic point. But what of more routine names of places and people? The suffixes on most Central Asian names are forms of Russification. The *ov*/*ev* ending on most surnames (for instance, Nazarba*ev*, Aka*ev*, Karim*ov*, Rakhmon*ov*, and Niya-z*ov*, the surnames of the current Central Asian presidents) are forms of Russification. Most Central Asians are indifferent to these suffixes. Some have dropped them, yet some insist on retaining them. Will they be dropped in historical references? In this book I have used a modernized, that is, a de-Russianized version of names of people, places, and things when it was clear to me that linguistic practice had changed. In references to published books or other works bearing a former name, I have retained the old spelling convention.

My pragmatic approach to these problems seeks to emphasize communication over aesthetics of symbol and style. To champion the protection of indigenous languages against the onslaughts of colonialism is a noble thing. In a colonized country, the defense of native languages is a means to advance the end of national liberation. After independence, however, the situation changes. The contemporary international community is dynamic and demanding. The facts that computers work in the Latin script and that most computer software commands are in English is hardly related to any deliberate neocolonialism. Yet in the computer age, many small societies feel a necessity to adopt the Latin script simply to stay abreast of technological change. The consequences are the same whether the transition was politically motivated or motivated by technological change.

G.G.

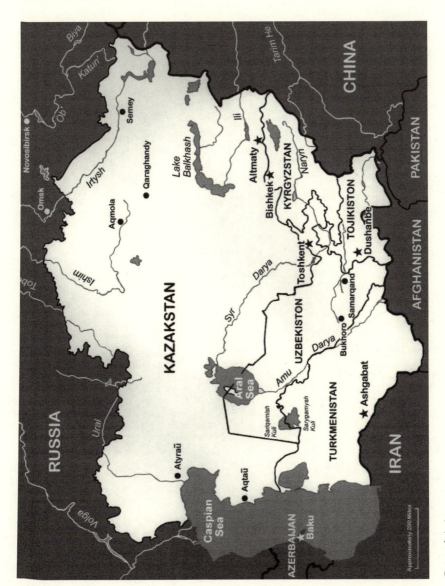

Central Asia

The Post-Soviet States

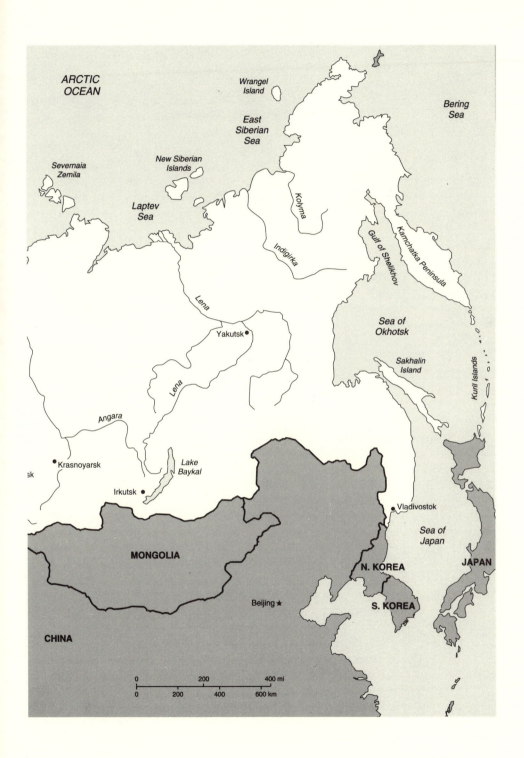

· ONE ·

New States and Ancient Societies

In the closing days of 1991 in a hurriedly arranged meeting in Alma-Ata, Kazakstan, eleven communist party officials signed a document declaring that "the USSR shall henceforth cease to exist."[1] No public referendum was held on the "Alma-Ata Declaration." No legislature was asked to ratify the agreement. No court was asked to rule on its constitutionality. No international forum was convened to discuss its global ramifications. Among the Soviet citizenry, the Alma-Ata Declaration gave rise to conflicting emotions. Surprise, resignation, and despair mixed with relief, elation, and celebration. The document was almost immediately accepted as legitimate by the international community. With this swift international acceptance of the Alma-Ata Declaration, the so-called Great Bolshevik Experiment—the seventy-year-long excursion into a new kind of civilization—came abruptly to a close. The world's largest country, a global superpower and what was very probably the most heavily armed state in history, dissolved into fifteen euphoric, anxious, confused, feuding, but at least nominally independent states.

Among these independent states were the five former Soviet socialist republics (SSRs) of Central Asia: Kazakstan, Kyrgyzstan, Tojikiston, Turkmenistan, and Uzbekiston. Each of the new states of Central Asia was a founding member of the Commonwealth of Independent States, the loosely defined coordinating structure for the post-Soviet community created by the Alma-Ata Declaration. Each of the new states of Central Asia sought and soon received diplomatic recognition as independent republics from major world powers. Each of the new states joined the United Nations (UN). Each of the states sought participation in leading international organizations such as the International Monetary Fund (IMF) and the International Bank for Reconstruction and Development

1

(IBRD). Each of the states pledged to uphold international standards of civil and human rights as specified in the principles of the Organization for Security and Cooperation in Europe (OSCE) (formerly the Conference on Security and Cooperation in Europe [CSCE]). Each of the new states entered the international community.

These were crucial steps toward political independence. But given the vast scale of political, economic, and even psychological changes resulting from the transition from the communist paradigm, it was soon clear that creating genuine and enduring political independence in these new countries would require more than merely announcing intentions and issuing declarations. One of Central Asia's most sophisticated political leaders, President Askar Akaev of Kyrgyzstan, rightly called attention to the scope of the challenge: "The empire has collapsed, yet sovereign and independent states have not been established. We are dealing with a far more important phenomenon than it may appear. This is probably the greatest political, social, and economic reorganization of the 20th century."[2] As Strobe Talbott noted, "The new states really are not independent at all. Their economies and infrastructures will take years, even decades, to disentangle."[3]

Exposed to the extraordinary centrifugal forces of the "end of empire" and the process of entering the ranks of the international community, the new Central Asian states quickly broke with their socialist-colonial past. And despite their common point of departure from within the Soviet system, the new states assumed very different trajectories as each set out on a path to independence. Kyrgyzstan determinedly set upon a course of rapid liberalization. Somewhat more cautiously, multinational Kazakstan set out to define itself as a liberal Asian democratic power. These countries won immediate praise from the international community.[4] Remote Tojikiston, impoverished and bordering war-torn Afghanistan, fell prey to vicious internal contests over power. Uzbekiston, the richest, most populous, but also the most diverse Central Asian republic, assumed a path of conservative and even authoritarian national consolidation.[5] Turkmenistan, ethnically compact and resource-rich, assumed an assertive and proud posture of national self-reliance.

INDEPENDENCE AND FREEDOM

An upheaval on the scale of the transition to national independence never takes place without it creating an enduring resonance in the lives of the people it affects. Great political events pass through peoples' lives like powerful storm winds. They arise suddenly and swiftly and sweep through the established order, leaving everyday life forever rearranged. As the thunder of great events recedes into the past, individuals are left to pick up their lives, to sort out the consequences on an individual level as best they can. The collapse of the USSR and the coming of independence swept through the lives of Central Asia's citizens with such force. Whether these people were accustomed to privilege or to deprivation, injustice or the largesse of the old order, the new order brought changes that affected their lives in fundamental ways.

For the journalist or the social scientist, these changes could be described as "economic" or "political" or "social." But for the people whose lives were transformed by these events, the important differences were mainly psychological. A whole civilization was swept aside. To be sure, the Soviet regime was a stagnant, brutal, corrupt, and corrupting system in many ways. But it was also a system based on values, morals, and mutual understandings that millions of people shared. It was a system that exploited people but also created its own beneficiaries, people who personally benefited from the established order. As the old order passed, these things too passed. In their place arose only questions.

The old order demanded conformity and regimentation. It specified what people could comfortably think and how they could safely behave. The new order demanded new values, new ideas, and new behaviors. The new Central Asian societies all emerged from the same Soviet mold, but these societies were very different in their relations with the outside world. The most advanced and promising country was Kazakstan. It was potentially rich but internally troubled, divided roughly in half by an indigenous population and a settler population of Russians. Kyrgyzstan, to the south, was small and remote and possessed little industry. More important, Kyrgyzstan was divided by mountains, with the country's southern half being more naturally connected to neighboring Uzbekiston. With the largest and best-educated population among the new Central Asian countries, Uzbekiston also possessed the most developed industrial, mining, and commercial structures. And throughout the Soviet period the Uzbeks had retained their cultural features, language, and sense of self more determinedly than had any of their ethnic neighbors.

Further to the south were Tojikiston and Turkmenistan. Tojikiston was the poorest of the states and, because of the continuing bloodletting of a brutal civil war, had few prospects for economic development in the near future. Turkmenistan possessed great potential natural gas wealth but suffered from its landlocked geographical position, lack of access to markets, and—most of all—bad government.

Independence did not arise in Central Asia as a result of indigenous forces. The Central Asian states were not "catapulted" to independence, they were subjected to it.[6] It is true that independence initially came with some nationalist euphoria and flag-waving, but its most profound aspect was disruption.[7] The implosion and fragmentation of the brittle Soviet economic system unraveled the mutual economic dependence of the regions. This meant that with the disintegration of the empire entire industries were without materials, supplies, and spare parts from their single-source suppliers. Central Asia's agriculture and mining enterprises were suddenly without their established markets. Transportation between regions ground to a standstill. New restrictions on travel and movement arose as states tried to protect their subsidized goods and services from "foreign" buyers. Russians who had occupied privileged positions in the apparat of the old regime suddenly found their careers in eclipse and their children's prospects for advancement almost nonexistent.

The changes that have taken place and taken hold in Central Asia were inevitable. But the way in which they took place was surely not. There were important choices for the societies of Central Asia along the way, just as there are important choices ahead. In a certain sense independence is not an end; it is only a means. Independence only implies that people have the opportunity to determine their futures free from the direct control of a colonial power. Albert Camus is attributed with having expressed this double-edged promise of liberty by observing that "freedom is a chance to be better." Freedom is surely not a guarantee of success and progress; it is an opportunity. Just as license by itself need not augment liberty, neither does independence assure advancement and prosperity. Whether the transition to independence in Central Asia actually liberates the peoples of these societies and contributes to the improvement of the human condition depends on many things. Above all, the pressure of the transition to independence invites people to define their goals and their aspirations. It invites people to define themselves. It raises the question: Who are the rightful citizens of Central Asia and the inheritors of this new freedom?

THE MANY FACES OF CENTRAL ASIA

First-time travelers to Central Asia often ask, "What are the different nations that live in these countries?" At first glance, this question seems to make a lot of sense in Central Asia. There are different groups speaking different languages, answering to different leaders, and, at the same time, referring in the abstract to the "unity and commonality" of Central Asian values, customs, and traditions. There are different Central Asian "communities."

The European and North American worlds have grown accustomed to thinking of communities in terms of "nations" and "states." Soviet ethnographers, who rejected analytical categories and concepts that they regarded as "bourgeois apology," preferred to use other terms. They spoke of groups in Central Asia not in terms of "nation" but as *etnos*, that is, as ethnic protogroups. But even this invention of ideological Soviet sociologists was basically a variation of Eurocentric ideas.

The idea of "nation" has its origins in the work of European scholars who in interpreting European history gave conceptual reality to these categories. In the 1940s, the great European scholar Hans Kohn could make pronouncements about the nature of nationalism with such force and power that scholars, political thinkers, and journalists began to interpret the desert peoples of the Middle East, the tribal groups of African states, and the compact, highly civilized societies of the Far East as typical European "nations" waiting for typical European "statehood."[8]

Eventually these categories were given life and meaning in the political practice of European societies. As Europe's influence spread around the world, so did the influence of these concepts and definitions. If "nations" were a part of the framework of the future, then the backward peoples of the world must surely have to find their natural national identities before they could join modernity. With the passing of time, the European categories were assumed to be universals. But the reality of ethnographic identity in the widely different cultural contexts of the world may be very different than what the convenient European model expresses.

One way to analyze the groups of people in Central Asia is to conceive of them not as nations on their way to statehood but rather in terms of their own natural history, which is connected to the physical features of Central Asia. When Central Asians reflect on their cultural experience, one thing that looms large in their background is the mountains. Geographers tell us that there is no comparable area on earth with "more topography" than Central Asia. The mountains of the Tien Shan, the Pamir, and the Altai Ranges fuse in Central Asia to create the greatest upwelling of earth anywhere on the globe. If we think in terms of the livelihoods that people pursued in traditional Central Asia, a picture of these groups emerges that emphasizes the prominence of the mountains.

Living high in the mountains were the sheep- and goat-herding peoples whose lives were always associated with the natural seasonal migrations. These were the high-mountain herders. Somewhat lower down from the mountain passes were the peoples of the high valleys. Yet farther down the great slopes were the settled peoples of the fertile valleys and oases. The nomads roamed the high plains extending to the north and the northeast of the great mountains. Finally, amid the vast expanses of the Kyzyl Kum (Red Sands) and Kara Kum (Black Sands) Deserts were the desert nomads.

It surely would be a Eurocentric mistake to conceive of these peoples and groups as nations. The peoples of Central Asia, before they were anything resembling "nations," were socioeconomic groups that had distinct styles of organization and distinct cultural features. The mountain people of what is now Kyrgyzstan and Tojikiston were closely tied to the cycles of nature. Their livelihoods depended upon mobility dictated by their need to follow the seasons. For mobile peoples, the mountains afforded natural protection from marauders. They found common-property conventions to be more important than private-property conventions. At the same time, their family structures were strong. Rather than empire, tribal confederation built around the family was the basic form of political organization.

The plains nomads of what is now Kazakstan had greater latitude of action but less protection from invaders. They too had little use for private-property conventions, since under conditions of abundance all natural resources were quite naturally regarded as belonging to everyone. The organization of their societies depended less upon the natural rhythms of wildlife than for those in the high-mountain areas and more upon their own capacities of organization. A tribal chieftain did not rule by divine mandate; he had to retain popularity among his followers—if only to keep them from simply wandering off. This gave rise to indigenous democratic traditions of consultation and advice. A chieftain's most important consultant was the *aq saqal*, the "greybeard" tribal elder whose authority was based in the clan structure.

The desert nomads of what is now the low valleys of the Syr Daria and Amu Daria Rivers and the great expanses of the Kyzyl Kum and Kara Kum Deserts endured by far the most difficult living conditions of all the Central Asian peoples. The desert is a demanding environment. Skilled at the techniques of survival amid extreme adversity—and necessarily skilled at the arts of war—the dwellers of the desert regions developed unique codes of behavior. Two principles dominated their internal relations. One, solidified over centuries of experience, emphasized loyalty within the group. The other emphasized unquestioned loyalty to one's own as opposed to outsiders. The outsider among the Central Asian desert peoples will come to recognize these "principles" to be the dominant feature of the desert societies.

Paradoxically the outsider may also note with surprise and pleasure that perhaps because of old traditions that grew out of the dangers of desert travel Central Asia's desert societies are among the most hospitable in the world. In the conditions of the desert, the offering of solace and protection to travelers was almost a law of nature. Today, an experienced world traveler is unlikely to find more friendly locals anywhere than in present-day Turkmenistan.

The traditions of tribal democracy and intertribal confederation that were strong among the nomadic peoples find their greatest contrast with the traditions of hierarchy and authoritarianism among the settled peoples of Central Asia.[9] The peoples of present-day Uzbekiston are the heirs

Central Asian *aq saqal* (graybeards) breaking bread and sharing tea. Photo by Maryanna Schmuki.

to the ancient settled civilizations of Central Asia. Their styles of behavior are very different from, for instance, their Tojik and Kyrgyz neighbors. These contrasts are clear when the settled and nomadic cultures come into contact. The outsider who sits down at the negotiating table to observe Central Asians from Kyrgyzstan interacting with Central Asians from Uzbekiston is likely to conclude that the cultural differences between them are far, far greater than they are, for instance, between the Central Asians and their European or North American friends.

This conclusion is unwarranted, because small differences between the Central Asian parties are magnified in their interactions. When Central Asians interact with people from the outside world they tend to be much more accommodating to the outsiders. But the important point to note is that Central Asia is composed of different societies with many different cultural styles.

In most societies that underwent "national consolidation" along the lines of the European experience, the establishment of cultural homogeneity took place as a result of the growth of one dominant culture in relation to minority cultures or, some might even conclude, at the expense of minority cultures. The Central Asian situation is much more complex.

Since Central Asian culture is polymorphic, in each of the republics there are competing claims as to what constitutes the core "national" culture.[10] The languages of the region are still not standardized to the extent that there is one simple, contemporary standard. Uzbek for instance, is looked at by many linguists as a group of closely related languages rather than as one language.

Even if Central Asian culture is varied and diverse, the logic of the contemporary political and economic situations binds these societies together in common endeavors. None of the new Central Asian countries can chart a future course without being influenced by its neighbors and without influencing its neighbors. At present, the Central Asian countries are interlocked in common undertakings not by motive or design, but by their situation. Consequently, these cultures and societies, as different from one another as they may be, cannot be considered in isolation. Central Asia is one community of many very different parts.

THE END OF EMPIRE

Once the Soviet republics emerged as separate and individual states after the breakup of the USSR, they found themselves subjected to a very different political logic than that which prevailed during the Soviet period. As newly emerging states, these countries found themselves antagonistically arrayed in terms of diverging security concerns and pressing economic tasks. The states found themselves thrown into a situation of intense pressure for rapid internal change and of mounting competition for influence over friends and foes in the outside world.[11]

In the past, as constituent Soviet republics of the USSR, these societies were forced to accept Moscow as the arbiter of internal and regional conflicts. Of course, during the Soviet period Moscow was hardly a benign and disinterested mediator, but Moscow did nevertheless serve in those days as something of a third party. As independent states the new countries of Central Asia are forced to find formulas to solve their domestic and regional problems without the help of Moscow and, in some cases, even despite Moscow's interference.

The new states of Central Asia found that in most cases they could accomplish this only by acting collectively, that is, by banding together to serve their common interests. They also found that they were not at all prepared to conduct the sophisticated foreign relations that collective action required. They had no professional foreign policy specialists and precious little resources to devote to solving internal and regional disputes. They soon discovered that international cooperation often implies a willingness to compromise and to bear sacrifices for a neighboring country. Since a compromising neighbor is one that can easily be taken advantage of in times of austerity, the new countries of Central Asia found themselves acting with increasing circumspection toward one another. They began to discover the laws of "collective action."[12]

There is nothing unusual about the pressures of national independence under these conditions. The situation involves challenges confronted by all newly emergent states. In the case of Central Asia, the problem may be stated simply: *The newly emergent states of Central Asia were linked in common endeavor in pursuit of common goals in such ways that the more energetically and enthusiastically they pursued those goals, the more likely they were to come into conflict with one another.* This challenge of independence has conditioned many of the choices that the Central Asian societies have made over the last few years and will face in the years immediately ahead. It is the classical situation of independence following the breakup of colonial empire, the so-called process of decolonization.

Decolonization is a big and ungainly word that simply refers to all the things that happen to a country that achieves independence through disengagement from an empire. It may be defined as the process of transition from colonial status to national sovereignty as well as the transition from foreign economic and political control to internal national control.[13] The history of decolonization is linked to the history of imperialism, a subject that was also closely connected from the very beginning to the "Great Soviet experiment."[14] It is no exaggeration to say that decolonization has been the single most significant and defining political feature of the global community in this century.[15] In terms of significance as measured by the number of people's lives directly affected, decolonization outranks in importance the two world wars, the superpower rivalry of the Cold War, and even the technological revolutions of the late twentieth century.

As we think of decolonization in Central Asia it is important to recall that the "Great Soviet empire" was never strictly speaking a typical empire. It is true that its borders were virtually identical to those of the tsarist empire that preceded it. But only in this geographical sense was it a direct descendent of nineteenth-century European Great Power colonialism. The "laws of motion" of the Soviet economic and political systems were very different from the mechanisms of imperialism of the more conventional brands.

The disintegration of the "Soviet empire" shares some characteristics with decolonization as it occurred in the Mongol, Arabic, Persian, and European empires, but in other respects Soviet decolonization was and is unique. The closest parallels to what is occurring in Central Asia are probably to be found in the "decade of decolonization" (1957–1967) on the African continent. These cases offer many suggestions regarding the pitfalls and promises of what could be called "typical" decolonization.

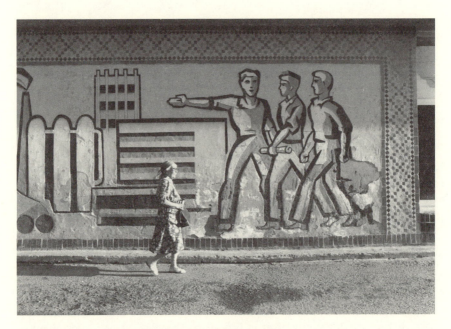

The path to socialism. Photo by Maryanna Schmuki.

This case of decolonization was typical in that the national boundaries of the former Central Asian states were artificial. In Central Asia the boundaries were adopted exclusively for the convenience of Moscow. And, as in typical decolonization, there were no preexisting national identities associated with the Central Asian states. Similarly, in Central Asia as in typical decolonization, there were nationalist movements stirring before independence. But unlike typical decolonization, in Central Asia the political opposition was not the key to political change. No powerful, charismatic, heroic leaders were swept into power with a moral mandate to oust a corrupted, quasi-colonial political elite.

And as in typical decolonization, in Central Asia there was a stratum of metropolitan settlers—"colonials"—in privileged social and administrative positions. Also typical was the strong sentiment among settler populations who protested the withdrawal of the metropole and the end of empire.[16] But unlike typical decolonization, in Central Asia the privileges these settlers possessed were not based in private-property rights. Since there were no private-property conventions in Central Asia, when the Soviet system collapsed the colonial settlers had only moral and not legal claim to what they possessed. As a consequence, the "foreign settlers" in Central Asia had little claim to privileges or special advantage after independence.

In the typical colonial pattern, Central Asia had grown dependent on the sale of raw materials to the industrial "core." But unlike most cases of colonialism, Moscow extended its basic physical infrastructure of communication, energy, transportation, and scientific research directly to these areas. To disrupt these linkages meant that both center and periphery would suffer. This is precisely what happened. In the Soviet collapse, decolonization was probably just as wrenching to the colonizers as to the colonized.

It is true that in some cases of independence from the European empires withdrawal encouraged economic prosperity, political stability, increased public participation, and a general increase in living standards and quality of life. Yet much of the decolonized world today continues to suffer from agricultural stagnation, chronic political instability, income inequality, low standards of living, and environmental degradation. As one critic of postcolonial development programs expressed it, "There is no story more common in human history than the betrayal of the promises inherent in revolution."[17] Decolonization and Third World nationalist movements ended the age of global European imperialism. In so doing, decolonization fundamentally altered the face of the world. "But [it] did not reverse the misery suffered by Third World peoples, and in some cases [it] added to it. Independence and revolution brought no easy solutions to the many fundamental problems facing the Third World."[18]

In light of this record of the decolonized world one should exercise caution in assessing the prospects of the Central Asian states to successfully manage their transitions to independence in the long term. One of the most pressing requirements of any successful transition is the establishment of a stable postcolonial political order. In most former colonized countries, attempts to transplant democratic political institutions—under the so-called Westminster system—were unsuccessful.[19] In Africa, for instance, the Westminster system has failed to survive in any of the countries in which it was originally adopted.

Similarly, in many countries the effort to create new postcolonial economic arrangements only resulted in a continuation of exploitation, fueling discouragement and resentment among the populace. In the typical case of decolonization, disengagement from the old colonial economic structures produced an immediate negative impact on the economy. In most decolonized regions of the world, postcolonial trade patterns tended to echo patterns that existed before independence. Long established trade patterns tended to endure. Francophone countries tended to trade with Francophone, Anglophone countries with Anglophone.

Major international organizations such as the World Bank established a presence in the decolonizing areas soon after independence. Before too long, however, these institutions were regarded in many countries as little more than instruments for the advancement of the interests of the power-ful developed countries.[20] Even direct foreign development assistance was often regarded with suspicion, resentment, or both.[21] Rejecting inter-national institutions and confronting the economic difficulties of decolo-nization, many decolonizing states sought withdrawal from an interna-tional community where, according to their calculations, it seemed the odds were against them.

For some newly decolonized states a strategy of withdrawal seemed to offer promise of economic "self-reliance" and "self-sufficiency," attributes that much of the populace often regarded as correlates of independence. If a country was "free" shouldn't it be self-reliant and self-sufficient? Economists tell us that the answer to this question in general is "No, ab-solutely not." Modern independence implies integration in the interna-tional community, not withdrawal and self-reliance.

There is a great deal of evidence that supports this. States that adopted strategies of self-sufficiency in the postcolonial world paid a high price. Efforts of governments in many of the newly independent countries to "go it alone" brought complete economic failure and governmental col-lapse.[22] The unwillingness of countries to participate in the international community combined with their inability to gracefully withdraw from it gave rise to complaints that they could not win. It seemed that many new countries could not participate in the international community on a fair basis, and yet they could not benefit from withdrawal. Under these cir-cumstances, theories were invented to explain how "neocolonialism" and "capitalist dependency" intentionally kept these countries in impover-ished and weakened positions.

In some respects the new states of Central Asia were less prepared to integrate into the global economy in comparison to many of the countries that underwent decolonization earlier. None of the Central Asian states had any direct experience in international negotiations, specialized diplo-matic staffs, or sophisticated understandings of market economics. These states had only primitive conceptions of the demands and requirements for participating in the international community and in international or-ganizations. Specialists in international affairs who had received their training during the Soviet period had been schooled to earnestly con-demn such international organizations as the IMF and the World Bank as instruments of Great Power political objectives rather than as organiza-tions of collective economic coordination.

The political and economic doctrines of the former USSR offered little guidance in the redesign of public and private institutions. Independence meant that new, post-Soviet institutions had to be designed. The mainte-nance of public order and economic survival required that these new po-litical and economic institutions had to be fashioned swiftly. Political leaders rhetorically embraced the idea of establishing market-based economies and civil societies modeled after those that existed in the developed world. Yet when these leaders consulted with Western specialists, they found that prevailing economic and administrative theories offered little guidance on how to grow capitalist markets and democracy from the soil of Soviet-style socialism.

In the absence of general principles to guide the process of transition, politics took precedence over principles. The urgent and the necessary took precedence over the beneficial and the desired. Since the former communist leaders of Central Asia commanded the only institutions capable of guiding the process of "destatification"—the dismantling of the state-run economies and Communist Party–dominated political system—these communist leaders themselves assumed the responsibility for engineering the transition to postcommunist rule. In each of the countries of Central Asia, for a variety of reasons and with widely varying degrees of success, the former communist officials began building national independence on the remains of nonexistent national communities.

TO BECOME A NATION

The idea of "nation" was anathema to communist doctrine. Marxism sought the creation of a new, universal, cosmopolitan, supranational community. As the *Communist Manifesto* had boldly proclaimed, the "worker has no country." The worker's allegiance, the communists reasoned, must be to the higher community of proletarians rather than to the nation. According to Marx, the theoretician of communist doctrine, and Lenin, the activist of communist practice and father of the Soviet state, nations were destined to die, passing into history and being replaced by a new form of socialist internationalism.

Consequently, nations had neither propitious bases in the indigenous cultures of Central Asia nor any reinforcement from seven decades of Soviet-style socialism. Yet the collapse of the USSR and the transition to independence thrust the societies of Central Asia on a European-style course of "nation-building." It was a course that was particularly beneficial to the entrenched party elite in Central Asia. Thus in this way Central Asia's "internationalist" party officials, wearing new hats, came to be the engineers of the transition to national independence.

When we reflect on the history of national consciousness, it is important to recall that before Europe had powerful states, it had influential supranational institutions. Such universal and catholic institutions as the Roman Church and, later, the tradition of intermarriage among the European cultural and political elite cut across national and state boundaries. The political importance of the European states was attenuated by cross-

TABLE 1.1   States, Population, Territory

	Population (millions)	Territory (thousand sq. km.)	Date of Independence
Kazakstan	16.9	2,717	December 16, 1991
Kyrgyzstan	4.5	198	August 31, 1991
Tojikiston	5.7	143	September 9, 1991
Turkmenistan	4.4	488	October 27, 1991
Uzbekiston	22.2	447	August 31, 1991

Source: Population figures are for January 1, 1994, from "Population Change in the Former Soviet Republics." *The Population Bulletin,* Vol. 49, No. 4 (December 1994), p. 7.

cutting cosmopolitan cultural, ideological, and political institutions. Eventually the psychological drive toward national unity overlapped with the principle of statehood. The modern nation-state came into existence.

Today when we use the concept of "national consolidation" we naturally call to mind the development of nation-states following the European experience. But it is important to keep in mind the reciprocal processes of nation-building and state-building. It is clear that "Frenchness" was not brought into being by the mere declarations of a monarch. The French state grew spatially, much in the way that cities typically do. French national identity was forged over centuries of gradual governmental centralization, with identity moving spatially from the "periphery" to a strengthening "core." Concentration in a "center" led to the establishment of economic and political communities united under the sovereign. The influence of the core cultural community radiated outward, enveloping peripheral communities, reinforcing a sense of national identity, and gradually laying the basis for the modern French state. Eventually, the state developed a rationale for existence separate from the monarch. It became a republic, a res publica. It became something that represented the people, a public, rather than being merely the embodiment of a monarch or the expression of an abstract ideology. Germany's national consolidation followed a similar course. The modern outline of the German state only came into being under the leadership of Bismarck in the 1870s, a result of a long process of incremental inclusion of "Germanic" peoples who inhabited areas at the periphery of the state.

In the pattern of European national consolidation, political institutions developed over decades of trial and error as societies sought out compromises and balances between the dominant culture and the minority cultures. As the power of nation-states grew, particularly after the French Revolution, nationalism rather than divine right became the principal basis of political legitimacy. Even when rulers ruled by fiat, they did so while championing symbols of national glory and destiny. The state became inseparable from the dominant national group that it represented. Peripheral ethnic and linguist groups were incorporated into the modern state principally through accretion at the periphery. Smaller and distinct communities lying at the periphery were incorporated either by arms or by the sheer weight of the cultural language, standards, and values of the dominant culture.

If we think of national consolidation while bearing the decolonizing world in mind, we get a very different picture from that of the European countries. Old World national consolidation established juridically what already existed politically, namely, national self-determination. It brought the state into line with preexisting cultural realities. It reaffirmed the legitimacy of an already existing political community. In contrast, New World nationalism was an attempt to create, forge, and mold new identities in the crucible of decolonization and independence. In the decolonizing world, national consolidation was compressed into a short amount of time and driven by the urgency of rapid integration into an already established and functioning international order. Nations did not create themselves gradually and through trial and error but were invented by external circumstances. Political leaders in the decolonizing world saw the strong state as an engine of development and rapid change. They also saw the strong, integral state as a means of preventing social disorder and averting border and territory disputes. Naturally, they also saw the state as a vehicle that would allow them to pursue their own political ambitions. The modern nation-state that emerged as a result of decolonization was drawn together as a consequence of independence, not by any inherent unity of the people.

The path to national consolidation in the Central Asian states more closely resembles the cases of "New World" nationalism. Language, religious creed, loyalty to the nation, patriotism to the state—these were the attributes that bound people together into the "nations" of the European world. In the new world of decolonization, the bases of national consolidation are different. The rationale of the strong state as an engine of development, the fear of social disorder, the danger of border and territory disputes, and the natural desire of the local political elites to retain power constitute the rationale for creating national communities in the circumstances of independence.

This fact represents the greatest irony of independence in Central Asia. By and large, independence came to Central Asia as had Soviet-style colonialism several decades before—it was imposed by Moscow. The leaders of the newly independent states of Central Asia were soon laboring to bring to life the "nations" that they previously had condemned as anticommunist. There was no public sense of patriotism, loyalty to nation, or devotion to the idea of a republic. Consequently, to succeed in forging independent states, the leaders of the new Central Asian states would have to create that loyalty, patriotism, and devotion.

Earlier, during the period of Soviet control in Central Asia, public officials expressed only contempt and disdain for the instruments of market economies and the institutions of democratic, representative government.[23] Officials throughout the Soviet Union shared these views in their public pronouncements, although their deeply held personal convictions may have been different. But after independence the leaders of the newly independent Central Asian states found themselves in the uncomfortable position of having to denounce their former convictions. In this way, the whole of Soviet ideology and doctrine, the intellectual bulwark of communism, evaporated with the collapse of the USSR. Only the state remained.

As the Soviet Union broke up, political leaders throughout its many regions attempted to stay in power.[24] In some areas, the collapse was accompanied by a generational change of leadership. In some areas, opposition figures were swept into power on waves of popular euphoria. In some areas, Soviet-era leaders proved to be very resourceful in maintaining control. The best examples of such Soviet leaders were Nursultan Nazarbaev in Kazakstan, Saparmurad Niyazov in Turkmenistan, and Islam Karimov in Uzbekiston. Previously committed communists and staunch supporters of the Soviet system, they made an ideological conversion quickly when the maintenance of power demanded it. With the coming of independence these leaders grasped the slogans of nationalism as their new doctrinal guides.

In Tojikiston, the former party head was brought back to power. In Kyrgyzstan, the respected head of the Kyrgyz Academy of Sciences was elected president. These leaders relied for advice and assistance upon high officials whose careers had been built on the Soviet ladder of advancement. These individuals likewise relied upon Soviet-era line-level officials and middle managers to manage the affairs of the bureaucracies. In virtually all cases, nonindigenous high-level managers were replaced with native managers. After considerations of nationality, the principal criterion of advancement was "experience." In a word, this meant little more than "Soviet-trained." In this way, the character of the managerial apparat that managed affairs after independence remained virtually the same as the one that managed affairs before independence. In each of the new Central Asian states, members of the well-established, official power structure remained in control.

These managers did not seek the destruction of the old system. They were trained in techniques and stratagems that enabled them to continually vie for power with central planners and politicians within the old system—but not to challenge the nature of the system itself. Once it was clear that the Soviet Union had come to its historical conclusion, the managerial class abandoned socialist formulas and Sovietisms and adopted many of the causes of the nationalist demonstrators that had begun, in the late 1980s, to develop nascent nationalist movements.

Many political leaders in Central Asia shifted their stance on key "nationalist" issues. They quickly became champions of local languages as official government languages. Karimov in Uzbekiston (who spoke Uzbek only haltingly before independence) took intensive training in the native tongue. He quickly and successfully learned to make speeches in Uzbek rather than Russian. The Central Asian leaders repositioned themselves as champions of the historical and cultural legacies of Central Asia. Having earlier condemned the nationalist opposition as politically naive, foreign-inspired and -financed, and antagonistic to the interests of the people and the republic, the leaders quickly attempted to buy off the most talented members of the opposition by offering them key jobs within the government. In this way, the sentiment of the opposition movements ended up, ironically, strengthening the new states of Central Asia.[25]

THE FUTURE AND THE PAST

There is a saying in Central Asia, "There is no need to predict the future, but there is a necessity to live it." In the spirit of this folk wisdom, this book seeks to explore some of the many questions looming in Central Asia's future that may have partial answers in past and current practices. This book is arranged first chronologically, then thematically. It begins with considerations of culture and background and then turns to some of the big questions in Central Asia's future.

Only a few years ago many people both within and outside Central Asia expected that if the Central Asian peoples gained the freedom to shape their own destinies, then appeals for establishing pan-Turanian or pan-Islamic communities would be irresistible. Most Western approaches to Soviet Central Asia were premised on the assumption that Central Asia was particularly susceptible to the rise of Islamic fundamentalist doctrines similar to those that brought about the downfall of the Shah of Iran in 1978.[26]

Many Central Asians did dream of establishing an "Islamistan" or "Turkestan," referring to the idea of a pan-Turanian fraternity of peoples that, depending on the context, might include all of the Turkophone regions of Asia and Asia Minor.[27] But with the first stage of independence behind us, it is clear that given the differences among Central Asians there is less reason to expect this outcome than say, for instance, a resur-

The Faithful in prayer. An Uzbek congregation bowing in prayer during *Rosakhait* in 1991 in Tashkent, Uzbekiston. Photo by Anvar Ilyasov.

gence of "pan-Africanism." Yet in many quarters sensationalism continues to dominate the approach to the Islamic world.[28] The question of the cultural unity and diversity of Central Asia's communities is one of the main themes of this book.

The creation of the independent states has exacerbated many of the social problems left over from the Soviet period. Central Asia's agricultural specialization created ethnic stratification as a result of a cultural division of labor.[29] Since independence, the promises of social support, health services, guaranteed incomes, and the other elements of "welfare authoritarianism" have come to be little more than that—promises. Corruption and organized crime continue to be pervasive and endemic problems in all of the Central Asian countries.[30] And the large numbers of people of Slavic and nonindigenous nationalities who remain in Central Asia in the aftermath of Soviet expansionism are concerned about the protection of their civil rights and their new status as "second-class citizens" of the states.[31] Many, of course, voted with their feet and returned to Russia or other parts of the former Soviet Union, but many have not found that to be practical or have remained in Central Asia, fearful of even worse difficulties elsewhere.

Boats stranded as a result of the desiccation of the Aral Sea—a legacy of years of mismanagement of Central Asian agriculture. Photo by Anatoly Rakhimbaev.

Another important question in Central Asia's future concerns the quality of the physical environment. Mismanagement during the Soviet period has left a legacy of daunting environmental problems that, at least potentially, could have a global impact. In particular, the Soviet agricultural development strategy placed the environment at risk: Soil exhaustion, salinization, and the accumulation of residues from agricultural by-products, pesticides, herbicides, and defoliants produced a public health crisis in the 1980s.[32] The upstream diversion of the waters of the Amu and Syr Rivers for irrigation purposes meant death for the Aral Sea, the largest standing body of water in Central Asia.[33] Slipshod mining and industrial practices produced environmental catastrophes in such places as Ekibastuz and Chimkent, Kazakstan, and Angren Basin, Uzbekiston. Years of nuclear testing left a legacy in Semipalatinsk, Kazakstan, that may linger for centuries.

The capacity of the Central Asian societies to work together is the best predictor of their ability to solve these environmental problems. Cooperation is the key to many of the modern world's problems. But cooperation is also a most difficult objective in a world in which economic forces tend to push countries into competition rather than cooperation. At the breakup of the USSR, Central Asia's aging industrial infrastructure was incapable of supporting its entering the highly competitive world market. Thus many outside observers reasoned that the Central Asian countries— with the partial exception of oil-rich Kazakstan and gas-rich Turkmenistan—consequently would be forced to continue to rely on agricultural development programs. Competing for access and market share in the intensely competitive international commodities markets could only mean regional tensions would grow among the new states.

Under both internal and external pressures to dispense with subsidies for inefficient farming practices and inefficient state-run industrial enterprises, the Central Asian countries lurched forward toward creating the legal and regulatory frameworks for market economies. But all the states have felt the temptation to adopt the export-led economic growth strategies of the successful "Little Tigers" of the Pacific—South Korea, Japan, Taiwan, and Singapore. Uzbekiston has gone even further, considering ways of tailoring a "Chinese model" to suit Uzbekiston's situation.[34] All of these pressures incline the new Central Asian states toward strategies that bolster rather than diminish the state's role in the society.

In the modern international community the capacity of countries to work together also depends on their interaction with the increasingly powerful international organizations—the UN, regional development banks, and international assistance organizations. As two informed observers of Central Asia put it, the "key question which will define the future of Central Asia, is whether countries of the region are able to become integrated into international structures beyond the borders of the former Soviet Union."[35]

The initial effect of the activities of international organizations in Central Asia was clearly to strengthen each of the new states and speed them on the course of national consolidation. International organizations initially had a powerful effect in conferring legitimacy on the existing governments. But international organizations have an inherent conservative bias. They prefer to work with officials who can actually succeed in implementing policies, so they naturally have a tendency to support leaders in power rather than to pose hard questions to them about internal political legitimacy. International organizations working with the new states of Central Asia tend to assume the legitimacy of existing bureaucratic institutions, state borders, and regional security arrangements. The international institutions consequently act in ways that reinforce the local institutions.

The ideas of the outside world that are siphoned into even closed communities by the international organizations, however, have a contrary effect. Concepts and ideas of universal standards in law and accounting practice—concepts hungrily sought after by the new Central Asian states—do not come without other universal concepts, such as the idea of the absolute dignity of the human being or the importance of civil protection against the arbitrary use of power by government. In Central Asia, international organizations quickly established a dialogue on technical and economic issues. They have just begun the dialogue on universal principles regarding civil rights, cultural survival, and international governance.

A thousand years ago, even a hundred years ago, rulers around the world could govern their kingdoms by fiat. In today's world, it is increasingly evident that coercion is a self-defeating instrument of management or government. Modern societies are defined by the fact that they depend upon the consent, the support, and even the enthusiasm of the governed. Human and civil rights are intrinsically, inherently, and absolutely valuable. But they are also instrumentally valuable: They are not mere luxuries of rich regions of the globe. But in the contemporary world, human rights also constitute the bulwark of a modern social order. They protect and make possible the commitment to the commonwealth that individuals and groups have to maintain if modern society is to prosper. No modern society can progress without recognizing and protecting these rights. The forms of recognition and protection may differ from place to place and culture to culture. How the challenges of establishing the rule of law and protecting human rights are met is one of the biggest questions of Central Asia's future.

These are the themes of this book. It is a book about the ancient societies of Central Asia and the new states that have been superimposed over them. It is about the past and future of the peoples, the fabric of the societies, and the politics of new states emerging on ancient soil. Chapter 2 traces the historical outlines of the Central Asian societies and their cultural institutions. Chapter 3 surveys the influences of the Soviet period. Chapter 4 describes the pressures of the Soviet collapse and the achievement of national independence. Chapter 5 considers the role of these new countries in the region and the world. Chapter 6 scans the horizon for the promise and possibilities—and the perils—that lie ahead.

NOTES

1. For a survey of the "great transformation," see Karen Dawisha and Bruce Parrott, *Russia and the New States of Eurasia: The Politics of Upheaval* (Cambridge: Cambridge University Press, 1994). The text of the "Alma-Ata Declaration" appears in Gregory Gleason, "The Federal Formula and the Collapse of the USSR," *Publius* Vol. 22 (Summer 1992), pp. 141–163. The Russianized version of the capital city's name, Alma-Ata, was replaced in 1992 with the Kazak language name "Almaty."

2. Ostankino television interview of 24 May 1992.

3. Strobe Talbott, "How to Keep Divorce from Leading to War," *Time* (2 March 1992), 34.

4. The first emergency assistance effort of the United States, Operation Provide Hope, was formally announced at the Coordinating Conference on Assistance to the New Independent States that took place in Washington, D.C., on 22 January 1992. At the conference, U.S. President George Bush noted in his opening statement, "In Central Asia . . . President Nazarbaev and President Akayev are leading the fight for reform." U.S. Department of State, *Dispatch* 3, no. 4 (27 January 1992): 57–60, quote at 57.

5. C (pseudonym), "One-Man Rule in Uzbekistan: A Perspective from Within the Regime," *Demokratizatsiya* 1, no. 4 (1993): 44–55.

6. Martha Brill Olcott, "Central Asia on the Catapult to Independence," *Foreign Affairs* 71, no. 3 (1992): 108–130.

7. Martha Brill Olcott, "Central Asia: The Reformers Challenge a Traditional Society," in Lubomyr Hajda and Mark Beissinger, eds., *The Nationalities Factor in Soviet Politics and Society* (Boulder: Westview Press, 1990), pp. 253–380.

8. Hans Kohn, *Nationalism: A Study in Its Origins and Background* (New York: Macmillan, 1944).

9. Michael Mandelbaum makes a similar anthropological argument regarding the influence of social organization upon political organizations: "Operating over huge territories in small, closely related units, the nomads developed loose governmental structures, requiring considerable consensus among individual authorities and permitting considerable autonomy. After all, within nomadic society, if conflict arose, there was always the option of simply moving on. The opposite was true within sedentary agricultural societies; dependent upon one specific piece of ground, which could grow only at the expense of someone else's land, the settled peoples required strong central control, to assure the stability of the entire group." Michael Mandelbaum, *Central Asia and the World: Kazakhstan, Uzbekistan, Tajikistan, Kyrgyzstan, and Turkmenistan* (Washington, D.C.: Council on Foreign Relations Press, 1994), p. 8.

10. Gregory Gleason, "Language, Culture, and Politics in Central Asia," *International Issues* 38, no. 6 (1995): 86–95.

11. Gregory Gleason, "Dynamics of National Independence in Central Asia: Implications for Russo-American Cooperation," in Sharyl Cross and Marina Oborotova, eds., *New Dimensions of Russian Foreign Policy* (Westport, Conn.: Praeger, 1994), pp. 193–210.

12. Two classic analyses of the logic of collective action are Mancur Olson, *The Logic of Collective Action* (Cambridge: Harvard University Press, 1965), and Russell Hardin, *Collective Action* (Baltimore: Johns Hopkins University Press, 1982).

13. It is traditional to distinguish between imperialism and colonialism along the following lines: Imperialism refers to a policy by a state to establish and maintain control over territories and peoples outside the state. Colonialism refers to a particular kind of imperialism where the annexed territory is not contiguous to the state and the peoples are ethnically different and economically less developed. See Arend Lijphart, *The Trauma of Decolonization* (New Haven: Yale University Press, 1966), p. 4.

14. Some observers view the invention of world communism as a reaction to the colonialism of the nineteenth century. The writings of Lenin indeed stressed that the Marxist program was above all a means to avoid the problems of an international order dominated by capitalism. In his major contribution to the theory of international relations, *Imperialism: The Highest Stage of Capitalism*, he relied heavily on an earlier work by the British scholar John Hobson. See John Hobson, *Imperialism: A Study* (London: Allen and Unwin, 1902).

15. A useful descriptive survey of world politics may be found in Peter Calvocoressi, *World Politics Since 1945* (New York: Longman, 1991). This book comprehensively and accurately describes the superpower rivalry but rightly argues that

decolonization was by far the more important long-term determinant of world politics.

16. Opposing complete abandonment of Russia's interests in Central Asia, Russian Foreign Minister Andrei Kozyrev argued forcefully that the Central Asian areas should remain under Russian "protection." Andrei Kozyrev, "Chego khochet Rossiia v Tadzhikistane," *Izvestiia* (August 4, 1993): 4.

17. John Isbister, *Promises Not Kept: The Betrayal of Social Change in the Third World* (West Hartford, Conn.: Kumarian Press, 1991), p. 135.

18. Isbister, *Promises Not Kept*, p. 135.

19. Democratic theorists typically distinguish between consensus democracy and majoritarian (or Westminster) democracy. The consensus system includes federalism, separation of powers, bicameral structure of legislatures with each house having a different electorate, state-based rather than nation-based political party systems, and executive veto power with provisions of the legislature to override given an extraordinary majority. See Robert G. Dixon Jr., *Democratic Representation: Reapportionment in Law and Politics* (New York: Oxford University Press, 1968), p. 10.

The majoritarian or Westminster system (which gained its name from the borough of London in which the British parliament is located) is commonly understood to describe a *constitutional democracy* in which all citizens, individually and through organizations, can participate and at least attempt to influence the workings of government. The system is based on the following principles. First, it is a system of *representative government* based upon the majority principle. A simple majority is sufficient to win a vote, but the minority is accorded by tradition and mutual understanding the right to seek to become the majority. The existence of a *two-party system* is founded on the idea of *loyal opposition*. The *separation of military and civil leadership* is based upon the idea of loyalty to the state and not to particular political patrons. Disagreement is over issues and policies, not over loyalty to the state. *Public accountability* is provided by an acknowledged latitude of freedoms of speech, assembly, and press. The principle of the *rule of law* implies the certainty of legal rules rather than arbitrary judgments in determining the rights of individuals and in prescribing the authorities of public officials. See Arend Lijphart, *Democracies: Patterns of Majoritarian and Consensus Government in Twenty-One Countries* (New Haven: Yale University Press, 1984).

20. See Robert L. Rothstein, *The Weak in the World of the Strong: The Developing Countries in the International System* (New York: Columbia University Press, 1977).

21. For an analysis, see Robert Cassen, *Does Aid Work?* (Oxford: Clarendon Press, 1986).

22. One of the best examples of this is Guinea in Africa. For an analysis of the strategy of withdrawal, see Donald Rothchild and Robert L. Curry Jr., *Scarcity, Choice, and Public Policy in Middle Africa* (Berkeley: University of California Press, 1978), pp. 135–142.

23. See Gregory Gleason, "Nationalism and Its Discontents," *Russian Review* 52, no. 1 (January 1993): 79–92.

24. Martha Brill Olcott, "Democracy and Statebuilding in Central Asia: Challenges for U.S. Policy Makers," *Demokratizatsiya* 2, no. 1 (1993/94): 39–50.

25. Roger D. Kangas, "Uzbekistan: Evolving Authoritarianism," *Current History* (April 1994): 178–182.

26. The leading interpretation of the Soviet decision to invade Afghanistan was that Moscow feared the "contagion" of Iran's revolution would spill into Central Asia. See Alexandre Bennigsen, "Muslims, Mullahs, and Mujahidin," *Problems of Communism* (November-December 1984): 28–44.

27. Some Central Asian intellectuals, at considerable personal risk, did publicly champion the idea of the establishment of a "Turkestan." At the same time, many Central Asians more quietly contemplated the idea. It is interesting to note, however, that the idea of a single, unified, overarching Turkestan political community was not an indigenous Central Asian concept, but one first introduced into the area by European thinkers in the nineteenth century. In this century the idea of "Greater Turkestan" was encouraged by the post–World War I Turkish nationalist leader Mustafa Kemal, the politician who engineered the creation of the modern Turkish state following the collapse of the Ottoman empire.

28. See Samuel P. Huntington, "The Clash of Civilizations," *Foreign Affairs* 72, no. 3 (1993): 22–49. A more balanced and informed perspective can be found in John L. Esposito, *The Islamic Threat: Myth or Reality?* (New York: Oxford University Press, 1992).

29. See Peter R. Craumer, "Agricultural Change, Labor Supply, and Rural Out-Migration in Soviet Central Asia," in Robert A. Lewis, ed., *Geographic Perspectives on Soviet Central Asia* (London: Routledge, 1993), pp. 132–180.

30. Gregory Gleason, "Corruption, Decolonization, and Development in Central Asia," *European Journal on Criminal Policy and Research* 3, no. 2 (1995): 38–47.

31. See on the Slavs and other groups in Central Asia Vladimir Shlapentokh, M. Sendich, and E. Payin, *The New Russian Diaspora: Russian Minorities in the Former Soviet Republics* (Armonk, N.Y.: M.E. Sharpe, 1994).

32. See Boris Z. Rumer, *Soviet Central Asia: "A Tragic Experiment"* (Boston: Unwin Hyman, 1989).

33. See Svetlana Nikanova, *Aral: Segodnia i zavtra* (Alma-Ata: Kainar, 1990); Kazakstan Academy of Sciences, *Problemy Aral'skogo moria: Sotsial'no-ekonomichekskie problemy razvitiia priaral'ia* (Alma-Ata: Nauka, 1984); Susan J. Buck, Gregory Gleason, and Mitchel Jofuku, "The 'Institutional Imperative': Resolving Transboundary Water Conflict in Arid Agricultural Regions," *Natural Resources Journal* 33, no. 1 (Winter 1993): 1–32.

34. In 1993 and 1994 one of the most popular themes in the local press in Uzbekiston was the success of the Chinese model. See, e.g., Adulkhafiz Dzhalalov, "Kitai: Plody reform," *Golos Uzbekistan* no. 25 (9–15 July 1994): 3.

35. Roald Z. Sagdeev and Andrei Kortunov, "Russia and the Commonwealth of Independent States," in Roald Z. Sagdeev and Susan Eisenhower, *Central Asia: Conflict, Resolution, and Change* (Chevy Chase, Md.: CPSS Press, 1995), pp. 1–14.

· TWO ·

Legacies of Central Asia

In the late spring of 1990, more than a year before the USSR began to break up, the leaders of the five Central Asian republics gathered in Alma-Ata (now Almaty) to contemplate a common response to what they described as the area's "social, political, economic, and moral crises." The meeting was the first official summit of Central Asian republic dignitaries in Soviet history. Observers expected the meeting to be more symbolic than substantive. But contrary to expectations, the leaders' communiqué issued after the meeting reflected a profound appreciation of the common problems facing Central Asian societies. It cast into sharp relief the conflicts among the republics while succinctly drawing attention to the common interests among the republics.

The communiqué asserted that Central Asia and the native peoples of Kazakstan stood united by common historical experience, shared cultures, and common values and by their closely linked destinies. At the same time, the communiqué asserted that the borders of the republics were inviolable and could not be changed "by anyone's will."[1] Nothing could summarize the problems facing the peoples of Central Asia more clearly than these two propositions. United in culture, divided in politics; united in traditions and heritage, divided by circumstance. The presidents seemed to be testifying to the "oneness" of Central Asia even as they insisted upon the distinctiveness of each of the separate republics. Central Asia, they reaffirmed, is "both one and yet many."

"Are you a Central Asian or a Kazak?" you may ask a citizen on the streets of Jambul, a city in southern Kazakstan. The reply that you may get is, "A Turk is a Turk." Yet in the next sentence the speaker may add that he or she is an Uzbek living in Kazakstan. And if you press the issue of national identity further, you may get a new explanation with each new question. A claim to multiple identities is apt to puzzle many an out-

25

sider who, armed only with Western sociological concepts, is trained to think in terms of "nations," "states," and "ethnic groups."

How great are the differences among the groups of Central Asia? How strong is the commonality among them? Can commonality be expected to defeat divisiveness in the long run? Answers to these questions can only be found by looking deeply into Central Asian values.

GEOGRAPHY AND DESTINY

At the heart of Eurasia—the globe's largest landmass—are the lands that compose Central Asia. Today, Central Asia includes the countries of Kazakstan, Kyrgyzstan, Tojikiston, Uzbekiston, and Turkmenistan as well as Xinjiang, the westernmost province of China. Parts of northern Afghanistan and parts of Iran are also included in Central Asia. For its size, Central Asia includes the world's greatest volume of geophysical uplift. Central Asia is an assemblage of towering mountains and deep valleys, of remote and impassable ridges, of high plateaus and glaciers. The Pamir, the Altai, the Tien Shan, and the Turkestan Ranges form a series of great radiating spirals in Central Asia. Their peaks are some of the highest in the world, rising to nearly 7,500 meters. No other inhabited landmass has so much sheer physicality, so many great mountains, so much earth thrusting into the skies. No other comparable area exists on earth. These physical features of the central region of the Eurasian landmass define more than the region's topology. They define its history.

"Geography is destiny," say some historians. But in the long march of history the "idea" of Central Asia may have been less a geographical one than a topological one. Central Asia's ancient past was determined not by its geography, that is, by its location at the heart of the Eurasian landmass, but rather by its topological features. In the ancient world, when humans lived close to nature and the cycles of their existence followed the cycles of the natural world, these mountains defined the livelihoods and shaped the patterns of life for all the inhabitants of Central Asia. For those who lived at higher altitudes, the mountains' high plateaus and high valleys were habitat to goats and sheep. The mountains also afforded their inhabitants protection from the nomads and warriors of the plains far below. For those who lived lower, in the great valleys and oases at the base of the mountains, the cycles of seasonal runoff made possible agriculture and animal husbandry. And even for those who lived on the plains and deserts far distant from the mountains, the mountains determined their area's climate. Those who roamed the great sloping plains and even the deserts were nurtured through the long winters and the short but severe summers by the rivers fed from the glacial melt of the mountains.

The ancient history of Central Asia is an epic that cannot be separated from the "prominence of the mountains." It is a history of conquest and migration, of nomadic pastoralism on the sweeping alluvial plains radiating from a center defined by mountains. Before they were "nations," before they were "workers," before there were oriental despots, before there were feudal slaves and lords, the peoples of Central Asia were the peoples of the highlands, river valleys, and oases of the great mountains. The economic and cultural life of Central Asian civilization has its sources in these mountains, the "ceiling of the world." The intellectual life of Central Asia—the "mind" of Central Asia—cannot be understood apart from the importance of the mountains.

Central Asia's original inhabitants were nomadic tribes who moved in and out of the high mountain valleys and down into the oases and plains that today are China, Afghanistan, Iran, and the new states of Central Asia. In ancient times, nomadism and pastoralism were superseded by agrarian societies. Agricultural communities developed in the rich river valleys and the oases that were fed by the snowmelt of the great mountains. The largest Central Asian populations today are located in the oases and the valleys associated with the major rivers, particularly the Amu Daria and the Syr Daria Rivers.[2]

Given the variation among the mountain, valley, and desert environments, Central Asian societies developed many distinct qualities, mixing local features and influences with those from outside. In broad terms, we can identify successive waves of cultural influences that over the past three millennia swept through Central Asia. From the north, the earliest influences were those of the early marauding tribes of the Kazak Steppe. From the south, the Iranian and Arabic influences began perhaps as early as the eighth century B.C. and continued through the Arabic suzerainty of the eighth century A.D. Mediterranean influence swept through for a brief period with the eastern campaigns of Alexander the Great, the famed warrior-general who for a time had been a pupil of Aristotle. From the east, the technologically advanced Chinese came for the purpose of trade. The Mongols swept through from the north and east, bringing destruction and domination—and a continuing cultural legacy. In the mid-nineteenth century Russians arrived from the north to establish foreign colonial control. In sum, these varying historical influences left a richly patterned, heterogeneous cultural community in Central Asia.

The detailed history of these waves of foreign influences is now being reinterpreted as the period of Soviet influence closes. No doubt many established historical truths are likely to be reevaluated as modern events begin to exert new pressures on the meaning of the past. Much of what has been repeated about Central Asian history was constructed by Soviet historians interested in sticking to regularities specified by the official doctrine of historical materialism, even when evidence for their interpretations was sparse or sometimes altogether missing. But some of the broad outlines of the different periods of Central Asian history and the waves of foreign influence are generally agreed upon.

CENTRAL ASIAN HERITAGE

At the dawn of recorded history, Central Asia belonged to Iranian peoples. A Persian-speaking people inhabited the valleys of the Jaxartes and Oxus Rivers (the Syr Daria and Amu Daria, respectively) probably as early as the eighth century B.C. The plains to the north of the Jaxartes were inhabited by the Scythians, also an Iranic-speaking people, and by numerous smaller groups of people such as the Tocharians, who were an uncivilized, warlike, nomadic people who left little historical trace. The lands north of the Oxus were known to ancient historians of the Persian and Arabic worlds simply as Transoxania—lands beyond the Oxus. By the sixth century B.C., there were two great kingdoms in Transoxania. The Persian monarch Cyrus the Great established the city of Cyropolis along the banks of the Jaxartes, and the Bactrian kingdom, centered in what is today Afghanistan, exercised influence north into the valleys of the Oxus.

In the middle part of the fourth century B.C. Alexander of Macedonia (Alexander the Great) passed through Central Asia on his march to conquer India. The Central Asia that Alexander found was composed of city-states. Sogdiana at this time was centered in Samarkand in today's Uzbekiston. Margiana was centered to the south around the city of Merv (today known as Mary) in Turkmenistan. Khorezm, situated on the banks of the Middle Amu River, was already an independent area. Alexander pressed as far as modern-day Hojent in northern Tojikiston, a city that then became known as Alexandria Eschate—the ultimate Alexandria. Many other Central Asian cities, including Merv and Herat, were renamed in honor of Alexander. Legend has it—inaccurately—that Alexander founded Samarkand. Although Alexander's stay in Central Asia was brief, it was significant. The influence of the Greek customs and ways lingered long after Alexander himself departed. He remains even today a folk hero in the area.

As Greek power receded after the death of Alexander in 323 B.C. in Babylon, Central Asia fell for a time under the influence of the Parthian empire. With the rise of the Samanid dynasty in Persia, the influence of Baghdad gave way to Persian influence. Bukhara grew to be a major trading area and eventually became the capital of the Samanid dynasty. At about this same time, the sporadic invasions of the Turks of the northeast plains grew more regular. Turkic warrior bands periodically flowed out of the northern plains and into Central Asia's valleys. These tribes engaged the Chinese to the east, the Persians to the south, and the Byzantines far to the west, but they found little organized resistance within Central Asia. Although these early Turkic intrusions were destructive, their lasting impact was minor. The major wave of Turkic influence came only later, in the thirteenth century, after the Arab influence.

Arab armies brought the word of Islam to Central Asia after the death of Muhammad in 632. In the century following the prophet's death, the Arab empire reached from North Africa and Spain in the west to Asia Minor and Persia in the east. The Arabs penetrated into Central Asia in the middle of the seventh century, reaching Merv in 651. But they did not drive farther into Central Asia for some period due to active opposition. Only by degrees and increments did Arab influence gradually grow over the next century to eventually encompass the major settled cities of Central Asia.

The Arabs brought science and culture in addition to the Islamic faith. Direct rule by the Arabs lasted only a short time; their real and enduring influence was in the ideas and the cultural legacy they left behind. Indeed, the Arabic language served as the local language of science and commerce in the region for the next 300 years. Central Asia became a center of learning. As the flames of learning flickered and were extinguished in the European and Mediterranean areas during the Dark Ages, scholarship and knowledge continued to burn bright in Central Asia. In the oases of Central Asian antiquity, particularly in Khorezm and Bukhara, Arabic learning left behind a rich intellectual legacy. The great Central Asian scholars of the Middle Ages, Al Khwarezm, Abu Rai Raihan Al Biruni (973–1048), and Abu Ali Ibn Sina (980–1037), produced their works during this period. Al-Khwarezm, from whose name derives the word "algorithm," is credited by Central Asians with inventing algebra.[3] Ibn Sina (known as Avicenna to the scholars of the Latin-speaking world) was a philosopher, mathematician, physician, and poet who had an influence in western Europe for centuries. He was regarded by European medieval thinkers as the successor to Aristotle. Ibn Sina is credited with keeping the works of Aristotle alive when Dark Age Europe had long since discounted the intellectual and cultural riches of ancient Greece as meaningless and useless.

By the turn of the millennium, Samanid rule had collapsed, and such power and authority that existed had passed to the hands of the Turkic warriors living on the frontiers. It was about this time that the great cyclone from the east descended upon Central Asia. The "Great Khan," the Mongol Chingis Khan, stormed through the valleys of the Jaxartes and the Oxus and attacked the ancient oases of Central Asia. He captured the great cities of Bukhara and Samarkand in about 1225. The Mongol Khan died a short time later, in 1227, leaving his empire in the hands of his de-

scendants, who divided up Central Asia (as well as other parts of the territory they conquered) and ruled directly.

Under the rule of Khan and his immediate successors, the ancient
world of Eurasia was united for the first time. From the Pacific Ocean in
the east to the Indian Ocean and Persian Gulf in the south to the edges of
central Europe, one political expanse was created. The skills of the Mongols in empire-building were not matched in the cultural sphere. The
Mongols destroyed many of the brilliant cities of Central Asia, including
Tashkent, Samarkand, and Bukhara. They destroyed the ancient irrigation system of the Fergana Valley. The Mongols are also said to have
rerouted the waters of the Amu River northward. The unity that Mongol
political control brought to Central Asia—that is, the *pax Mongolica*—may
be oddly named, for it largely left destruction in its wake. As one anthro-
pologist put it, it was the "peace of the desert."[4] But it also left a common
political space. In this way it paved the way for the growth of commerce
that took place during the two succeeding centuries.

Before the Mongol presence, there had been earlier trading groups,
such as the Sogdians. Some historians argue that the Sogdian language
was once the common language of Central Asia.[5] The Chinese, Greeks,
and Persians were also active in Central Asian trade routes during the
early history of Central Asia. But it was only after the establishment of the
pax Mongolica that trade began to flourish richly along Central Asia's
Jibek-joli or Great Silk Route. When Marco Polo journeyed to Cathay in
1271 it was along the Silk Route. Probably, the golden days of transasiatic
commerce were brought to a close by global circumnavigation. In 1497,
Vasco da Gama rounded the Cape of Good Hope on the southern tip of
Africa on his way from Lisbon to India. A century later the land routes
across Central Asia had fallen into disuse. The Silk Route never regained
its former vitality.

Chingis Khan's *Orda* (horde), under the leadership of his sons, also left
the continuing legacy of the Turkic languages. Turkic languages were already widely used in Central Asia. And although the Mongol rulers and
warriors themselves spoke Mongol, they brought in their wake waves of
Turkic-speaking populations. Moreover, their destruction of the Arabic
and Persian centers of learning and commerce created a vacuum that
drew in the Turkic vernacular, which became the dominant language
group of the area. Persian and Arabic nonetheless continued to be the languages of science and learning. Moreover, even as the Turkic languages
gained popular ascendancy, the cultural traditions of Islam, left as a
legacy by the Arabs, proved more enduring than the weak cultural influences of the Turks and Mongols. During this period, the Turkic tradition
was fused with the Islamic tradition in a process of mutual assimilation.
By the fifteenth century, the Mongol language, adopted by the ruling

Tamerlane's tomb in Samarkand. Photo by Gregory Gleason.

Mongol warriors but no one else, was entirely displaced by Turkic languages. The father of Uzbek literature, Alisher Navoii (1441–1501), wrote during this period.

A descendant of Chingis Khan, Timur the Lame (Tamerlane), moved his rule over the city of Kish in about 1350 to Samarkand. Timur assembled a great army and set out, like Chingis, to conquer the world by force of arms. He invaded Persia; he invaded the Siberian plains lying to the north; and he swept eastward far into Anatolia, for a time even capturing Ankara (1402). But Timur was the last of the leaders who managed to unify Central Asia. After Timur's death, Central Asian leaders were unable to reunite the area into one "Turkestan." Timur's grandson, Ulughbek (Muhammad Taroghoi, 1394–1449) was one of the exceptional Mongol leaders. He was not only a ruler but also a scientist. He created an observatory that measured the heavens more exactly than any until the twentieth century. Zahiriddin Bobir (1483–1503), a Timurid leader whose imperial designs were continually frustrated by the tribal fragmentation within Central Asia, turned to the south. Bobir marched through Afghanistan and on to India, where he founded the Mughal empire.

The Mongol influence was in eclipse by the fourteenth century, but during the fifteenth century a new Mongol threat arose from the Jungarian federation situated on the northern slopes of Kazakstan. Central Asia at this time was an assemblage of small principalities with shifting coalitions unable to cooperate with one another. There was constant expansion and contraction at the local level and little regional cooperation. Political rule was not personalized; it was in the hands of the entire clan of the Khan (the senior member of the clan being known as the Khan). Sultans were mainly autonomous; subordination was based on tributary or tax relations, not a presumption of infallibility. During this period, power passed from the more nomadic Kazaks in the north to the settled Uzbeks along the Syr Daria. The tribes to the south, in what is today Turkmenistan and Tojikiston, were mainly peripheral and local-minded. Early in the sixteenth century, Central Asia came under the control of Uzbek tribes from the steppes led by Muhammad Shaibani Khan. The Shaibanid invasion further accelerated the decay and fragmentation of the area.

By the beginning of the nineteenth century, many of the tribes of Kazakstan were subordinated to Tashkent rule. The crucial distinction in this period was not national identification but economic association. The nineteenth-century observer Eugene Schuyler noted that according to the native population, the whole society was divided into two classes, settled and nomad. The nomads were called Kazak, and the settled people went by the name Sart.[6] These were economic groups, not ethnic, much less "national" ones.

Among the settled population, the glories of the ancient civilization had long since faded. A cruel slaveholding feudalism was the dominant form of society. The Bukhara of that day has been described as a "land of poverty and persecution and slavery, of oppressive taxes, of public tortures and drawn-out executions, a place where curious non-Muslim visitors could be (and sometimes were) clapped into the emir's *siyah chah*, his black hole, and eventually put to death."[7] The area was roughly divided into three khanates, each led by an all-powerful, local Khan: Kokand in the Fergana Valley; Bukhara in the Zerafshan Oasis; and Khiva downstream on the Amu River. The Bukharan Khan, because of the enduring Persian influence, also maintained the title of emir.

Unlike island kingdoms or many of the culturally defined lands of Europe, the Eurasian continent was a great expanse of land that seemed to invite periodic redefinition via the ebb and flow of invasion and retreat. Perhaps for this reason, the Russian empire has never had clearly defined boundaries. Starting from its origins in the European plains, it grew in a series of great, expansionist waves radiating out in the directions harboring the least opposition. The history of the Russian state begins in the middle of the ninth century with the establishment of a government in the city of Novgorod by Rurik the Dane. Rurik's successor, Oleg, moved the capital south to Kiev, located on the Dnepr River. The Kievan state expanded until the eleventh century. At that point, it reached from the Baltic

Sea in the north to the Black Sea in the south, from the Urals in the east to Romania in the west.

In 988, Prince Vladimir made peace with the Byzantine empire centered in Constantinople. Vladimir adopted Christianity. By the thirteenth century, Kievan Russia consisted of an assemblage of city-states. This left it easy prey to the Mongols who swept in from the east, and in 1236 Kiev fell to the Mongols. Ivan Kalita, named grand prince by the Mongol Khan in 1328, persuaded the head of the Russian Orthodox Church to move the Church to Moscow, which thereafter became the political capital as well. Ivan's grandson, Dmitri, attempted to overthrow the Mongols, defeating them in 1380 in the famous battle of Kulikovo. But Mongol overlordship lingered for another century. In 1480, Ivan III, known as Ivan the Great, refused to recognize the authority of the Khans. Russia began to unify.

The troops of Ivan IV, better known as "Ivan the Terrible," captured the Turkic city of Kazan in 1552. Russian vistas swept to the south. Soon afterward the Turks of the Volga region were added to the Russian empire. Siberian expansion in the seventeenth century added other Turks, Mongols, and smaller Siberian groups. Over the next two centuries, Russia pushed eastward and southward across the Central Asian steppes. Russian troops advanced to the edges of the Siberian forest lying on the north frontier of the Kazak Steppe by the 1820s. Gradually the local tribes were integrated and displaced as Russian settlers moved into the regions that the growing Russia had annexed.

Russia moved into Central Asia by the early 1850s to counter British gains on the Indian subcontinent. Russian troops conquered the city of Kokand in the important Fergana Valley as early as 1853, but Russia considered Central Asia to be of only marginal economic or strategic value—until the great defeat in the Crimean War (1854–1856). After that, Russia's competition with Britain appeared to be much more urgent. Russia accordingly set out to capture as much of Central Asia as possible. The last Central Asian area brought under Russian control was the desert region that today is Turkmenistan. A fierce battle in January 1881 at the ancient fortress of Geok-tepe near present-day Ashgabat ended with the massacre of the native population by the invading Russian army. Following the siege of Geok-tepe, resistance to Russian control consisted mainly of suicidal rebellion rather than organized opposition.

In 1867, General K.P. von Kaufman was appointed the first governor-general of Turkestan.[8] Von Kaufman had been operating out of Orenburg, in present-day Kazakstan. But the city of Tashkent, lying on the alluvial plains of the western edge of the Tien Shan Mountains, was easier to maintain logistically, easier to supply, and more easily linked by rail than other cities. It became the seat of the governor-general and later grew to be the most important city in Central Asia. At first, the Russian government did not demand unconditional surrender of its protectorates, letting the local leaders rule in a tributary relationship. The khanates retained their native rulers and a degree of political autonomy.[9] Meanwhile, the Kazaks to the north and the tribes of the Kara Kum Desert were subjected, at least in principle, to direct Russian rule. The Russians initially maintained these relationships with the three dependencies in Central Asia—the Bukharan emirate and the Kokand and Khivan khanates. Soon, the Kokand khanate, which proved the most difficult to rule—and also commanded the best agricultural land in the entire Russian empire—tempted Russian colonial settlers. The Kokand khanate was subjugated directly to the Russian governor-general.

The first formal administrative structures of the tsarist government in Central Asia were established shortly after the tsarist Decree of 1867, which created the *guberniia* of Turkestan. The decree specified a two-tiered administrative arrangement that was fairly typical for Russian imperial colonies, recognizing a firm border between the cultural lives of the indigenous Muslims and the colonizing Russians. As a rule, the Russian overlords sought not to interfere with local customs. Communication between the natives and the Russians was discouraged; natives were not encouraged to learn Russian unless necessary for purposes of communication. In general, the Russians remained ignorant of and indifferent to the culture of the locals, and vice-versa.

Events toward the end of the nineteenth century fueled apprehension among Russia's central military officials and administrators that the Turkestan provinces were too distant to be effectively governed with this two-tiered system. A series of scandals involving the Russian administration led to a government commission of inquiry, which found that flagrant abuses of authority were extensive.[10] In the Turkestan area, as Helene Carrere d'Encausse has observed, "Each local Russian leader tended to behave as a petty king whose power was not limited by any authority; this provoked frequent clashes with the Muslim populations."[11] A series of popular revolts broke out in 1889. The revolts resulted in a commission of inquiry that produced a report criticizing the Russian policy of noninterference in cultural affairs for abetting the growth of pan-Islamic propaganda.[12]

Europe during the nineteenth century was in the heyday of empire. Imperialism was a political system with economic motivations. But there were many complex economic and political sources of imperial designs. For instance, British supremacy on the seas and the doctrine of free trade facilitated the textile boom of the first half of the nineteenth century. With demand for cotton constantly increasing, the disruption of the world cotton market caused by the U.S. Civil War created a panic. The effect, of course, was to incline European governments that had already accepted the colonial principle to support the development of new imperial holdings for cotton cultivation. More than anything else, the demand for cotton drove the British into Egypt. It also drove the Russians south, where they looked for steady supplies of cotton fiber and other raw materials. Although Central Asia was on the distant periphery of the Russian empire, the Russians nevertheless brought with them technological change, which was already transforming Europe and the Americas. Trains and telegraphs reached Central Asia, compressing space and time.

Ironically, the influence of modernizing Europe gave new impulse to earlier Central Asian traditions. As European political and economic concepts were introduced in a much-reinterpreted Russian form, the intellectuals of Central Asia responded not by adopting these new ideas but by rehabilitating their own ideas. Under foreign political domination, the ancient Central Asian traditions of "family dialogue" and "tea house discussion circles" enjoyed a new life. Young Central Asian intellectuals awoke to the glories of their past even as they awoke to the humiliation of the foreign domination of their present. The Central Asian writers who emerged in this period were the intellectual children of the West but also champions of native culture. These writers and thinkers, including Muhammad Amin Mirzakhuzha ughli Muqimii (1850–1903), Zokirzhon Kholmuhammad ughli Furqat (1858–1909), and Hamza Haqimzoda Niezii (1889–1929), continue to be revered in Central Asia as intellectual and moral forerunners of the best in contemporary Central Asian culture.

The chief intellectual conflict during the first decades of the twentieth century was between representatives of the modernist movement and Central Asian conservatives. The most influential of the modernists were the *jadid*-ists. So named from the Arab expression *usul jadid* or "new method," these intellectuals argued in favor of incorporating some elements of Western, even Russian values to bring about the transformation of Central Asia. But ironically, the Russian authorities saw the civil unrest that erupted in Central Asia after the 1905 revolution as having originated in the communities most influenced by Russia. Thus central officials came to view the modernists as a threat to the maintenance of the Russian imperial administration. The long-standing Russian principle of noninterference, consequently, was superseded by policies that sought to ally the Russian imperial presence with the most conservative elements of the local power structures. By the end of the empire, the tsarist regime had been led by its own ignorance and fears into supporting those least friendly to the continuation of Russian administration.

THE MEANING OF *HURMAT*

Central Asian history offers some insight into the historical and political factors that have helped to shape Central Asian political culture. And the past lives on in the present in innumerable factors and forces that con-

Elder Uzbeks in prayer. Tashkent, 1990. Photo by Anvar Ilyasov.

tinue to shape the future. A situation—any situation—is always an inheritance. Moreover, what may act to define a situation even more profoundly than the "objective features" of the situation—that is, the persons, places, things, and ostensible choices the situation presents—are the habits of thought and practice that are inherited from the past. The ideas of the past are the greatest legacy. In this way, life flows from ideas.

The collective effect of habits of thought and practices of the past might be referred to simply as "culture." The habits of political thoughts and actions that have their source in history, tradition, public values, common remembrance of the past, and shared vision of the future might be referred to as "political culture." Cultural theory draws attention to postures, values, beliefs, styles of functioning, attitudes toward authority, and rational calculations of self-advancement. Culture is difficult to define because it appears both malleable and resilient. Cultural theory asserts that even as culture acts as an "action frame of reference"[13] that appears to be subjective and internal, it is actually a product of the public sphere of activity. Some cultural theorists have argued that "meanings are shared; they are conferred on objects or events through social interaction."[14]

The perspective of cultural theory encourages us to ask, How has the political culture of Central Asia been formed? Which aspects of it are adventitious and which are essential, permanent, and enduring? According to a leading proponent of cultural theory, the "cultural hypothesis is that individuals exert control over each other by institutionalizing moral judgments [that serve to justify] their interpersonal relationships."[15] What are the most prominent forms of institutionalized moral judgments in Central Asia?

Some observers say that particular features of Central Asian society, ranging from the Oriental despotism of ancient Central Asia to the resilience of Islamic tradition, have shaped a unique Central Asian sensibility. Some say that authoritarianism is inevitable under these circumstances. Other observers, however, point out that Central Asia is a land whose history is rich in poets and astronomers, mathematicians and physicians, traders and warriors. They say that Asian authoritarianism is in the eyes of the beholder. To say that Central Asians have failed to adopt and conform to the democratic institutions of western Europe and North America, contend these defenders of Central Asia, is not to misunderstand Central Asia, but to misunderstand the very nature of democracy.

The authoritarianism of the settled peoples of Central Asia has long been apparent to outsiders. Some scholars have sought explanation for these cultural differences by noting that the regimentation and centralization required for the peaceful functioning of the society inhabiting the irrigated oasis shaped the structure of power. In a famous although now frequently discounted interpretation of the origins of "Oriental despotism," Karl Wittfogel argues that the demands that emerged from the necessity to centrally manage an irrigation system produced a sociopolitical organization that Wittfogel characterizes as the "hydraulic society."[16] Wittfogel's thesis is that unlike the individualistic political culture that develops in many water-rich agrarian societies, semiarid agricultural societies often require a high level of centralized decisionmaking. These demands on the hydraulic society result in the emergence of the "managerial state." The economic, administrative, and political functions of the managerial state are concentrated in a ruling class consisting of landowners, land managers, and the military.

In the semiarid oases and valleys of Central Asia, the value of land was always closely linked to its water supply. In ancient times, the success of local political officials often hinged on their skill at managing local water resources. Streams, irrigation canals, and wells had to be maintained, kept clean, and protected from external threats. Highly political decisions regarding the distribution of water had to be made and enforced, and "free riders"—appropriators attempting to use more than their allotted share of water—had to be monitored and sanctioned. The *mirab*, the watermaster of the Central Asian societies, was responsible for more than simply managing an economic resource; he was responsible for channeling the lifeblood of the society.

The importance of the traditional watermaster in Central Asian society is illustrated by an anecdote. Traditional lore has it that when the *mirab* position fell vacant by death or some other exigency, a new *mirab* was chosen through a trial by fire. Candidates who declared their interest in the position were given a test in which they were required to build a small demonstration canal from one point to another. The engineer whose canal guided the water to its destination first won the test and became the new *mirab*. Other contestants suffered more than merely the ignominy of defeat—they were put to death. This practice reduced the contenders for this important societal post while ensuring that the science of irrigation engineering was pursued with a fitting seriousness of purpose. This legend, of course, may be largely apocryphal, but it nevertheless illustrates the importance that Central Asians attached to the management of irrigation systems.

To outsiders, Central Asian political practices often seem idiosyncratic and subject to mysterious unwritten protocols, secretive mutual understandings, and subtle but powerful local political idioms. Central Asian traditions of patriarchy, popular submissiveness, deference to authority and to elders, and weak democratic institutions would seem to impel Central Asian societies toward an authoritarian future. Within the old USSR, Central Asia was the area most unaffected by Mikhail Gorbachev's reforms under perestroika. It was the area most resistant to democratic change. Outsiders, even if sensitive to the great differences among the groups of Central Asia, often assess Central Asian values in terms of their distinctive acceptance of hierarchy. Perhaps the most visible aspect of the public culture of these countries is the great importance associated with *hurmat*, the idea of "deference" or "respect."

In present-day Central Asian life, the origins of *hurmat* are not hard to find. *Hurmat* begins in the family. Personal life is family life in Central Asian societies: Property is communal, *palov* (the preferred Central Asian dish) is shared, elders are given deference without question, and women are subordinated. Authority is personalized. In some northern portions of Tojikiston, many people referred to Uzbekiston's president, Islam Karimov, whom they regarded as their protector in Tojikiston's civil war, as *Islam-aka* (Father Islam). Also, the structure of authority is emphatically patriarchal. In many regions of Central Asia, the elder or most respected man represents the head of the family; the family's women are positioned in a separate hierarchy. In some regions of Uzbekiston, for instance, there is literally no word for "wife"; it is the same word as that used for "women." In some regions, the word for "sister" is the same word used to refer to an older woman, whether she be a mother or older sister. The hierarchies of political life are merely a natural extension of the structures of the family. Several examples may underscore this point. For instance, fu-

Village elders in the daily tea ritual. The elders gather informally in the daily Central Asian ritual of tea-drinking and discussion in a small village in the Fergana Valley. Photo by Gregory Gleason, 1992.

nerals are quite naturally the most important political gathering. When a responsible figure in the community dies, an important social position is vacated. The filling of that position initiates a "vacancy chain" that influences all positions of lower order throughout the hierarchy in the community.

In Central Asia, power is often vested in the person, not the post. The terminology of European languages suggests the roots of this practice in European societies as well. For instance, words that designate official posts have associate words denoting the official's "administration" or "jurisdiction": Thus we have emperor/empire (or imperium), king/kingdom, ambassador/embassy (*posol/posolstvo*), hakim/hakimiat, emir/emirate. But this terminology only suggests the vestiges of the past. In contemporary society, we tend to think of counties as purely administrative jurisdictions; rarely does the word "county" bring to mind the idea of a ruling count. We know of a country's president, but probably few of us have ever contemplated the idea of *presidentia*—which would be the area over which a president presides. In other words, steeped in liberal democratic traditions, we tend to automatically distinguish between the post and the person who fills it, between the position and the jurisdiction under its control.

KINSHIP, CULTURE, AND WORSHIP

Reflected in the arts, lifestyles, and behaviors, the common culture of Central Asian societies is distinctively different from those of surrounding countries. The process of defining Central Asian culture is thus certain to raise as many questions as it answers. The ideas, the medium, and the context of Central Asian culture can be discussed within the context of the most important Central Asian institutions. The intellectual life of Central Asia is closely bound up with Islam. The culture of Central Asia is closely intertwined with the linguistic communities of the region. And the sense of community is always associated with the "fellow-feeling," the sense of "weness" that Central Asian groups experience. Those groups are based in family associations. The community of Turkic speakers, based in the Central Asian comprehension of Islam and bound together by close family ties, is the defining feature of Central Asian institutions.

The profession of Islam is deeply rooted and profoundly articulated throughout Central Asian society. The high level of civilization that is characteristic of Islamic societies is unmistakably present in Central Asian society. "Islamic consciousness"—the idea of being a Muslim that requires communication with Allah and that imposes an obligation for right action—continually surrounds one in Central Asian societies. Islamic consciousness is everywhere present; Central Asian Muslims routinely refer to Allah in their speech, ask for forgiveness or divine intercession, praise Allah's mercifulness, and seek Allah's guidance in their daily deliberations over business or family matters. At the same time, however, Islam is not followed in the way it is in other parts of the Muslim world. The differences in forms of profession say much about the roots of Central Asian culture and the influences of the Soviet period.

Islam came to Central Asia with the Arab conquest in the early eighth century. The Islamic confession brought the ideas of Islam as well as the teachings of the Islamic world. Islamic influence spread throughout the Central Asian region until, by the end of the tenth century, Islam was the only formal religion of the territory. However, the greatest influence of Islam was in the highly politically organized areas of the oases and the river valleys. Later, Islamic practices spread into the steppes and the deserts and, to a lesser extent, into the mountains. In these areas, Islamic practices were never as strong as they were among the peoples of the settled areas. The best way to appreciate the importance of Islam in the role of ideas in Central Asia is to view Islam in terms of the history of the influence of the core Islamic practices and beliefs.

The prophet Muhammad was born in Mecca ca. 570 A.D. and died in 632 A.D., the first year of the Muslim calendar. The basic teaching of Islam is that there is one God, Allah, and Muhammad is his Messenger. The

Qur'an is the holy book of Islam. Islam teaches that the Qur'an is the will of God, revealed through the apostles. The Qur'an exists on earth, but it is an exact copy of the text that also exists in Paradise. The Qur'an is not a revelation of a miracle; it is itself the miracle. In the first two centuries after the life of the prophet Muhammad, a number of divisions appeared among the Muslim faithful. Two of the most important today are the Sunni and Shia.

The teachings of the Qur'an specify the rules of life, the wages of sin, and the rewards of Paradise after life. The Qur'an, say its followers, does not contradict the earlier holy writings of Judaism and Christendom, but completes these. The God of the Qur'an is both "compassionate and merciful" and a punisher of evil and wrongdoing. The God of the Qur'an prohibits injustice, cruelty, and evil and enjoins the faithful to practice right living, kindness, charity, and good deeds. The good Muslim need not fear death, for death is merely the door into Paradise.

Muslim believers stress that Islam is not only a religious doctrine but also a way of life. Islam does not make distinctions between doctrine and life, between thought and action, between word and deed. Islam demands total commitment of the individual, for it is a living doctrine. The Western doctrine of separation of church and state, therefore, seems to many Muslims to be artificial. Muslims point out that Islam is democratic. Prayer or supplication to demigods or to a divinely inspired clergy would diminish the relationship between God and man. In Islam, there is an immediate relationship.

A Muslim is a person of principle. A Muslim society is one of a high level of civilization. The relationship between principle and practice in Islam is simple. Human beings are creatures of habit. Rituals are a way in which people routinize and institutionalize habit. Islam, with an emphasis on the unity of thought and action, assigns a special importance to habit. In Islam, rituals have a seriousness of purpose that gives order and meaning to individual life. The shared observance of rituals serves to bind the community together through establishing if not common purpose itself, at least common expectations about the behavior of one's fellow-believers. In the end, common purpose emerges from common practice. Ritual in Islam has a teleological purpose.

The important ritual duties are prayer, almsgiving, fasting, and pilgrimage. Prayer in Muslim countries is conducted five times per day, at sunset, night, dawn, noon, and afternoon. The faithful are called to prayer by the muezzin, the crier who calls from the minaret at the appointed hours: "God is most great. I testify that there is no God but Allah. I testify that Muhammad is God's apostle. Come to prayer, come to security. God is most great." The faithful gather at the mosque, and facing the mihrab—thus facing Mecca—they begin to recite *rakas* or prayers from the Qur'an.

The faithful are led in prayer by a leader, the imam. Almsgiving originally involved tithing a fortieth of a man's income but has since become voluntary. The Qur'an orders that fasting be observed in the month of Ramadan, the lunar month in which the holy script was revealed. No one may eat, drink, or smoke during the day throughout the month of fasting. The pilgrimage requires that every good Muslim make the trip to Mecca at least once. Wine and pork are forbidden. While all Muslims believe in these principles, those of the Shia confession also profess that an imam appears to each generation, and it is the obligation of the faithful to follow him.

The practice of Islam within Central Asia has been affected by the historical conditions under which Islam was adopted, the destruction of the Islamic heritage brought about by the Mongol conquest, and the influence of official, state-enforced atheism during the period of Soviet overlordship. Most Central Asian believers are Sunni, although many Muslims in Tojikiston belong to the Shia confession. Virtually all indigenous Central Asians consider themselves Muslim, although a large number of Central Asians have only a vague idea about what that implies. Most Central Asians simply observe that being Muslim distinguishes them from the peoples of the north (whom they regard generically as Christians) and that to be Muslim means to live in their traditional style and to practice rituals related to their beliefs. The Central Asian faithful agree on five pillars of Islamic practice: *imonlik* (confession); *salat* (daily prayers); *haj* (pilgrimage); *zakat* (charitable contributions); and the observance of Ramadan.[17]

From its earliest days, Russian colonial policy in Central Asia favored segregation rather than integration; consequently, there was little attempt under the tsarist Russian government to supplant Islam with Orthodoxy. Soviet Marxist ideology, of course, was antagonistic to religion, but Marxism comprehended religion primarily in terms of organized religious structures such as those of the Russian Orthodox Church rather than the ritual practices that define Islamic consciousness.[18]

The Islamic faith became the target of Bolshevik antireligious zeal after Lenin's death. An all-out assault was launched in 1928, when the Soviet regime closed the Islamic courts (*shariat*) and the religious schools (*medresses*) and terminated the economic basis of the clergy by redistributing the clerical landholdings (*waqf*). The pilgrimage to Mecca (*haj*) was prohibited. Traditional patriarchy was attacked. Polygamy and the wearing of the veil were outlawed. The Arabic script was replaced by the Latin script, and copies of the Qur'an could not be published.

The efforts of the Soviet government to eradicate the influence of Islam had mixed success. The cultural aspects of Islam remained influential; its "official" aspects, however, were attacked. In its cultural aspects, Islam continued to serve as a guide and a source of solace for the moral person. At the same time, the official structures of Islam were either destroyed or captured by the Soviet regime. Perhaps the vitality of cultural Islam during this period may be attributed to a popular backlash against Soviet atheism; perhaps it may be attributed to the proselytizing of Islamic movements in Iran and elsewhere; or perhaps it may have resulted from an anticolonialism conjunction of Islam and ethnicity, the idea of the emergence of an "Islamistan."[19]

LANGUAGE AND IDENTITY

The idea of a large community within Central Asia may have its source in such common values as those promoted by Islam. But the practicality of the idea has much to do as well with the fact that the native language of 90 percent of Central Asians is one or another form of a Turkic language. (See A Note on Languages in Central Asia.) The Turkic languages are all genetically related. They belong to the non–Indo-European group.[20] In terms of structure and lexicon, they are every bit as far from Russian as they are from English.

The three main groups of languages in use in Central Asia are Turkic, Persian, and Slavic. Turkic is the most widely spoken group of languages in Central Asia. The Turkic languages are related to modern-day Turkish as spoken in Turkey, but they are far enough removed from Turkish that most educated speakers would not normally find their speech mutually comprehensible. The variants of Turkic spoken within Central Asia are also closely related. In most cases, they are too close to be linguistically described as separate languages but too distant to be described as dialects. A well-educated Turkmen, for instance, would not normally understand the speech of an Uzbek but would find written Uzbek relatively easy to read. At the same time, the Turkmen would have little difficulty in understanding a Turk from Ankara but would have difficulty reading the Turkish language, because it is written in Latin letters.

The Turkic languages of Central Asia consist of three branches: the Karluk or East Turkic group (e.g., Uzbek); the Kipchak or central group (e.g., Karakalpak, Kazak, Kyrgyz); and the Oguz group (e.g., Azerbaijan, Turkmen). Many local variations of the Turkic languages exist. Since these languages were used mainly for domestic purposes, the terminology of twentieth-century science, commerce, and technology in these languages consists principally of Russian loan words. Illustrating the differences among the Turkic languages, the expression "New Day" is *Janga Kun* (Kazak), *Jangï Kun* (Kyrgyz), *Täze Gun* (Turkmen), and *Yängi Kun* (Uzbek); compare *Rûzi Nav* (Tojik).

The most widely spoken language of Central Asia is Uzbek (the Karluk group). Modern Uzbek has a number of major dialects. The main dialects have six vowels and no vowel harmony. The minor dialects have up to ten vowels and preserve the vowel harmony that is found, for instance, in modern Turkish. The dialects have some grammatical peculiarities but are mainly distinguished by lexical differences. There are many Arabic, Persian, and Russian loan words in modern Uzbek.

The Persian language (Farsi) dialects spoken in Central Asia include four groups: the Samarkand and Bukhara dialects; the Zerafshan dialect; the Badakhshan dialect; and the Darwaz dialect spoken in Tojikiston. All of these dialects are intelligible to the educated Iranian speaker, although lexical differences exist.

The third major language is Russian. Russian has been spoken among the upper classes in Central Asia for more than a century. Although it is the language of the "colonial occupier," the Russian language is also the common tongue for many Central Asians. It is the language of science, technology, and politics. Russian is widely spoken in the large cities. Moreover, members of the political and economic elite speak Russian fluently.

Determined efforts by the Soviet government to sponsor greater popular reliance on Russian, especially among the peasantry, met with either opposition or indifference from the local populations. Soviet sources claim that the 1979 census showed the number of native-speaking Uzbeks fluent in Russian rising from 13.5 percent to 49.3 percent during the period 1970–1979. Such claims were no doubt greatly exaggerated. In rural areas in Central Asia today, Russian is spoken poorly and infrequently. With the transition to national sovereignty in the Central Asian states, the privileged position of the Russian language is changing swiftly. For instance, in Tashkent in December 1991 most street signs and subway signs were written in Russian. By the spring of 1992, however, despite the fact that there was still a large Russian-speaking population in Tashkent, Russian-language signs in public places virtually disappeared in favor of Uzbek-language signs. Turkic languages and dialects of Persian are spoken in Afghanistan, China, Iran, and Pakistan. There are few Arabic speakers in Central Asia.

Today the writing system widely used in Central Asia is based upon the Cyrillic alphabet, the one used for Russian. A runic alphabet was used in the seventh century in the eastern reaches of Central Asia, but apparently it never penetrated into modern-day Central Asia. When the Arabs conquered Central Asia, they brought with them the Arabic script. The Chagatai language, once used as the educated language of Central Asia, was written in this form of Arabic script. Over the years, Chagatai grew far removed from common speech and was used only in formalistic documents. It was replaced by the vernacular languages of Central Asia in the early 1920s. In 1925 a decree was issued that established a ban on the import of materials printed in the Arabic alphabet. Today there is disagreement over the status of the Arabic script. Some Central Asians regard it as every bit as much of an external imposition as the Cyrillic script. Others, however, insist on a return to Central Asian classicism. For instance, the 1989 Tojik language law and the program of the Rastokhez (Revival) popular front both called for a return to the Arabic script in modern-day Tojikiston.

After the consolidation of Soviet power in Central Asia, language policy played a key role in Moscow's deliberate efforts at social engineering. Between 1927 and 1930, a Latin script was adopted for the spoken languages of Central Asia. Between 1934 and 1940, a new version of the Latin script was introduced by the Soviet government. However, in 1940 the Soviet government, fearing direct communication between the Turks of Turkey and the Turkophone populations of Central Asia, introduced yet another language reform, replacing the Latin script with Cyrillic script. With the disintegration of the USSR and the transition to national independence in the Central Asian states, sentiment in favor of a return to the Latin script throughout much of Central Asia has grown considerably. The governments of both Turkmenistan and Uzbekiston have announced official plans to complete a return to the Latin script within the decade.

If Islam provides a shared community of values and the Turkic languages provide a shared medium of communication, it is the family that provides the real locus of socialization and acculturation. The term "family" in Central Asia does not mean a "nuclear family" of single sets of offspring from a single set of parents. It is a much broader concept that includes progenitors as well as progeny. There is a link with the past that is almost as important as the link with the future. One's ancestors seem often, in the calculations of a typical Central Asian, to reckon just as palpably as one's contemporary family members.

By European and North American standards, Central Asian families do not seem to have clear boundaries. An outsider being hosted by a rural Central Asian may be introduced in sequence to a surprisingly large number of people with the explanation that they are the host's "brother." At some point the puzzled outsider may pause to ask, "Just exactly how many brothers do you have?" What this puzzlement reflects, of course, is the fact that the concept of "brother" in one language does not always translate well in another. The same outsider may find it impossible to travel anywhere within a 100-kilometer radius without his host providing a cheerfully receptive household for the purposes of finding tea, lunch, dinner, or a night's lodging. The "branches" of the typical Central Asian family appear to be almost infinite.

What this suggests is that the Central Asian family is related to large kinship structures, namely, to clans or even to tribes. A tribe is an extended family, that is, a genetically related network. The tribe stresses affective sentiments, the personalistic quality of loyalties, and the obligations that accompany family relationships. Clans are yet larger, extended family relationships that encompass real or putative blood ties. In the Fergana Valley of Uzbekiston, in Mary Oasis in Turkmenistan, and in numerous other regions of Central Asia, clan affiliation—not national affiliation—is the most important source of a person's identity. In Turkmenistan, there are said to be thirty-three major clans. The main clans are the Yomud, located in the western and northern parts of the country; the Tekke, located around Ashgabat; the Goklan, located in the area west of Ashgabat; the Sariq and Salor, located in the Tejen and Murgab Valleys; and the Ersari, located along the upper reaches of the Amu River.

Clantocracy is a term sometimes used to denote the relationship between strong clan identification and political control. Clan identification is very different from national identification. Language has always been the principal bearer of national identity. Of course, there are groups of people who think of themselves as one nation but who do not speak a common language. These exceptions only prove the rule—in this case a historical language is resurrected and preserved, in part to maintain the national identity. Clan identification, however, is not language-based since it assumes a common language. Clans may function within large communities that appear, because of the language similarity, to be national communities. In reality, however, a clantocracy is the foundation of the national consensus. In Central Asia, nations are relatively recent constructs superimposed on the much more important and fundamental clans.

NOTES

1. "Zaiavlenie," *Pravda Vostoka* (24 June 1990): 1.

2. The two great rivers of Central Asia are the Amu Daria and the Syr Daria ("daria" in Turkic meaning "river"). Most geographical sources refer to the "Amu Daria" or the "Amudari'a" or some other version of the word, transliterated from one of a number of languages. It is slightly redundant, of course, to speak of the "Amu Daria River." However, one hears reference frequently enough to the "Rio Grande River," a similar redundancy. In this book I have departed somewhat from conventional usage and am using the simple form of "Amu" when I speak of the "Amu Daria" river.

3. Historical sources identify Al Khwarezm of Baghdad (780–850) with having written the *Book of Integration and Equation*, the foundation of algebra.

4. See Lawrence Krader, *Peoples of Central Asia* (Bloomington: Indiana University Press, 1963), p. 85.

5. See Krader, *Peoples of Central Asia*, pp. 74–77.

6. Eugene Schuyler, *Turkistan: Notes of Journey in Russian Turkistan, Khokand, Bukhara, and Kuldja*, vol. 1 (New York: Scribner, Armstrong, 1876), p. 104.

7. James Critchlow, "Caravans and Conquests," *Wilson Quarterly* 16, no. 3 (Summer 1992): 20–32, at 30–31.

8. See David MacKenzie, "Turkestan's Significance to Russia," *Russian Review* 33, no. 2 (1974): 167–188, and David MacKenzie, "Kaufman of Turkestan: An Assessment of His Administration, 1867–1881," *Slavic Review* 26, no. 2 (1967): 266–285.

9. Seymour Becker, *Russia's Protectorates in Central Asia: Bukhara and Khiva, 1865–1924* (Cambridge: Harvard University Press, 1968).

10. Schuyler, *Turkistan: Notes of Journey*, vol. 2, p. 210.

11. Helene Carrere d'Encausse, "Organizing and Colonizing the Conquered Territories," in Edward Allworth, ed., *Central Asia: A Century of Russian Rule* (New York: Columbia University Press, 1967), p. 154.

12. Carrere d'Encausse, "Organizing and Colonizing the Conquered Territories," pp. 157, 170.

13. Talcott Parsons and Edward Shils, *Toward a General Theory of Action* (Cambridge: Harvard University Press, 1951), p. 4.

14. Aaron Wildavsky, "Choosing Preferences by Constructing Institutions: A Cultural Theory of Preference Formation," *American Political Science Review* 81, no. 1 (1987): 4.

15. Wildavsky, "Choosing Preferences by Constructing Institutions," p. 8.

16. Karl A. Wittfogel, *Oriental Despotism* (New Haven: Yale University Press, 1957).

17. Ramadan is the ninth month of the lunar calendar. It extends for thirty-seven days.

18. Alexandre Bennigsen and Chantal Lemercier-Quelquejay, *Islam in the Soviet Union* (New York: Praeger, 1967).

19. Azade-Ayse Rorlich, "Islam and Atheism: Dynamic Tension in Soviet Central Asia," in William Fierman, ed., *Soviet Central Asia* (Boulder: Westview Press, 1991), pp. 186–218.

20. Most historical linguists argue that there are six major language groups on the Eurasian landmass. These are Afro-Asiatic, Dravidian, Kartvelian, Indo-European, Uralic, and Altaic. The Indo-European group includes the Indic, Iranian, Slavic, Germanic, Baltic, Romance, Celtic, Armenian, and Anatolian languages. The Uralic languages include Finnish, Estonian, and Hungarian. The Altaic includes Mongolian and the Turkic languages. Russian historical linguists have argued that these six groups can be traced to a common proto-Eurasian language, which they called Nostratic.

· THREE ·

The Soviet Socialist
Republics of Central Asia

According to Karl Marx, human history proceeds in a succession of logical stages driven by laws of social development. These laws maintain that society has to pass through a feudal stage before reaching a capitalist stage and through a capitalist stage before reaching the socialist stage. The Leninist variant of Marxism, however, introduced a modification to the theory. Lenin maintained that with the right leadership it was possible to "skip stages," proceeding directly from feudalism to socialism. Since Lenin regarded nationalism as a feature of the capitalist stage of development, he thought that nationalism too ultimately would be transcended through socialism. In place of the nationalist values of capitalism, the socialist community would substitute the universalist values of "proletarian internationalism."

For those societies in which proletarianism was not well developed, Lenin championed the principle of national self-determination on the grounds that national self-promotion, if directed by the Bolsheviks, would accelerate the transition to socialism. Lenin believed that the elemental forces of nationalism could be harnessed to the goals of socialist revolution. Since it was based on these premises, the Marxist-Leninist rationale for the Bolshevik takeover of power in Petrograd in 1917 anticipated little role for peasants and nomads in the new socialist society. Yet Central Asia eventually fell to the Soviet state as a spoil of war in the revolutionaries' victory over the monarchist opposition. For these reasons, Lenin saw the creation of artificial national communities as a stage-skipping step toward revolutionary transformation in Central Asia.[1]

In theory, the socialist construction of national communities may have been an intellectually interesting and even elegant concept. But in practice, it was very unclear exactly what it entailed in the circumstances of Central Asia, presenting leaders with several questions. What should be the size and the shape of the new socialist states of Central Asia? Should language or clan affiliation be the determining factor in defining these new "socialist nations"? The simplest option was to incorporate all of Central Asia into Russia, declaring its peoples to be proletarians. Another was to replace the leaders of the Central Asian emirate and khanate with pliant pro-Bolshevik surrogates while retaining the existing territorial divisions. A third was to fit the ethnographic map of Central Asia with congruent political institutions. A fourth was to unite all of Central Asia into a greater "Turkestan."

The first option was quickly rejected by the Bolsheviks. The second was entertained for a period but then also was rejected. (The retention of the existing territorial boundaries would suggest continuity with the previous political order. The Bolsheviks, intent upon overturning the nineteenth-century nation-state system, reasoned that the territorial structures would have to be changed to prevent political structures from being captured by the former privileged groups.) The third possibility, that of duplicating ethnographic divisions with political institutions, posed more practical difficulties: The true ethnographic contours were difficult to ascertain, and who could decide who constituted the legitimate nations of Central Asia?[2] The fourth option, that of uniting the entire region under one Turkestan nation, seemed the most compatible with Lenin's plan for a transition to socialism.

Thus the Turkestan Autonomous Soviet Republic was established.[3] In the period between the Bolshevik Revolution and 1924, the peoples of Central Asia were treated by the Bolsheviks as one nation, a Turkestan nation. Moscow officials grew increasingly apprehensive that nationalism in Turkestan might present a greater challenge to socialist unity than the Leninist formula envisaged. The popular appeal of champions of pan-Turanian national unity, charismatic figures such as Sultan Galiev, Turar Ryskulov, Mustafa Chokay, and Enver Pasha, made Moscow leaders fearful that if they allowed national sentiment to further develop in Turkestan, they might not be able to rechannel it into proletarianism. Moscow thus resolved to break up the unification movements of the Bashkir and Tatar nationalists. Increasingly, the Bolsheviks began to think in terms of preventing the formation of pan-Turanian sentiments by establishing smaller national units. The communist theoretician Ian Rudzutak explained the change in Moscow's perspective, saying, "I cannot agree with the decision to create a Turkic republic. This decision was reached under the influence of nationalists. In any event, a single Turkic people does not exist; there are Turkmen, Kazaks, Kyrgyz, and Uzbeks."[4]

TABLE 3.1   The Constituent Soviet Central Asian Republics of the USSR (prior to independence)

	Population (millions)	Territory (thousand sq. km.)	Date of Formation
Kazakstan	16.538	2,717	Dec. 1936
Kyrgyzstan	4.291	198	Oct. 1924
Tojikiston	5.112	143	Oct. 1924
Turkmenistan	3.534	488	Oct. 1924
Uzbekiston	19.906	447	Oct. 1924

* These are the official dates of entrance into the Union of the republics of Central Asia. The shape and status of these units changed considerably over the years. Tojikiston and Kyrgyzstan were first admitted as autonomous republics.

Source: Narodnoe khoziaistvo SSR v 1985, pp. 12–17. The 1989 population figures are from Trud (April 30, 1989).

Shifting his course, Lenin set about dividing the Turkic peoples into smaller segments in an effort to prevent the development of a nationalist coalition antagonistic to socialism.[5] This policy came to be known as "national delimitation." Among Central Asians, fear began to grow that Moscow's strategy was designed purposely to split the Turkic peoples and to fragment the economy in an effort to divide, conquer, and rule.[6] Despite objections, however, national delimitation won the day: Central Asia was divided into several "Soviet socialist republics"—the SSRs—none of which had an independent existence prior to Soviet power. Essentially, it was these boundaries that the new states inherited upon the breakup of the USSR.

Whereas the Central Asian socialist republics had a common institutional framework within the USSR, each of the republics had a different character and experience under socialism.

Keeping track of the multitude of parties, personalities, and events leading to the revolutionary transformation of tsarist Russia to the communist USSR, in addition to the party name changes that occurred later during Soviet rule, is a tall task. For the sake of clarity, "communism" here is used as the generally accepted name for the ideology of Marxism-Leninism. Likewise, the acronym "CPSU" will be used in reference to the Communist Party of the Soviet Union, although that formal title was not adopted until 1952; in discussing the final days of the Soviet Union we also refer to it as the "Party." The five Soviet socialist republics of Central Asia are identified by their common acronyms: Kazakstan (Kazakh)—KaSSR; Kyrgyzstan (Kirgiz)—KiSSR; Tojikiston (Tadzhik)—TaSSR; Turkmenistan (Turkmen)—TuSSR; and Uzbekiston (Uzbek)—UzSSR.

TABLE 3.2   Principal Ethnic Groups in Central Asia by Size and Concentration by Titular Republic, 1989, in "USSR"

	Size (millions)	Population (millions)	Titular (millions)	Density I*	II*
Uzbek	16.697	19.906	14.124	84%	70%
Kazak	8.136	16.538	6.532	80%	39%
Kyrgyz	2.529	4.291	2.228	88%	52%
Tojik	4.215	5.112	3.168	75%	75%
Turkmen	2.729	3.534	2.524	92%	92%

Key: Size is total ethnic group. Population is of titular republic. Titular is the total ethnic group within titular republic. Density I: percent of group in titular republic. Density II: percent of republic population of titular group.

Source: Journal of Soviet Nationalities, Vol. 1, No. 2 (1990), pp. 157–159. These figures are based on the January 1989 Soviet census.

DEVELOPMENT AND RUSSIFICATION IN THE KAZAK REPUBLIC

Kazakstan statehood dates from 1920, when the territory of Kazakstan was established as an autonomous Soviet socialist republic (it became a union-republic of the USSR at the end of 1936). The KaSSR was the second largest republic in the USSR and was often treated separately from the other Central Asian countries because its northern border extended into southern Siberia. Until the 1990s, the standard reference was to "Central Asia and Kazakstan," suggesting that Kazakstan territory was physically and conceptually located midway between Central Asia and Russia.

The KaSSR shared common borders with China, the Kirgiz Soviet Socialist Republic, the Uzbek Soviet Socialist Republic, and the Russian Federated Soviet Socialist Republic (RFSSR). Its borders made up almost a fifth of the Caspian Sea shoreline. Half of the shoreline of the Aral Sea lies within Kazakstan. The KaSSR occupied a very large territory, totaling 2,717,300 square kilometers (1,049,000 square miles). By way of comparison, its area was larger than the area of the U.S. states of Arizona, California, Colorado, Nevada, New Mexico, Texas, and Utah combined. The borders of present-day Kazakstan mirror those of the former KaSSR.

Kazakstan had more nonindigenous peoples than did any of the other Central Asian SSRs. The population of Kazakstan in 1991 was roughly 40 percent ethnic Kazak and 40 percent Slavic and European. Modern Kazaks tended to be concentrated in the southern part of the republic, whereas Russians and, more generally, non-Asians tended to inhabit the northern regions. A relatively large German population, deported by

Stalin from their homeland and former German-occupied lands during and after World War II, was situated in the northeastern part of the republic.

The KaSSR's economic development was influenced by two postwar rapid-modernization programs. One was the Virgin Lands agricultural campaign initiated by Nikita Khrushchev in 1957. Although the territory was relatively dry and thus often unsuitable for many kinds of farming, the Virgin Lands campaign was predicated on the proposition that wheat-growing areas of Ukraine were geographically positioned such that they were approximately one-half wavelength of the standing waves of the upper atmosphere away from Kazakstan. This implied that under normal conditions a drought in Ukraine could be expected to coincide with heavy rainfall in Kazakstan. Between 1954 and 1961, the USSR brought 47 million additional hectares into production under the Virgin Lands campaign, almost 90 percent of which was in the KaSSR.

A second important aspect of the KaSSR's economic development was the establishment of major research and industrial facilities. From the point of view of Soviet economic planners, the northern border of the KaSSR existed only on the political map; in economic reality this border was unimportant. The highly centralized Soviet electric grid included major trunk lines servicing the eastern reaches of the republic that went through the northern part of it. Major primary commodity processing centers, such as the Karaganda coal facilities, were located in the KaSSR. Baykonur, the largest Soviet space-exploration center and launchpad, was located there. One of the USSR's most important nuclear weapons testing facilities was located at Semipalatinsk, where the first Soviet hydrogen bomb was detonated in 1953.

Kazak intellectuals and political leaders historically have downplayed the significance of ethnic differences between the Kazaks and the peoples of the Slavic north. (Central Asian leaders to the south, in contrast, tend to play up the differences between indigenous and nonindigenous peoples in their countries.) Nineteenth-century Kazak intellectuals such as Chokan Valikhanov (1835–1865) and Abai Kunanbaev (1845–1904), for instance, defended secular and pro-Western views that encouraged Kazak development, rather than ethnic exclusivism, within one Eurasian community. However, just prior to the Bolshevik revolution, many Kazak intellectuals adopted the idea of purposeful Kazak national unity or even pan-Turanianism. Their premises, ironically, were not indigenous concepts but were imported largely from European thinking toward nationalism and national unity.

In June 1916, under the pressures of World War I, Tsar Nicholas II issued an edict in an attempt to dragoon 390,000 Central Asians into the war effort. The tsar's order provoked uprisings throughout Central Asia.

Armed resistance in the northern part of Kazakstan was particularly heavy. Eventually, the uprising was put down by Russian troops. A tense standoff between rulers and ruled persisted after the revolt. When news of the Bolshevik revolution in Petrograd reached Kazakstan, it was greeted by relief on all sides.

Immediately following the collapse of the Russian empire, native intellectuals took the opportunity to establish the national party Alash Orda to unify indigenous Kazakstan. Alash Orda entered into a coalition with promonarchist White forces and fought actively for independence during the Russian civil war. But the coalition was an uneven one. White forces were not interested in Kazak independence, only the restoration of the monarchy. Toward the end of 1919, with the White offensive in disarray, the Kazak nationalists signed a truce with the Bolsheviks.

At first the Bolshevik government was puzzled by the adamant conservatism of the Kazaks regarding its plans for political and economic reorganization. But the Bolsheviks chose not to embark on major social transformation efforts because of the severity of the national economic situation and the fact that the Bolshevik government possessed the most limited capabilities. Consequently, early Bolshevik plans for land reforms in Kazakstan were shelved. The Soviet administrative system was simply superimposed over the existing local power structures, in which local elites occupied the leading positions. The new Soviet government tried persistently but unsuccessfully throughout the 1920s to encourage a Kazak transition from nomadism to settled agriculture. The Bolshevik program of collectivized agriculture was finally forcibly imposed on Kazakstan in 1928.

The forerunner to the Kazak Communist Party, the Kirkraikom of the RKP(b), was formally created in January 1920. The party apparatus split into several factions during the 1920s. Some Kazak communists argued that Bolshevism was a continuation of Kazak values, since Kazak *aul* (village) organization was essentially a simple form of communism. Others argued in favor of a more nationalistic version of Kazak communism that was implicitly less sympathetic to the Bolshevik definition of the internationalist communist future. During the 1930s, the leaders of the Kazak party were accused of nationalist deviations—"wrecking"—by attempting to rehabilitate the Alash Orda. Many were purged, many others killed.[7]

The Stalinist purge of the 1930s introduced a new generation of leaders in the KaSSR, as it did elsewhere in the USSR. Their careers had been tied to the Russian Communist Party rather than to local nationalist causes. They were more beholden to Moscow and less eager to promote the interests of local peoples. The job of such leaders in the party—for instance, N.A. Skvortsev and, between 1946 and 1954, Zh. Shaiakhmetov—was essentially to carry out Moscow's wishes. When change came to the top communist leadership with de-Stalinization in the late 1950s, change came to local leadership as well.

As a part of the Virgin Lands campaign, Khrushchev appointed the Russian P.K. Ponomarenko first secretary of the Kazak party. Ponomarenko, however, was closely associated with Khrushchev's leading rival, Georgii Malenkov, and was replaced in July 1955 with Khrushchev protégé Leonid Brezhnev. Brezhnev ruled in Alma-Ata for only a short period. The second secretary, I.D. Yakovlev, replaced Brezhnev when he was called back to Moscow in March 1956. Yakovlev was in turn replaced in December 1957 by N.I. Beliaev, whose term in the post was also short-lived: He was replaced in December 1959 by Dinmukhamed Akhmedovich Kunaev. Kunaev stayed in power as first secretary until December 1962, when he was replaced by I.Iu. Yusupov.

After Khrushchev's ouster in October 1964, Brezhnev worked out a personnel policy emphasizing political loyalty above all other criteria. Under the rubric of his "stability of cadres" policy, Brezhnev encouraged continuity and party loyalty. Local leaders that could promise unquestioned support for the existing socialist order were rewarded with virtually unlimited tenure in office. (In December 1964 Brezhnev reappointed Kunaev as party boss. He maintained the post until December 1986, when the Gorbachev government, ostensibly through its anticorruption campaign, replaced him with Gennadii V. Kolbin, an ethnic Russian. This resulted in a major public demonstration on December 17, 1986, and riots thereafter.)[8]

Regional personnel policy in the USSR typically maintained that the leader of each republic had both a management and a representational role. For this reason, CPSU leaders in Moscow tried to select republic party leaders who ethnically represented the republic and also had managerial skills. From Moscow's point of view, the first requirement was more important, because the managerial skills could always be supplied by a circuit official and a shadow administration provided by the CPSU. As a rule, first secretaries in the Central Asian republics tended to be indigenous representatives of their republic, whereas second secretaries tended to be Slavic representatives of the center.[9] Officials of the security services, the leaders of border troop units, and the commanders of the Turkestan Military District were generally Russian or perhaps Slavic.[10] But during the late 1970s, the gradual maturation of the indigenous political elites in Central Asia brought them increasingly closer to the real seat of power.[11]

The career and political style of Kunaev illustrates the compromises involved in the role of intermediary leader. Kunaev was born in Alma-Ata in 1912 and graduated from the Moscow Institute for Nonferrous Metals in 1936, later receiving a doctorate in technical sciences. He worked as a mining engineer before the war, joined the party in 1939, and as a deputy chairman of Kazakstan's Council of Ministers during wartime was active in the relocation of factories from western urban areas to Kazakstan. He became a member of the Kazak party's Central Committee in 1949 and, while still a young man, became the president of the Kazak Academy of Sciences. Kunaev became a CPSU Central Committee member in 1956 and, in 1960, became the first secretary of the Central Committee. Two years later he left this post to become chairman of the Council of Ministers of Kazakstan but returned to head the party organization in 1964. He was brought into the CPSU Politburo as a candidate member in 1966 and, in 1971, became a full member, a position he retained until 1986.

In the mid-1980s rumors, fueled by increasingly strident personal attacks on Kunaev in the Moscow central press, circulated in Kazakstan claiming that the CPSU leadership was preparing to dismiss Kunaev in favor of a more pliant appointee.[12] In an extremely controversial move, the Russians brought in Gennadii V. Kolbin, a Russian-born engineer, to replace Kunaev. Kolbin had spent five years on circuit assignment in Georgia and three in Ulyanovsk before being appointed to head the party in the KaSSR. Kolbin held the head party post until June 1989, when he was transferred back to Moscow.

In the KaSSR as in the other republics, the economic administration was directly connected to the political administration. The connection was officially known as the "combined branch-territorial principle." According to this principle, territorial interests were represented by the territorial decisionmaking units, principally the party organizations at the oblast and raion levels. Branch (or what Western economists would call "sectoral") interests were represented by the decisionmaking hierarchies of the economic production and service ministries. The Soviet regime consciously adopted the principle of combined branch-territorial management to prevent two things. On the one hand, it was designed to prevent territorial organs, for instance, the oblast party organizations, from becoming localistic fiefdoms of the oblast party chiefs. On the other hand, it was designed to prevent the economic ministries from attempting to run the entire country by *diktat* from Moscow.

The KaSSR managerial leadership was divided along the lines suggested by the branch-territorial principle. One group of leaders consisted of branch officials, the other of oblast officials. The oblast officials tended to be the link between the KaSSR's government and the localities. The oblast party head was simultaneously a representative of Alma-Ata in the local area and the local chieftain.

The principal forums for discussing the political agendas were the republics' party congresses, held every five years. The Kazak party's Congress, like all the other SSR party congresses throughout the USSR, in recent times always slightly preceded the CPSU Congress held in Moscow. For instance, the 16th Congress of the Kazak party was held in Alma-Ata just in advance of the 27th Congress of the CPSU held in February 1986 in Moscow.

While the party concentrated on the political agenda, the economic apparatus concentrated on the implementation of policy. The economic ministries were the responsible organs for carrying out policy. Particularly important officials were likely to have had some experience in both the economic and the political organs. For instance, Kazakstan's soon-to-be president, Nursultan Nazarbaev, was promoted to chairman of Kazakstan's Council of Ministers, a key position of power at the zenith of the economic ministries. Previously, Nazarbaev had been a party secretary for industry. Born in 1940, Nazarbaev spent most of his life working in the Karaganda Metallurgical Combine in Temirtau. He received his education from the combine's Higher Technical School. He moved into party work, was identified as a successful manager, and was brought to Alma-Ata as party secretary for industry in 1977. Nazarbaev became party chief in June 1989 when Gennadii Kolbin was transferred out of the republic.

Democratization throughout the republics formally began with the March 1989 elections for the USSR Congress of People's Deputies. But in a wider sense, the processes of democratization had already begun within Kazak intellectual and professional circles long before. Such celebrated Kazak writers as Olzhas Suleimenov had already begun the public discussion of a national consciousness for Kazaks and Kazakstan. Suleimenov's book *Az i Ya*, first published in 1975, caused a sensation when it appeared. Condemned by some for its heretical views of the legacies of Great Russian Chauvinism and championed by others as a defense of national cultures, it catapulted Suleimenov to political prominence. By 1983, Suleimenov was elected president of the Kazak Writers Union.

Another strong force pushing democratization in the KaSSR was the public concern over the deteriorating condition of the environment. Many of the large industrial enterprises in the northern region had been routinely dumping untreated wastes into the environment during the 1970s and 1980s virtually without regulation. An explosion in September 1990 at a factory making nuclear fuel at Ulba, in the east, led to the contamination of a large area by toxic gases. The nascent environmental movements of the 1970s and 1980s were unbridled by Gorbachev's glasnost policy in the mid-1980s. The Semipalatinsk-Nevada organization, for instance, dramatized the scope of environmental damage caused by the nearly unregulated testing of nuclear devices in the republic. In response to the public outcry, in 1991 Nazarbaev announced a moratorium on testing at the Semipalatinsk facility.

The March 1989 elections for the Congress of People's Deputies—the first freely elected deliberative assembly in the USSR since 1918—gave ninety-nine seats to the KaSSR. Of that total, seventy-three seats came from territorial and national-territorial districts; twenty-six were elected from social institutions. The majority of the candidates who were elected had run in uncontested races.

This new popularly elected parliament in Moscow passed new legislation in September 1990 that provided for open elections to the republics' legislatures and also reorganized the administrative system, shifting power from the party first secretary to the chairman of the Supreme Soviet. Nazarbaev was elected chairman of the KaSSR's parliament in February 1990. In March 1990, the republic's first free elections took place, but since many of the seats were unopposed and the preelection meetings were used to manipulate districts where races were contested, the communists won an overwhelming majority of the seats in the parliament.

The new parliament first convened in April 1990 and, in one of its first actions, elected Nazarbaev president. In October the parliament passed the Kazak declaration of sovereignty. The republic took part in the March 1991 referendum on the retention of the Soviet Union and overwhelmingly voted in favor of retaining the union. More than 88 percent of the eligible voters cast ballots, with 94 percent favoring the proposal.

"KIRGIZIA": SOVIET MOUNTAIN OUTPOST

During the early Soviet period the area popularly known for many years as "Kirgizia" existed in different forms: first as an "autonomous oblast," later as an "autonomous republic." Its last territorial form was that of a full-status "socialist republic"—the Kyrgyz Soviet Socialist Republic came into being in December 1936. In 1991, the republic's parliament changed the name to Kyrgyzstan, thereby bringing the name into closer conformity with the pronunciation in the native Kyrgyz language.

Most of the territory is situated high in the mountainous eastern reaches of Central Asia in the Tien Shan Range. Its remote location and marginal economic significance made it one of the least "political" of the Soviet republics. The KiSSR had a territory of 198,500 square kilometers (76,640 square miles), about the size of the U.S. state of Nebraska. Present-day Kyrgyzstan's borders mirror those of the KiSSR.

The territory contains rare natural beauty and is often referred to as the "Switzerland of Asia"; at 7,439 meters, Peak Pobeda is the second-highest mountain in the area that composed the former Soviet Union. It traditionally also has had a sensitive border with China—the high mountain passes had been used by nomadic peoples for centuries. Even during the

Soviet period and during the height of Sino-Soviet antagonism, these remote mountain passes remained difficult for Soviet officials to control.

The Kyrgyz have an ancient culture. The *Manas*, the 1,000-year-old Kyrgyz epic trilogy, sings of the traditions of these pastoral and nomadic people. In the nineteenth century, as pastoral and nomadic ways of life were threatened by agriculturalism, the Kyrgyz came into conflict with farmers encroaching on their lands. In 1898, during the Andijan rebellion, the Kyrgyz fought the incursion of Russian colonial settlers into the best lands of the Fergana Valley. In 1916, another local rebellion was put down by Russian troops, forcing as many as 150,000 Kyrgyz to cross the mountains into what today is China. The Kyrgyz also played a prominent role in the Basmachi revolts in the Fergana Valley during the 1920s.

At the start of modern Kyrgyz statehood in the early Soviet period, the boundaries of the KiSSR were very disadvantageously drawn. Most of the fertile land of the Fergana Valley was given to the settled and agriculturally oriented Uzbeks. This may not have seemed a great tragedy in the early 1920s, as land was still available for grazing by nomadic groups wandering down from out of the high mountain passes. But by the time the extensive irrigation projects of the Fergana Valley were developed in the 1960s and 1970s, this land was no longer available to the Kyrgyz for grazing.

The KiSSR, like other republics, was governed by a succession of officials appointed by Moscow.[13] There is some evidence, though, that the republic's remoteness gave its officials greater latitude in local action and encouraged them to be more protective of their people.[14] The Kyrgyz party's first secretary for more than three decades, Turkdakun Usubaliev, seemed to balance his obligations to his native people and to his Moscow overlords rather precariously. That he was successful from one perspective is indisputable; his tenure in office, from 1961 until 1985, was remarkably long. On the one hand, Usubaliev was criticized by his own people for being too pro-Russian, for promoting Russian culture and language, and for having a Russian view of his country's heritage.[15] On the other hand, he was criticized by Moscow for being too lenient and for permitting localism and backwardness.[16] Ostensibly this was the reason for his removal in November 1985; he was replaced by Absamat Masaliev.

Usubaliev's style says much about internal politics. Usubaliev began his career as a teacher and gradually entered party life, working his way up through a number of lesser posts in the Kyrgyz party. In 1955–1956, he served as editor of the Kyrgyz-language republic daily newspaper, *Sovettik Kirgizstan*. He published a number of pamphlets on Soviet nationality policy. After his retirement, his successor, Masaliev, unleashed a vitriolic attack at the 18th Congress of the Kyrgyz party in February 1986 on the "dictatorial manner" in which Usubaliev ruled the republic.[17]

Lenin pointing to the south in Bishkek. The statue of Lenin was ironically left standing on the main square in the capital of Kyrgyzstan—long after his statues had been removed from the main squares of all the other former Central Asian capitals. Kyrgyzstan, the most liberal and democratic of the Central Asian states, was more willing to live with its past as it set out upon a new future. Photo by Gregory Gleason, 1993.

The movement to rediscover traditional Kyrgyz values gathered momentum during the 1970s, led by the national intelligentsia in the KiSSR. Such figures as Kyrgyz writer Chingiz Aitmatov, whose remarkable works were written sometimes in Russian and sometimes in his native Kyrgyz, represented the modern, cosmopolitan Kyrgyz intellectual, a champion of national values but an opponent of ethnic exclusivism and chauvinism.[18]

As in the other republics, democratization began with the March 1989 elections for the USSR Congress of People's Deputies. The KiSSR received thirty-two seats on the basis of ethnicity and nine seats on the basis of population. Twelve additional seats were filled by public organizations. During the summer of 1989, new legislation on language and a new electoral law were passed in the republic's parliament. The new parliament was initially to be a bicameral house, but later legislation changed it to a single body of 350 people's deputies. A variety of electoral principles were discussed, but the one finally chosen was a simple population formula rather than a consociational (ethnic) formula or a formula that would give disproportionate influence to social organizations (and thus to the communists).

The republic's parliamentary elections in February 1990 were carefully managed by the party apparat through the preelection meetings and the nomination process to ensure the continuation of the communists' leading role. Over 80 percent of the deputies were party members. All of the raikom first secretaries, both of the obkom secretaries, and four leading republic party secretaries won seats in the parliament. The first meeting of the new parliament was on April 10, 1990. The parliament elected Masaliev as the new chairman of the Supreme Soviet.

Riots in the southern regions of the KiSSR and in the Fergana Valley of the UzSSR during the summer of 1990 did much to discredit party leadership and to create general fears among the populace of party retaliation and a new wave of authoritarianism. Official inquiries into the cause of the riots pointed to mismanagement by the established party elite. At the republic's Central Committee plenum in August 1990, Askar Akaev cited press accounts blaming the party leadership for the problems that led to the riots. He questioned why nothing had been done to rectify the situation. Continuing struggles with the central authorities in Moscow and internecine political conflict in the KiSSR led to the scheduling of an extraordinary session of the Kyrgyz Supreme Soviet. Members of an opposition group called Kyrgyzstan staged a public demonstration on the steps of the Supreme Soviet building on the eve of the extraordinary session in October 1990, demanding a declaration of sovereignty and the establishment of presidential rule.[19]

That parliamentary session changed the character of Kyrgyz politics permanently. As expected, the parliament voted to introduce presidential rule in the republic, but the parliament produced a surprise in rejecting the candidacy of Masaliev for president. The initial round of voting was split, with 154 votes for Masaliev, 96 for Prime Minister Apas Dzhumagoluv, and 83 for Dzhumgalbek Amanbaev, party first secretary for Issyk-kul Oblast. Masaliev did not receive a majority of votes; the required second round of voting also failed to produce a majority. This reopened the nomination process. On October 27, 1990, Askar Akaev, then president of the Kyrgyz Academy of Sciences, emerged after the fourth round of voting as the first president of Kyrgyzstan.

Pushed to the sidelines, the party organization continued to fight for power, but by the winter of 1990–1991 it had lost support in its primary power base, Moscow. Even *Pravda*, still the official newspaper of the CPSU at the time, referred to the "hard-headed conservative" communists of the Kyrgyz apparat.[20] In April 1991 a party plenum reorganized the party, replacing virtually the entire leadership. Only one party secretary retained his position after the leadership change. Dzhumgalbek Amanbaev, expressing support for the republic's new president, Akaev, was elected first secretary under the new organization.

Given that the political machine was dominated by party officials, the choice of Akaev as the first president of Kyrgyzstan was indeed exceptional. Akaev was born in 1944 in the village of Kyzyl-Bairak. He graduated from Leningrad Institute of Mechanics and Optics and worked in Leningrad before returning to the capital of Bishkek (then named Frunze to honor the Red Army military commander who captured the town). Akaev entered party work very late, becoming a member only in 1981. He was elected vice president of the Kyrgyz Academy of Sciences in 1987 and, two years later, became its president.

"Kirgizia" was always a special case. During the years of Soviet power, the central Soviet government seemed less concerned about the KiSSR than any of the other Soviet republics. It was probably not accidental that there was never a Kyrgyz leader on the CPSU Central Committee Secretariat or Politburo.

"TADZHIKISTAN": ACROSS THE CULTURAL DIVIDE

Two generalizations characterized Tojikiston (a former Soviet socialist republic then known by its Russian-language pronunciation, "Tadzhikistan") as the Soviet Union began to break up: It was the most physically beautiful and ethnically cosmopolitan of the Soviet republics; and it was the republic that experienced the most tragic withdrawal from the Soviet Union. It is a high-mountain territory on the southeastern frontier of the former Soviet Union.[21]

The Tadzhik Soviet Socialist Republic was created in roughly its present form in 1929. The TaSSR covered 143,100 square kilometers (55,251 square miles), making it larger than the U.S. state of Florida. The TaSSR had a 2,000-kilometer (1,240-mile) external border with Afghanistan and China.[22] The TaSSR also shared internal borders with the KiSSR, the UzSSR, and the TuSSR. Present-day Tojikiston's borders mirror those of the TaSSR.

Today situated at the junction of China, Afghanistan, and Pakistan (which comes close but does not quite touch the border), Tojikiston is the nexus of a number of major mountain ranges, the Tien Shan to the north, the Hindu Kush, and the Karakoram. These ranges merge into the Pamir Knot. The southeastern region, known as Badakhshan, is a high region with some of the largest glaciers in the world. The Pamir-Alay Ranges radiate westward through much of the territory. The height of the Pamir Range makes overland travel impractical during winter months, and the

range divides the republic between north and south. The north of Tojikiston is primarily composed of Leninabod Veliat (Leninabod Oblast), with
its capital in the ancient city of Hujand (Khojent). The south is further divided between east and west, with the major towns located lower in the
valleys to the west.

During the Soviet period, the TaSSR's economy was primarily agricultural, accounting for about 38 percent of the net material product and
about 43 percent of employment. Like Kyrgyzstan, Tojikiston is a mountainous country with substantial hydroelectric generating capacity. With
the exception of a large aluminum plant at Regar (Tursunzoda), near
Dushanbe, most local industry in the southern part of the republic was
low-technology cotton-cleaning mills, sewing shops, and food-processing
plants. The northern part of the republic possessed the bulk of the industrial facilities. For instance, the town of Chkalovsk near Hujand was the
administrative center for a number of metallurgical factories scattered
around northern Tojikiston and eastern Uzbekiston. The Chkalovsk facility was opened in 1946 to carry out primary processing of the uranium
that fueled the first Soviet nuclear explosion in 1949.

The fact that Iranian was the predominant language group in the TaSSR
resulted in the development of a more concrete national identity. There
were numerous other Persian-speaking areas in Central Asia, particularly
in Bukhara and Samarkand and in parts of the Fergana Valley. But the fact
that the TaSSR was situated in a remote corner of the Soviet Union no
doubt contributed to its integrity as a national unit.

The sequence of leaders in its high party positions leaves little doubt
that the TaSSR was always an unusual republic in comparative terms.[23]
There was never a Tojik leader on the CPSU Central Committee Secretariat or Politburo; Moscow chose to rely upon local cadres to run the
government and administrative apparatus. As a result of this unusual degree of autonomy the Tojiks managed to develop a political and administrative apparatus that was apparently far removed from Moscow's administrative scrutiny. The apparatus reportedly tended to develop under
its own momentum and in its own direction. Occasionally, the top CPSU
leaders in Moscow intervened to reestablish their control through personnel appointments. For example, in 1961 a major scandal, ostensibly a result of falsification of reported cotton deliveries, gave Leonid Brezhnev an
excuse to purge virtually the entire high-level TaSSR leadership and to
appoint Dzhabar Rasulov to head the party (where he remained until
1982).

Rakhman Nabiev was elevated to the post of first secretary of the party
in April 1982, vacating his position as chairman of the TaSSR's Council of
Ministers. After a little more than three years, in December 1985, he was
removed from the post and replaced by Kakhar Makhamov, the man who

had earlier taken the chairmanship of the Council of Ministers when Nabiev vacated it. Nabiev was trained as an irrigation engineer but spent most of his career in party work.

Democratization is too idealistic a concept to accurately describe the disintegration of party control and the rising currents of regionalism that swept Tojikiston following perestroika. Four aspects of the perestroika period in Tojikiston stand out: increased nationalist tensions over land and language issues; increased competition for political control of the republic, played out both within the party and between the party and other political movements; the mass exodus of Russians and other members of nontitular nationalities; and political polarization leading to gridlock in economic administration.

Beset by severe social and economic problems, the TaSSR experienced political unrest earlier than the other Central Asian republics. The regional conflicts centered on the distribution of land, particularly in the disputed border regions, and the use of the Tojik language in the republic. In February 1989, a disturbance involving 3,000 people broke out in Dushanbe. A group of local youths had beaten up a member of a Byelorussian youth group visiting with a cycling team. Other Tojik and Byelorussian youths then reportedly became involved in the fracas and drew in hundreds of people on the streets. And in June 1989, Tojiks from the Isfara area near Leninabod confronted neighboring Kyrgyz farmers in a dispute over the ownership of land. Troops were called in and violence was first averted, but the peace lasted only a month.

In July 1989, the republic's Supreme Soviet approved a new language law specifying Tojik as the official language. The law, considered discriminatory by some non-Tojik-speaking residents, provoked mass demonstrations in the capital. Party boss Makhamov responded by pledging to fight all manifestations of nationalism and chauvinism.[24] Political opposition groups formed to champion many of the nationalist causes. The group Rastokhez (Revival) was established in October 1989 in Dushanbe. Rastokhez and the other groups, formally or informally, played an important role in the debates over nationality policies.

In February 1990 a joint Tojik-Kyrgyz commission was established to conduct a formal inquiry into the border disputes between the two republics. But within days the commission was disbanded over disputes about its charge and composition.[25] Nationalist passions were further inflamed during Black February. On February 11, 1990, a major disturbance erupted in Dushanbe. Rumors regarding the government's intent to distribute apartments to Armenian refugees provoked demonstrations, which soon erupted into riots. The government declared a state of emergency, and troops fired on demonstrators in the streets. The events polarized segments of the opposition. By the following April, demonstrations were started by *fidai*-ists.[26] Competition over access to housing in the larger cities led to conflict between the local population and the Russian speakers and to conflict among the local groups themselves.

Election reform began with the Supreme Soviet's passage of a new election law on November 24, 1989. Elections were held in two stages. Local elections were held in December 1989 and were followed in February 1990 with elections to fill the 230 seats in the republic's Supreme Soviet. Although communists dominated the election process, from the campaigning and preelection meetings to the elections themselves, and won a large number of the seats (roughly 94 percent), this did not strengthen communist control of the country. The communist designates quickly fell into serious disagreement among themselves once the electoral process had changed the rules of the game.

The Islamic Revival Party (IRP) appealed for recognition late in 1990, but the parliament declared the IRP to be illegal. The IRP confronted the government directly with a demonstration that lasted for two weeks. The government lifted the ban. By mid-1991, the communist-backed government found that it was one of a number of competing political organizations—and that it was losing the competition.

"TURKMENIA": SOVIET BORDERLAND

Formed in October 1927, the Turkmen Soviet Socialist Republic (known today as Turkmenistan) occupied the southernmost position of all the Soviet republics, possessing a 1,100-kilometer (680-mile) border with Iran and a 900-kilometer (560-mile) border with Afghanistan. Larger in size than the U.S. state of California, the territory actually possesses little hospitable land, most of it being covered by the sands of the Kara Kum Desert. The valleys of the low-lying Kopet Dag Range, along the southern frontier, had been the home of ancient trading and nomadic civilizations. The oases and valleys around the Murgab and Tejen Rivers also supported ancient civilizations. The Caspian shoreline, which extends from southern Kazakhstan southward to the frontier of Iran, makes up the westernmost border of the territory. The area adjoining Iran enjoys one of the few semitropical climates in the USSR. Present-day Turkmenistan's borders mirror those of the TuSSR.

The largest city and capital, Ashgabat, lies on the 38th parallel, in line roughly with San Francisco and Cordoba, Spain. A major earthquake in 1948 destroyed much of the city and the architectural monuments. Virtually all the old buildings that remained standing afterward were then destroyed in the process of the Soviet reconstruction of the city.

Although there have always been strong proponents of Turkmen fraternal unity, such as the eighteenth-century Turkmen poet and philosopher

Magtumguli, the primary political allegiances of the Turkmen have been to the tribe, not to any nation. The traditional Turkmen political system was a tribal confederation, rather than a national republic.[27] The largest tribes are the Tekke in central Turkmenistan, the Ersari near the Afghan border, and the Yomud in the western region. The most influential tribe today is the Hoja. The influence of tribal politics has often been decried as leading to factionalism and as hindering the political development of the republic. As the former party first secretary and current president of Turkmenistan, Saparmurad Niyazov, expressed in 1989, "We will never establish complete order in the republic if we don't rid ourselves of clan and tribal disagreements once and for all."[28]

The TuSSR had a large and important natural-gas industry. Most of the gas was shipped northward through Uzbekiston, Kazakstan, and then further west for markets in Russia and Ukraine. However, during the Soviet period, the TuSSR realized little of its profits from gas sales. The exact extent to which Turkmen natural-gas resources subsidized the rest of the USSR is a matter of conjecture, but sales surely represented a subsidy provided to the central government. After the breakup of the USSR, President Niyazov referred to the prices that were paid out by the central Soviet government as preposterously low, not even representing "symbolic" prices.[29]

The bulk of the TuSSR's national income was generated by agriculture, especially cotton production. The great lifeblood of the TuSSR was the water that it siphoned off of the Amu Daria River. The TuSSR was (as Turkmenistan is today) a downstream semiarid republic with one of the most expansive irrigation projects in the world. Its agriculture was (and is) virtually totally dependent on this irrigation system.

The political leadership, like that of TaSSR and the KiSSR, played an insignificant role in Soviet politics. There was never a Turkmen leader on the CPSU Central Committee Secretariat or Politburo. Soviet nativization (or "rootification") campaigns that sought to staff the administrative systems in minority republics with native personnel were never strong or very successful in the TuSSR. This was due in part to Moscow's view that the natives were inadequately prepared to hold responsible positions and in part because the TuSSR was on a politically sensitive southern frontier. The Russian and Slavic presences in the TuSSR were dominated by the military functions of border protection.

The TuSSR was administered essentially as a distant province of the USSR. Turkmen leadership was appointed by Moscow. Party second secretaries made the key economic and political decisions. Security interests dictated by the fact the TuSSR occupied the sensitive southern frontier were paramount in Moscow's eyes. If members of the republic leadership were willing to support these interests, Moscow cared little for its internal affairs. The republic leadership thus learned to live with this political contract, and successive generations of leaders carried out its terms successfully.

The transition to the current leadership began with the appointment of Saparmurad Niyazov as the head of the party organization in December 1985. Although Niyazov spent much of his career in party work, he represented a generational change from his predecessor, Mukhamednazar Gapurov. Gapurov was trained and worked as a teacher before entering party work. Niyazov, as a member of the younger technical elite, was trained as an electrical engineer. Niyazov's power base was in Ashgabat, where he served as a secretary for industry in 1980 before becoming first secretary of the Ashgabat city organization. In 1984 Niyazov became an ideological instructor for the CPSU Central Committee. A short time later, he was appointed chairman of the Turkmen Council of Ministers and became party first secretary in December 1985.

The democratization campaign in the TuSSR was more closely controlled than in any of the other Central Asian republics. In the autumn of 1989 the Supreme Soviet amended the TuSSR's constitution and passed changes to the electoral laws. The size of the Turkmen Supreme Soviet was decreased from 330 to 175 deputies, now meeting in one chamber instead of two. The electoral districts were solely territorial, not consociational; particular seats were not reserved for the party or other organizations. Preelection meetings and the nomination process were carefully managed by the party organization.

Party members represented 78 percent of the candidates, a fact, according to the local party newspaper, that testified to the "strong faith among the general population in the Communist Party."[30] Balloting was secret and universal but not necessarily competitive. A candidate had to receive a majority of votes to be elected. There was some discussion of direct presidential election, but the legislation eventually adopted established presidential election from within parliament.

The general election was held in January 1990. Party members filled 88 percent of the seats. Native Turkmens filled roughly 75 percent of the seats; Russians and other Slavs captured no more than 20 percent. Thus the elections did not represent a significant step in democratization; they did represent a significant step in nativization. The first session of the new Supreme Soviet convened in January 1990. The session elected Niyazov chairman of the Supreme Soviet.

PARTY FIEFDOM IN UZBEKISTON

The Uzbek Soviet Socialist Republic was the most dynamic of the Central Asian republics during the Soviet period. Formed in 1924, the UzSSR shared a small portion of international frontier with Afghanistan. It also shared internal borders with the TuSSR, the TaSSR, the KaSSR, and the KiSSR. It possessed the southern half of the Aral Sea. It extended from the Pamir Mountains in the east to the Kara Kum Desert in the west. It included the Fergana Valley, one of the most productive agricultural regions in the world. The UzSSR's territory covered 488,100 square kilometers (172,742 square miles), making the UzSSR more than twice the size of the U.S. state of Kansas. Uzbekiston's present-day borders mirror those of the UzSSR.

The UzSSR was the most populous republic of Central Asia and commanded the largest economic resources as well as a position of great status. It possessed (as Uzbekiston does today) significant reserves of oil, gas, coal, uranium, and gold.[31] The eastern reaches in the mountains possess hydroelectric facilities. The central parts possess fertile river valleys. The western parts are arid. The UzSSR's industrial production was based primarily on processing of agricultural raw materials, and most industry was linked to the agricultural specialization of the economy. But the large cities also had some production facilities for aircraft and defense-related industries. Tashkent served as a regional hub of commercial and military activity for all of Soviet Central Asia. Much of the military infrastructure of the Turkestan Military District was located in Tashkent, headquartered in a building on Gorky Street referred to as the "Pentagon" of Central Asia.

The most important ethnic divide in the country was and is between the Uzbek-speaking majority and the Persian-speaking minorities in Bukhara and Samarkand. There are long-standing disputes between the Uzbeks and the Karakalpak peoples near the Aral Sea, as well as the Kyrgyz in the eastern part of the country.

The UzSSR was heavily populated with Slavic and other non–Central Asian immigrants retreating to the hinterlands during World War II. Many stayed behind after the war, and still more joined them in the 1950s and 1960s, drawn either by the area's remoteness from the political oppressiveness of the European regions or by the occupational mobility provided by the expanding economy. During the 1940s and early 1950s, the UzSSR was mostly administered by Russian-speaking settlers. But by the 1960s, with the native population growing and the economic base expanding, a gradual accretion in the authority and, eventually, the power of local political and economic managers was unmistakable.[32]

The architect of this localist impetus was party boss Sharaf Rashidov. Rashidov served as first secretary from 1961 until his death in 1983. It is quite likely that Rashidov initially served as a figurehead upon assuming that role. But by the time of his death, the party apparatus—securely in the hands of native Uzbeks—had become the real locus of power. During

Rashidov's tenure, the party organization garnered the power to win friends and punish enemies primarily through its control over party organization, but the Uzbeks also managed to gain a commanding position within the republic's economic administration.

Rashidov was the archetype of the Soviet-appointed Central Asian leader. Born just a few days before the October revolution in a remote village on the Jizaq Steppe, he attended the Jizaq Pedagogical Technicum and began working as a teacher at eighteen. He became an editor of the Uzbek language newspaper *Lenin Iuli* (The Lenin Path). He did not join the party until 1939, after the Great Purge. He entered Samarkand University, but his studies were interrupted by the war. He joined the Red Army as a political officer and was wounded in combat near the city of Porfino in 1943. He returned to Samarkand and was appointed party secretary for the Samarkand Oblast. He soon returned to editorial work as head of the staff of the daily Uzbek-language newspaper *Qizil Ozbekiston*, and a short time later he became chairman of the Uzbek Writers Union. At age thirty-three, he was selected chairman of the UzSSR Supreme Soviet Presidium, an honorary post.

Rashidov was named a candidate member of the CPSU Central Committee at the 20th Congress. After the 22nd Congress, he became a full member of the CPSU Central Committee, a post he retained until his death in October 1983.[33] In 1960, he was named deputy chairman of the Presidium of the USSR Supreme Soviet. In March 1959, he was appointed first secretary of the Uzbek party's Central Committee, another post that he held until his death. The highest post that he held was that of candidate member in the Politburo of the CPSU Central Committee (called the Presidium from 1952 until April 1966) from 1961 until his death. Rashidov was heavily decorated, twice named a Hero of Socialist Labor, and variously awarded the Order of Lenin, the Order of the October Revolution, the Red Star, and the Mark of Respect.[34]

Rashidov's power structure seemed to collapse under the pressure of the Moscow-based anticorruption campaign of the mid-1980s. Throughout the republics of Central Asia, as in the rest of the USSR, the spring of 1990 saw a great deal of discussion regarding the implications of the republics' "sovereignty." As the republic legislatures were preoccupied with formal declarations of sovereignty, many local areas decided to take the issue literally. Some local Soviets interpreted the new *arenda* reform that would legalize the private holding of land to mean that local Soviets would now be empowered to reassign property in their region's collective farms and state farms.[35]

In June 1990 a decision by local Soviet officials in the city of Osh, located in the KiSSR and adjacent to the UzSSR border, resolved to take away the land of the Lenin kolkhoz that ethnic Uzbeks had been farming for years in order to give it to ethnic Kyrgyz. The decision precipitated a riot that left 300 people dead and over 1,000 injured in June and July 1990. Red Army troops were called to the area to quell the violence. The first reports of the incident suggest that it was a spontaneous outburst of ethnic conflict. Later reports, however, stressed the premeditated character of many of the attacks and the fact that preparation had been made well in advance of much of the violence.

Even as UzSSR officials were locked in these conflicts with the center, they were responding to social pressures from below. There was an acute awareness of a "background of mounting social tension." The tragedies of earlier violence in the Caucasus, Tojikiston, and Georgia and the fear of growing chauvinistic feelings formed a backdrop to the ethnic tensions within Uzbekiston. The new "platform" of the Uzbek party, published a short time before the elections, referred darkly to the "appearance of forces" that were "speculating on the difficulties of this transitional period" in an effort to "capture power." These forces were attempting, the document warned, to "drive a wedge between the people and the party" by "intentionally aggravating the difficulties of the current situation."[36]

By late 1988, vocal opponents of the current government had emerged. A national unity movement called Birlik (Unity) was established in November 1988 and gained the attention of Western audiences.[37] Antigovernment social movements such as the Committee in Defense of the Aral Sea stridently opposed environmental mismanagement. Public dissatisfaction propelled the movement for open critical movements. The party and government fought back by narrowing the range of permitted discussion and debate. Birlik was criticized by both the Uzbek party and the UzSSR government,[38] which accused it of being manipulated by "those who would divide the country and stir up ethnic antagonisms."[39] One government-sponsored social organization, for instance, asserted that the leaders of Birlik "have appointed themselves representatives of the people and try to discredit everything positive that is done in Uzbekiston. They appeal to the people to nominate the leaders of Birlik to the post of Peoples' Deputy. Their actions cannot be described as anything other than the lust for power."[40]

In response to the restive atmosphere, public officials responded with decrees. In February 1990 the UzSSR Supreme Soviet Presidium issued an order setting out penalties for fomenting public disorder.[41] The order referred to "provocational rumors which were inciting the public to panic." The order set a fine of 200 to 500 rubles or two months of hard labor for anyone circulating material calling for pogroms or the use of violence, threatening the public order, or spreading panic among the population.[42]

In this political climate, the party apparat sought to manage the election to ensure that it would not lose control of the reins of power. The last hurried session of the old UzSSR Supreme Soviet, meeting for only two days, passed a series of amendments and decrees that paralleled the changes in the USSR electoral system that were adopted in December 1988. New draft election laws, one for republic elections and one for local elections, were introduced and then, following a brief discussion, were spirited through the UzSSR Supreme Soviet in October 1989. A new language law naming Uzbek as the official language was passed.[43] The last decrees issued by the departing parliament were the resolutions establishing the timing of the republic and local elections.[44] Both the republic and local elections were set for the same day, February 18, 1990.

With the exception of the actual vote, the most important aspect of the elections was the nomination process. (The case could be made that the nomination process was actually *more* important than the actual vote since the outcomes could easily be determined in advance through its careful orchestration.) Individuals had the right to nominate from within recognized organizations or institutions. Some groups, the so-called "informals" (*neformaly*), for instance, were excluded.

The UzSSR Central Electoral Commission formally met for the first time in October 1989.[45] It was clear that a good deal of work had already been done because the draft election law had been drawn up and circulated, and the new law was passed by the time the commission met. The commission had already solicited proposals from the Karakalpak Autonomous Soviet Socialist Republic (KKASSR) Supreme Soviet Presidium, the *oblispolkoms*, and the Tashkent *gorispolkom* for the formation of the electoral districts. The commission announced the creation of 500 districts in Uzbekiston.[46]

Voters received three ballots, one for republic elections, one for oblast elections, and one for raion elections. Each voter was required to mark off the names of the candidates he or she did not want, leaving not more than one name unmarked. The ballots were printed in dual Russian-Uzbek–language versions. There were 86,635 candidates registered for the posts in the city, village, raion, and oblast parliaments. Most of the republic's attention, however, was devoted to the competition for the UzSSR deputy positions. In the general election, voter turnout was high, especially in the rural areas.[47] A total of 9,385,740 people, or 93.5 percent of eligible voters, cast ballots.[48]

Accusations of incompetence and mismanagement among party personnel are hardly unprecedented, especially in Uzbekiston. Willful and overt insubordination among lower party officials is, however, unusual. Toward the conclusion of his remarks to a Central Committee Plenum held late in 1989, about three months before the February 1990 elections, Islam Karimov accused the party leaders in Andijan Oblast of manipulating public discontent for their own purposes.[49] He noted that there were

Protecting Lenin. Uzbekiston's militia in riot gear cordon off the statue of Lenin in April 1990. Photo by Anvar Ilyasov.

many cases of posters of a "nationalistic and anti-Soviet" character that had been posted in public places. Meetings were being held at which open appeals were being made for the advancement of nationalist aims. The local party officials, Karimov charged, were tolerating these developments. He implied they were encouraging them. One can also read Karimov's allegations as suggesting that some of the lower party officials were themselves acting as agents provocateurs in these events.

In the UzSSR, as in the other southern Central Asian republics, the process of de-Russification started with the rise of nationalist disturbances. Russian-speaking technical specialists were reported to be fleeing the minority nationality regions in Central Asia, for fear of anti-Russian ethnic pogroms, and leaving inadequately trained personnel in many key positions. For instance, it was reported that the drain of specialists from the Syrdar thermal station, the largest in the republic, had left the two 300,000-kilowatt generators without adequate supervisory personnel. Energy output was reduced as a result.[50]

In the view of Moscow, the UzSSR was the most significant political entity in Central Asia. Its political figures were customarily accorded a position of secondary importance in Moscow, but at least they were always included in discussions. Uzbek party secretary Rashidov even managed to hold a seat on the CPSU Central Committee Politburo for eleven years.

CENTRAL ASIA AND THE DEMISE OF THE USSR

In Russian history, revolutions were often sparked by attempts at reform, and the collapse of the USSR is evidence of that proposition. The demise of the USSR began with Gorbachev's perestroika, an attempt to rehabilitate the USSR. In an effort to form political constituencies for his reform, Gorbachev announced major political changes at the 19th Conference of the CPSU in June and July 1988. But the accelerating pace of perestroika afterward only encouraged supporters of independence movements in the Baltic states to press for concessions from Moscow.

In November 1988 the legislature of the Estonian republic adopted changes to the republic's constitution, reserving the right to veto all-union legislation passed in Moscow. The new legislation declared the land, natural resources, industrial plant, banks, and general capital located within Estonian territory to be property belonging solely to the Estonian republic.[51] The executive chamber of the USSR legislature in Moscow quickly acted to invalidate the "Estonian Clause."[52] But the transition had already begun.

The decentralization process gathered speed in 1989. Elections for the USSR Congress of People's Deputies were held in March 1989. Despite the fact that the Communist Party had done everything possible to manipulate the returns in its favor, some of the communist functionaries were rejected. Elections to the republic legislatures were held on different dates, beginning late in 1989 and staggered throughout 1990. As the new, popularly elected republic legislatures convened, many of the new representatives (deputies) openly began to challenge Moscow's historical dominance.

Republic legislatures vied with the USSR legislature on a series of issues ranging from language, migration, and economic sovereignty to citizenship and, in a few cases, to the subject of political independence. The republic legislatures began to discuss, pass, and—in very rare cases— even implement new laws, not all of which were consistent with the all-union laws or even with each other. Soviet citizens, many of whom clearly were in a state of delighted amazement at these developments, began to speak of a "war of laws."

Central officials offered a succession of plans designed to placate localist sentiment while keeping the old structure essentially intact. To dampen the growing nationalist fervor, the Party stepped forward with a much-touted "Nationality Platform" in September 1989.[53] To mollify local complaints that the economy was excessively centralized, the government offered a plan called the General Principles for Restructuring the Management of the Economy and Social Sphere in the Union Republics.[54] To head off separatist attempts, the government offered the Law on the Order of Questions Connected to the Secession of a Union Republic from the USSR.[55] The Law on the General Principles of Local Self-government and Local Economy in the USSR was passed in April 1990.[56] At the same time, the Law on the Basic Economic Relations of the Union SSR, Union Republics, and Autonomous Republics was passed.[57] But these laws had virtually no discernible effect on the mounting economic deterioration. If anything, the laws provoked public resentment as people began to see them as little more than bureaucratic maneuvering in the face of an impending crisis.

Toward the end of 1989, the process of decentralization began to take on the character of devolution. A key event in this transition was the split in Lithuania's party in 1989. The split precipitated that party's formal withdrawal from the CPSU in December 1989, symbolizing the end of Party hegemony in the USSR. Secessionist movements surged ahead following the decision of Lithuania's party to secede. Gorbachev adopted the view that the union must be further decentralized, but he was unwilling to recognize that the Lithuanians would no longer be satisfied with Soviet-style "autonomy" and were demanding full political independence.

Under the circumstances, Gorbachev reversed his earlier opposition to a new Union Treaty, viewing it instead as a means of "rescuing" the Soviet state. He announced at the February 1990 CPSU Central Committee Plenum that it had become necessary to negotiate a new Union Treaty.[58] At the same time, Gorbachev countered Lithuania's attempt to "go it alone," instituting an economic blockade. But following the election of Boris Yeltsin to the post of president of the Russian republic—and Yeltsin's suggestion that he was prepared to negotiate independently with the Lithuanians—Gorbachev was forced to retreat on the blockade.

In the spring of 1990 a committee was established to draft the new Union Treaty.[59] Anticipating a renegotiation of the basic contract, the republics quickly formulated their negotiating positions through declarations of sovereignty. The results were even more dramatic than the "war of laws." By the end of 1990, each of the republics had passed legislation on sovereignty. The legal meaning of the declarations was none too clear. Government officials, intent on propping up the central government, referred mockingly to a "parade of sovereignties." Provisions of the declarations varied widely. For instance, the June 1990 resolution of the Russian republic allowed the central government to retain control of defense, state security, aviation, communication, transportation, energy, and space; other areas of policy belonged to the republic. In contrast, the July 1990 Ukrainian declaration went further, asserting the right to establish an independent militia and security force.

To counter the growing movement for republics' rights, Gorbachev attempted to redefine the relationship between the all-union government and the republic-level governments. A new version of the Union Treaty was proposed to combine self-sufficiency, independence, and sovereignty of the republics with an effective center. "A Strong Union means a Strong Center and Strong Republics," said the slogan. Gorbachev maintained that the union should be held together by mutually advantageous economic relations in an all-union market. He emphasized the importance of maintaining some key all-union economic institutions, in particular the concept of a "single economic field."[60]

This draft of the Union Treaty was approved by the USSR Supreme Soviet (the upper house) in December 1990 and was introduced in the Congress of People's Deputies (the lower house) later that month. But many deputies were not satisfied with the provisions of the treaty. Latvia's delegation refused to attend the Congress. Estonia's delegation attended but marched out in protest on the first day. Gorbachev retreated from his reform agenda in response, swinging away from the political positions of the early perestroika supporters such as Alexander Yakovlev and Eduard Shevardnadze in favor of party conservatives.[61]

Facing this opposition to his proposed Union Treaty, Gorbachev attempted to undercut his opponents by calling for a popular referendum on the concept of the union. At the same time, he began promoting yet another revised version of the Union Treaty, one that he claimed would give even more authority to the republics. The referendum was held on March 17, 1991.[62] The question put to voters was, "Do you consider necessary the preservation of the Union of Soviet Socialist Republics as a renewed federation of equal sovereign republics, in which the rights and freedoms of an individual of any nationality will be fully guaranteed?" Several republics (Lithuania, Latvia, Estonia, Georgia, Armenia, and Moldova) boycotted the vote. According to the official results, voter turnout was 80 percent, with 76.4 percent voting yes and 21.7 percent voting no. In Moscow only slightly more than 50 percent favored the union, and in Leningrad (now St. Petersburg) voters also split evenly. A majority of voters in such large cities as Kiev and Sverdlovsk voted against the preservation of the union.

By the spring of 1991, observers began to speak openly not only of devolution, but of "disintegration." In June 1991, Boris Yeltsin was elected president of the RFSSR by a strong majority. The election greatly strengthened his hand in negotiations with Gorbachev, who, although technically the Soviet president, had been elected only by the Congress of People's

Deputies, a body whose numbers had been carefully stacked in 1989 with Party officials. By mid-August 1991, Gorbachev had produced four versions of the Union Treaty, each one progressively giving greater powers to the republics.[63] But Party conservatives were aware that a new Union Treaty, if adopted and implemented, would represent the end of the old Soviet Union. In a desperate last-minute effort to preserve the old structure, an eight-man committee of the country's stalwart Party conservatives announced the creation of an "emergency committee." While Gorbachev was in the Crimea on summer vacation, the emergency committee declared that it had taken control of the government to save the country. Most Western governments quickly denounced the emergency committee. In the ensuing fray, Boris Yeltsin emerged as a courageous defender of democracy. Gorbachev returned from his vacation to resume his position as president of the USSR. The coup collapsed.

The leaders of the Central Asian states responded to the coup very differently. Nazarbaev in Kazakstan was initially cautious; he offered neither support nor condemnation. On August 20, however, he issued a statement denouncing the emergency committee as illegal. As the coup collapsed, he resigned from the Politburo and the CPSU Central Committee. Akaev in Kyrgyzstan was among the first to openly denounce the coup, claiming it to be illegal. Tojikiston's Nabiev, Uzbekiston's Karimov, and Turkmenistan's Niyazov all avoided explicit commitment, although Karimov appeared to favor the coup, withdrawing his support only as the union visibly collapsed.[64]

The parliamentary deputies returned to Moscow after the coup to find themselves in a new country. The August events had completely transformed the political landscape in the USSR. Yeltsin immediately pressed for greater sovereignty for Russia. In October negotiations on the formal provision of an "economic association" began on neutral territory in Alma-Ata, Kazakstan, at the invitation of Nazarbaev. The Treaty of Economic Association was signed by eight republics as a result of the meeting, but Ukraine's leader, Leonid Kravchuk, refused to sign, saying that Ukraine's consent must await the outcome of the December 1991 elections in Ukraine.

In fact, it was the outcome of those elections in Ukraine that tipped the scales in favor of the republics. Many had argued that Ukraine, with its substantial Russian and Russian-speaking population, would not break away from Russia without splitting internally. The election results showed differently. More than 84 percent of registered Ukrainian voters turned out to vote on December 1, 1991. In a field of five contenders, Kravchuk, a proponent of an independent Ukraine, captured more than 61 percent of the vote for the presidency.[65] The elections seemed to demonstrate that the winning coalition was outside the unified Soviet Union that Gorbachev supported.

Drawing the lesson from the vote in Ukraine, the leaders of the three large Slavic republics, Leonid Kravchuk from Ukraine, Stanislav Shushkevich from Belarus, and Boris Yeltsin from Russia, took a bold step. After a discreetly arranged meeting in the historic border town of Brest, they gathered in the Belarus capital of Minsk on December 8, 1991, to sign a resolution asserting that a new formation, the Commonwealth of Independent States (CIS), would serve as successor to the USSR. The document declared that the "Soviet Union henceforth ceases to exist."[66]

The Minsk Declaration took the Central Asian presidents by complete surprise. Whether by accident or design, it described a new political compact that was exclusively Slavic. Kazakstan's Nazarbaev was the only one of the Central Asian leaders who had been invited to attend the Minsk meeting, but the invitation came late and apparently only as an afterthought. The Minsk Declaration defined a moment of decision for Central Asia.

In an interview in *Nezavisimaia Gazeta* in May 1992, Nazarbaev later recounted the events leading up to the dissolution of the empire. He claimed that Yeltsin had phoned him to invite Kazakstan to join in the new Commonwealth, but he declined. Nazarbaev noted that after the Minsk meeting there was talk of a broader, Slavic-based political community. This would imply that the Muslims of Central Asia should now also form a political community. As Nazarbaev recalled, "We were very close to a dangerous confrontation between the two at that time. We had a draft on the establishment of an Asiatic confederation. . . . Then, at Saparmurad Niyazov's invitation, we met in Ashgabat to discuss the situation."[67]

The five Central Asian leaders met in Ashgabat on December 13, 1991. The outcome of that discussion was to opt for continued participation in a political community that was geographically defined by the political space of the former USSR. The resulting public announcement claimed that the Central Asian presidents were in fundamental agreement with the concept of the Commonwealth but were taken by surprise by the Minsk Declaration.

The Central Asian leaders asked that they be brought into the Commonwealth, but only on the condition that they be included as founding members. The three Slavic leaders agreed to this condition. Arrangements were hurriedly made for yet another summit. On December 21, 1991, the representatives of eleven of the former republics gathered in Alma-Ata to sign a new agreement to form a broader-based Commonwealth. The meeting produced a new agreement—not a treaty—that described a larger Commonwealth of Independent States, listing eleven states as original cosignatories.

The Alma-Ata Declaration was rapidly acknowledged by the international community. It sealed the fate of the Soviet Union. Thus without a referendum, without a popular mandate, without parliamentary advice or consent, the Soviet state ceased to exist. USSR President Mikhail Gorbachev, simply acknowledging the inevitable, resigned on December 25, 1991. The Soviet flag ceased to fly over the Kremlin. It ceased to fly over the USSR. It ceased to fly over Central Asia.

NOTES

1. James Critchlow is right in pointing out that the very idea of nationalism is foreign to Central Asian societies in noting that nationality "was a European concept imported to the territory by outsiders operating in the framework of the new Soviet regime." James Critchlow, *Nationalism in Uzbekistan* (Boulder: Westview Press, 1991), p. 4.

2. For many years Russian-language sources delicately avoided any discussion of how the boundaries of the Central Asian states were actually determined. There were no published discussions of the composition of the committees, how many people were consulted, whether public meetings were held, whether tsarist-era anthropological studies were used, and so on.

3. Although the Turkestan Autonomous Soviet Republic was not at first referred to as a "socialist republic," the abbreviation customarily used in Soviet sources was Turkestan ASSR.

4. G.A. Ian Rudzutak, *Turkan* (rpt. Moscow: Academy of Sciences, 1963), p. 62.

5. Alexandre Bennigsen and S. Enders Wimbush, *Muslims of the Soviet Empire* (Bloomington: Indiana University Press, 1986), p. 33.

6. Tsentral'naia partiinaia arkhiva IML pri TsK KPSS, F. 17, op. B/n, ed. khr. 394, l. 26. Cited in A. Agzamkhodzhaev and Sh. Urazaev, "Natsional'no-gosudarstvennomu razmezhevaniiu respublik Sovetskoi Srednei Azii—60 let," *Sovetskoe gosudarstvo i pravo* no. 10 (1984): 29, n. 11.

7. A description of the scope of the Kazak purge may be found in Martha Brill Olcott, *The Kazakhs* (Stanford: Hoover Institution Press, 1987), pp. 218–219.

8. Kunaev's account of the events of December 1986 may be found in A.D. Kunaev, *O moem vremeni* (Alma-Ata: RGZhI, 1992), pp. 267–283.

9. For empirical analysis of this point, see in particular Grey Hodnett, *Leadership in the Soviet National Republics: A Quantitative Study of Recruitment Policy* (Oakville, Ontario: Mosaic Press, 1978).

10. The Muslim republics seem to have been singled out for special treatment in the security area. Whereas in the non-Muslim borderland republics a member of the titular nationality usually occupied the post of KGB chairman, in the Central Asian republics this post usually went to a member of European nationality. See Timur Kocaoglu, "The Chairmanships of the State Security Committees of the Soviet Muslim Republics," *RFE/RL Radio Liberty Research* RL 34/84 (19 January 1984).

11. Bess Brown found that in each of the Central Asian republics the proportion of Muslims to Slavs in government positions was increasing during the period 1970–1980. Bess Brown, "The National Composition of the Governments of the Central Asian Republics," *RFE-RL Radio Liberty Research Bulletin* RL 313/82 (4 August 1982).

12. Bess Brown, "Kunaev Remains Largely Unreconstructed," *RFE/RL Radio Liberty Research* RL 348/86 (14 September 1986).

13. The list of surnames of the top Kyrgyz Communist Party officials is illustrative: M.D. Kamenskii (1924–1925); N.A. Uziukov (1925–1927); V.P. Shubrikov (1927–1929); M.M. Kulkov (1929–1930); A.O. Shakhrai (1930–1933); M.L. Belotskii (1933–1937); M.K. Amosov (1937–1938); A.V. Vagov (1938–1945); N.S. Bogoliubov (1945–1950); I.R. Razzakov (1950–1961); T. Usubaliev (1961–1985); A.M. Masaliev (1985–1990); Dzhumgalbek Amanbaev (1990–1991).

14. One observation that has been made along these lines is that Sultan Ibraimov, the Kirgiz Council of Ministers chairman in the late 1970s, was murdered by his opponents in December 1980 for his outspoken defense of Kyrgyz national advancement. See Bess Brown, "Deceased Kirgiz Premier Receives Belated Honors," *RFE/RL Radio Liberty Research* RL 223/86 (6 June 1986).

15. Usubaliev frequently criticized the more nationalist-minded members of the local intelligentsia. He took a personal hand in offering historians guidance on the correct interpretation of Kyrgyz history. See Ann Sheehy, "Usubaliev Scores Kirghiz Historians and Cultural Figures for Nationalistic Errors," *RFE/FL Radio Liberty Research* RL/216/83 (1 June 1983).

16. *Pravda* (26 February 1986).

17. Bess Brown, "Eighteenth Congress of the Communist Party of Kirgizia: An Attack on the Past," *RFE/RL Radio Liberty Research* RL 88/86 (20 February 1986).

18. One of Aitmatov's best-known works, *The Day Lasts More Than a Hundred Years*, recounted the legend of the Juanjuan people, a nomadic tribe that made *mankurts*, mindless slaves, out of its captives by placing caps made of the wet skin of camel udders on the victim's heads. As the caps dried and constricted, the victims lost their memories and thus their national identity. The moral of the tale is that "remembrance of the past is key to the future."

19. See Bess Brown, "Liberalization Reaches Kirgizia: Profile of the New President," *Report on the USSR* 2, no. 48 (30 November 1990): 17–20.

20. Yu. Razguliaev, "V chem skazyvaetsia zloba dnia," *Pravda* (5 July 1991): 2.

21. In Russian-language sources the republic's name was spelled "Tadzhikistan," a consequence of the fact that Russian orthography has no letter *j*.

22. In 1985, a treaty on the state border was signed by Afghanistan and Tojikiston.

23. First party secretaries of the Tojik party included: Bobodzhan Gafurov (1946–1956); Tursunbai Uldzhabaev (1956–1961); Dzhabar Rasulov (1961–1982); Rakhman Nabiev (1980–1982); Kakhar Makhamov (1982–1985); Rakhman Nabiev (1985–1991).

24. "O prakticheskikh merakh po realizatsii v respublike reshenii sentiabr'skogo (1989) plenuma TsK KPSS," *Kommunist Tadzhikistana* no. 2 (February 1990): 19.

25. *Kommunist Tadzhikistana* (11 February 1990): 1.

26. The word *fidai* means someone who is willing to give their life for their views.

SOVIET SOCIALIST REPUBLICS OF CENTRAL ASIA ■ 79

27. Ruth I. Meserve, "A Description of the Positions of Turkmen Tribal Leaders According to 19th Century Western Travellers," in Barbara Kellner-Heinkele, ed., *The Concept of Sovereignty in the Altaic World* (Wiesbaden, Germany: Harrossowitz Verlag, 1993), pp. 139–147.

28. *Turkmenskaia iskra* (2 December 1989), as quoted in Annette Bohr, "Turkmenistan Under Perestroika: An Overview," *Report on the USSR* 2, no. 12 (23 March 1990): 21.

29. Vitalii Portnikov, "Ritm reform my dolzhny opredeliat' sami," *Nezavisimaia gazeta* (20 October 1992): 2.

30. *Turkmenskaia iskra* (17 December 1989).

31. The major uranium and gold deposits are located in the middle section of the republic, close to the town of Zarafshan.

32. For an analysis of the early generations of Soviet leadership in the UzSSR, see Donald S. Carlisle, "The Uzbek Power Elite: Politburo and Secretariat (1938–1983)," *Central Asian Survey* 5, nos. 3/4 (1986): 91–132; Michael Rywkin, "Power and Ethnicity: Regional and District Party Staffing in Uzbekistan (1983/1984)," *Central Asian Survey* 4, no. 1 (1985): 3–40.

33. Rashidov's predecessor as first secretary, Nuritdin Mukhitdinov, was also a candidate member of the Politburo (then called Presidium) from 1956 until 1957. This prompted some expectations that there was an "Uzbek seat" on the Politburo that Rashidov merely filled.

34. See Gregory Gleason, "Sharaf Rashidov and the Dilemmas of National Leadership," *Central Asian Survey* 5, nos. 3/4 (1986): 133–160.

35. *Pravda Vostoka* (17 March 1990): 1.

36. "Osnovnye napravleniia natsional'nogo, sotsial'no-ekonomicheskogo i dukhovnogo razvitie Uzbekskoi SSR i mestnyi sovety: Platforma kompartii Uzbekistana k vyboram narodnykh deputatov uzbekskoi SSR i v mestnye sovety," *Kommunist Uzbekistana* no. 1 (1990): 39.

37. The full name of Birlik was Unity Movement for the Preservation of Uzbekiston's Natural, Material, and Spiritual Riches. At the first public demonstration in March 1989, the group called for a reduction in the cotton target and an end to cotton monoculture in the UzSSR. For a more full description of the group, see Bess Brown, "The Role of Public Groups in Perestroika in Central Asia," *Report on the USSR* (26 January 1990): 20–25.

38. For example, *Pravda Vostoka* printed an explanation why the Tashkent *gorispolkom* refused to issue a permit for a Birlik-sponsored public meeting to be held on 18 March 1990. The *gorispolkom* turned down the permit at the request of many workers who opposed it. *Pravda Vostoka* (16 March 1990): 4.

39. Unsigned commentary, "K chemu prizyvaiut lidery `Birlika?' *Pravda Vostoka* (10 March 1990): 1.

40. Ibid.

41. "Ob usilenii otvetstsvennosti za deistviia, napravelnnye protiv obshchestvennogo proiadka i bezobpasnosti grazhdan," *Pravda Vostoka* (11 February 1990): 1.

42. "Ob uporiadochenii organizatsii i provedeniia sobranii, mitingov, ulichnykh shestvii i demonstratsii," *Pravda Vostoka* (22 February 1990): 1.

43. Both laws were passed on 20 October 1989. The text of the laws was published in *Pravda Vostoka* on 24 and 25 October 1989. See "O vyborakh narodnykh deputatov Uzbekskoi SSR," *Pravda Vostoka* (24 October 1989), and "O vyborakh deputatov mestnykh sovetov narodnykh deputatov Uzbekskoi SSR," *Pravda Vostoka* (25 October 1989).

44. These decrees were passed on 19 and 20 October 1989, respectively. See *Pravda Vostoka* (21 October 1989): 1.

45. *Pravda Vostoka* (29 October 1989): 1.

46. The descriptions of the electoral districts were published in *Pravda Vostoka* and other local newspapers on 30 and 31 October and 1 November 1989.

47. Some questions were raised with respect to high voter turnout. One newspaper reporter observed that the reported turnouts of over 98 percent in some areas were surely fictitious. As he put it in terms that Uzbek citizens could easily appreciate, "Even if they sold meat and oranges at the voting booths you couldn't get that kind of turnout." I. Khisamov, "My vybiraem, nas vybiraiut," *Pravda Vostoka* (3 March 1990): 2.

48. This is a high voter turnout by cross-national comparative standards. In comparison with previous Soviet elections, however, it is low. The turnout for the 1987 local elections in the UzSSR, for instance, was 99.84 percent. See *Pravda Vostoka* (27 June 1987): 1.

49. "Itogi sentiabr'skogo (1989 g.) plenuma TsK KPSS i zadachi partiinykh organizatsii respubliki," *Kommunist Uzbekistana* no. 1 (1990): 35.

50. Timur Pulatov, "Dogonim i peregonim Angolu!" *Moskovskie novosti* no. 41 (14 October 1990): 7.

51. See *Sovetskaia Estonia* (17, 18, and 19 November 1988).

52. *Pravda* (18 November 1988).

53. "Natsional'naia politika partii v sovremennykh usloviiakh (Platforma KPSS)," *Pravda* (24 September 1989).

54. A draft version of this document, prepared by the USSR Supreme Soviet Presidium, was published in all the Soviet central newspapers on March 14, 1989. It was announced that a draft law on the subject would follow.

55. See "O poriadke resheniia voprosov, sviazannykh s vykhodom soiuznoi respubliki iz SSSR," *Izvestiia* (6 April 1990): 1.

56. See "Ob obshchikh nachalakh mestnogo samoupravleniia i mestnogo khoziaistva v SSSR," *Izvestiia* (14 April 1990): 1.

57. See "Ob osnovakh ekonomicheskikh otnoshenii Union SSR, soiuznykh i avtonomnykh respublik," *Pravda* (17 April 1990): 1.

58. *Pravda* (6 February 1990): 4.

59. Although provisions of the treaty had been under public discussion for months, the final draft form of the new treaty was not published until late in 1991. For a text, see *Izvestiia* (24 November 1990): 1.

60. These remarks were made by Gorbachev at the televised press conference of 31 August 1990 on Moscow TV channel 1. Transcribed in "USSR Today: Soviet Media News and Features Digest," compiled by Radio Liberty Monitoring, 706.01 (31 August 1990).

61. Shevardnadze indeed resigned as foreign minister in December 1990, warning of an impending government takeover by party hard-liners.

62. For materials relating to the referendum, see Staff of the Commission on Security and Cooperation in Europe, *Referendum in the Soviet Union: A Compendium of Reports on the March 17, 1991 Referendum on the Future of the U.S.S.R.* (Washington, D.C.: April 1991).

63. Texts of the documents may be found in *Izvestiia* (24 November 1990; 9 March 1991; 27 June 1991; and 15 August 1991).

64. Karimov would later jail or deny press credentials to journalists who observed this in print.

65. The closest contender, Vyacheslav Chornovil, won about 23 percent of the vote.

66. The text of the Minsk Declaration was reprinted in the *New York Times* (9 December 1991): A4.

67. Interview with Aleksandr Gagua, "Idei i liudi," *Nezavisimaia gazeta* (6 May 1992): 5.

· FOUR ·

Central Asian States Emergent

As the Soviet Union receded into history during the fateful autumn and early winter of 1991, Central Asian leaders lost the luxury of indecision. They would have to act. Should the Central Asian states define a new future for themselves as independent states? Should they unite into a Greater Turkestan? Should they merge with their ethnic brethren to the south and become part of the Middle East? At the invitation of Turkmenistan's Saparmurad Niyazov, Central Asian leaders met in the city of Ashgabat in December 1991 to discuss their destinies. The outcome was a compromise: They would maintain their identities as separate states, maintain close relations with the peoples to the north, and seek to redefine their countries as members of the international community. They voted to enlarge the Commonwealth of Independent States, but only as an umbrella organization and not as a "government" or "supranational organization."

The Central Asian leaders made hasty arrangements with Russia's Boris Yeltsin, Ukraine's Leonid Kravchuk, and Belarus's Stanislav Shushkevich—the Slavic leaders—to meet in Alma-Ata. In a very important sense, the formation of the CIS was a product of the intentions of the Central Asian leaders to remain linked to the countries to the north.

In each of the Central Asian states old Soviet symbols were abandoned in favor of new ones. Even the names of the countries were changed: Kazakhstan became Kazakstan, replacing the *kh* with a *k*; Kirgizia became Kyrgyzstan; Tadzhikistan became Tojikiston; Turkmenia became Turkmenistan; and Uzbekistan became Uzbekiston.[1]

From common starting points within the old Soviet administrative structures, the newly independent countries of Central Asia set out on very different paths. Styles of leadership, forms of administration, economic development strategies, steps toward liberalization, and the roles of ethnic minorities evolved differently in the five countries. In some cases, the unique features of individual states made a crucial difference. For instance, the impact of Kazakstan's status as a nuclear power and the role of the Islamic opposition in Tojikiston turned out to be much more important than the preexisting commonalities among the countries.

ASIAN LIBERALISM IN KAZAKSTAN

Kazakstan was the last of the Central Asian republics to declare political independence. By the time Kazakstan's Declaration of Independence was adopted on December 16, 1991, the USSR had already officially been brought to an end by the Minsk Declaration (see Chapter 3). Kazakstan's unique position among the Central Asian countries made it a particularly important player in the disintegration of the USSR and the formation of the CIS. Nearly 40 percent of the population of Kazakstan consisted of ethnic Russians. Many educated Kazaks were more fluent in Russian than in their native Kazak, making Kazakstan's intellectual elite more fully Russianized than the elites of the other Central Asian states. Kazakstan was also more closely integrated into the Soviet physical infrastructures of communication, energy, and transportation than were the other Central Asian states. Indeed, Kazakstan was thought of by many Central Asians as the northern borderland periphery of Central Asia rather than the core. In times past, it was conventional in all Russian publications to refer to "Central Asia and Kazakstan," symbolically placing Kazakstan somewhere between Central Asia and Russia.

Today Kazakstan's economy, like the economies of all the Central Asian states, is structured around the production of raw materials and primary commodities. Kazakstan is a major wheat supplier as well as a major oil and coal supplier. In 1991, Kazakstan produced an average of 532,000 barrels of crude oil per day and a total of 130 million metric tons of coal. To a greater degree than any of the other Central Asian states, Kazakstan is equipped with major industrial facilities. But during the Soviet period Kazakstan's industry was structured to rely on subsidized petroleum, coal, and natural gas. Therefore, large sections of northern Kazakstan remain linked to the former Soviet Union's centralized energy grid, making Kazakstan's northern factories and cities dependent upon Russian energy supplies.

The president of Kazakstan, Nursultan Nazarbaev, was a man of great political influence and prestige in the old USSR, and he was the only ethnic minority figure to be seriously considered as a successor to Mikhail Gorbachev. According to popularity polls, ethnic Russians approved of Nazarbaev's politics even more than did ethnic Kazaks. As one notable

Table 4.1 Presidents of the Republics of Central Asia

Country	President	Elected by Parliament	Popularly Elected
Kazakstan	Nursultan Nazarbaev	Apr. 24, 1990	Dec. 2, 1991
Kyrgyzstan	Askar Akaev	Oct. 27, 1990	Oct. 12, 1991
Tojikiston	Rakhman Nabiev	Nov. 24, 1991	n/a
	Akbarsho Iskandarov	Sept. 7, 1992	n/a
	Emomli Rakhmonov	Nov. 19, 1992	Nov. 6, 1994
Turkmenistan	Saparmurad Niyazov	Oct. 27, 1991	June 21, 1992
Uzbekiston	Islam Karimov	May 24, 1990	Dec. 29, 1991

political commentator put it, intending a compliment, Nazarbaev is "an Asian who thinks like a European."[2] Nazarbaev was careful to avoid alienating the large Russian constituency in Kazakstan. In the presidential election of December 1991, Nazarbaev won 98 percent of the vote, an indication that he had support among the native population as well as among the Russian-speaking population.[3]

Nazarbaev's immediate response to the Soviet breakup was cautious. Two days after the outcome of the August 1991 Moscow coup attempt was clear, Nazarbaev denounced the coup as illegal and announced his support for further liberalization. Given Nazarbaev's stature as all-union figure, he was a man whose judgments were closely watched during the transition. This may have made Nazarbaev cautious in responding to the uncertainties involved in the breakup. The fact that Kazakstan alone among the Central Asian republics possessed nuclear weapons also played a part.

After the breakup, Nazarbaev emerged as a clear-thinking, businesslike cosmopolitan with an interest in economic efficiency and good government. He portrayed himself as someone who "knew industry from the inside" and was known among managers as "someone who could listen as well as talk." He managed to be a representative of Kazak traditions while not appearing doctrinaire or a champion of exclusivist nationalist causes.

However noble a leader's intentions, theory and practice in government often are two different things. Although on the one hand there are formal constitutions, on the other there are established patterns of thought and practice. Bureaucracies can be given new program objectives, but what they do in the process of implementing them often depends upon the interests of the implementers as much as the pronouncements of the leaders. Perhaps these two categories should always be the same, but in fact they rarely are.

Kazakstan's experience during the first years of independence clearly illustrated the gulf between theory and practice. Kazakstan's constitu-

Nursultan Nazarbaev, former Kazakstan Communist Party leader and independent Kazakstan's first popularly elected president. One of the most popular political leaders in the Soviet Union, Nazarbaev quickly became a champion of national independence after the breakup of the USSR. Stressing market reform and democratization, Nazarbaev won the confidence of the international diplomatic and commercial communities. Photo by Kaztag (Kazak Press Agency).

tions have acknowledged in theory a division between three branches of government—executive, judicial, and legislative. In practice, Kazakstan's government organization is referred to popularly as a "presidential system." In reality, however, it is closer to a traditional monarchy, subordinating legislative and judicial authority to the president. The prime minister, who heads the Cabinet of Ministers and represents the interests of the entire executive branch, reports directly to the president. The judiciary, consisting at the highest level of the Constitutional Council and the Supreme Court, is essentially dependent upon the Ministry of Justice, an organization directed by the executive branch. The legislature functions almost as an advisory committee.

In 1992, the first year of independence, Kazakstan's legislature functioned essentially as it did during the Soviet period. The 360-seat unicameral legislature adopted laws and resolutions that were prepared by executive-branch agencies. The deputies, or parliamentarians, were essentially representatives of entrenched interests—party organizations, large state-owned enterprises, government-funded public sector institutions, and other groups that were inimical to real political and economic reform. The unwillingness of the parliament to endorse reform legislation drove many observers to the conclusion that the Soviet-style legislature would have to be replaced by a democratically elected one. In close collaboration with Nazarbaev's aides, a leading contingent of proreform parliamentarians contrived to disband the parliament. In December 1993, a majority of the parliamentarians voted in favor of new elections, and Nazarbaev—also supporting new elections—ordered that the legislative chambers be locked.

Nazarbaev scheduled a new parliamentary election for March 17, 1994, which turned out to be more closely managed than the previous communist election. It included nominations from three categories: the president's state list (accounting for about 8 percent of the candidates), nominations from registered political parties and public organizations (accounting for about 44 percent of the candidates), and independent candidates (accounting for about 48 percent of the candidates). The election took place across twenty-one electoral regions overseen by Kazakstan's Central Electoral Commission and witnessed by a large cadre of international election observers. A total of 176 deputies were elected, forty-one of whom had served in the previous legislature, twenty-one of whom were women; the overwhelming majority were engineers by profession.

The election process was sharply criticized by some international observers as flawed, particularly by the Conference on Security and Cooperation in Europe (CSCE, now officially known as the Organization for Security and Cooperation in Europe, or OSCE). Other observers, however, argued that under the circumstances of independence and in terms of comparative standards of measurement the elections were free and fair.

This election resurfaced as an important political issue one year later when Kazakstan's Constitutional Court ruled the parliamentary elections were illegal and thus invalid. At first Nazarbaev vetoed this decision, but the court then overruled his veto. Yielding to the court decision, Nazarbaev dismissed the parliament and appointed a new prime minister, Akezhan Kazhegeldin, to form a new government. Nazarbaev retained the deputy ministers for defense, interior, finance, and foreign affairs as well as the secret service chief. A new draft constitution for the country was drawn up by Nazarbaev's trusted Minister of Justice. The constitutional draft was published early in August 1995 and approved by an overwhelming margin (90 percent) in a national referendum later that month.

The so-called Nazarbaev Constitution greatly expanded the powers of the executive. According to the constitution, presidential decrees essentially have the force of law. And although the president is not empowered to introduce legislation into the bicameral parliament, it can give the president lawmaking powers for one year by a two-thirds vote at a joint session. Parliament also has the authority to impeach the president by a three-quarters vote at a joint session. The president has the right to choose the prime minister and to appoint seven members of the forty-seven-member Senate. The remaining members of the Senate are elected from Kazakstan's nineteen regional parliaments, the *maslihats*. Elections for the new upper house took place on December 5, 1995. Popular elections for the national assembly took place on December 9, 1995. Many opposition groups, claiming the elections to be illegal, refused to participate.

Kazakstan's new judiciary has a two-tiered system consisting of the Supreme Court and Arbitration (Commercial) Court. The Constitutional Council, whose members are appointed jointly by the president and parliament, has jurisdiction over cases of constitutional interpretation. In the new constitution the Supreme Court's jurisdiction was extended to general cases on appeal. The Arbitration Court's jurisdiction was limited to cases of disputes regarding the interpretation of the commercial code. In the past, the constitutional court was widely seen as a protector of human rights. It was repeatedly the focus of widely publicized appeals for resolution of outstanding issues between ethnic Russian and ethnic Kazak groups.

The parliamentary elections of December 1995 established a new upper chamber of Kazakstan's parliament, the Senate. The election involved deputies from the nineteen *maslihats*. Each oblast elected two deputies to the Senate. Seven additional members of the Senate were left to presidential appointment. Two parties, the Party of National Unity of Kazakstan and the Democratic Party, dominated the election. Opposition groups protested the elections, calling them illegal.

There are many indications that the constitution's three-branch system of government does not represent the actual distribution of power in Kazakstan. Although executive, judicial, and legislative authorities no doubt play important roles in Kazakstan, there is evidence that the most important "branch" of government is actually the system of local governments. In Kazakstan's far-flung regional political administration, the traditional post of *Akim*, the chief regional officer legally subordinated to the president, is actually the locus of most power. The *Akim*'s jurisdiction is essentially that of the former oblast party secretaries.

The euphoria associated with independence led to some symbolic and substantive changes in policy. In 1992, symbolic steps were taken toward the nativization of the republic. Many oblasts were renamed: Tselinograd

Oblast became Akmolinsk, Chimkent became South Kazakstan, and Uralsk became West Kazakstan. In September 1992 the parliament passed legislation returning many cities to their traditional names. Tselinograd city became Akmola, Gurev became Atyrau, Kirovo became Zhanalyk, and Pugachevo became Ushbulak. The president announced that the capital of the country would be moved north to Akmola. Kazakstan's free-wheeling press carried long and involved discussions of the pluses and minuses of a capital move; parliamentary factions debated the idea; and the president argued publicly for it before announcing, in the summer of 1995, that the capital, for most government purposes, would be moved over a nine-year period to Akmola.

Most citizens saw the capital move as a response to the problem of cultural and regional division within the country. Many of Slavic origin felt they had awoken at independence in a foreign country. Others insisted that Kazakstan was a multinational country, home to all groups and races. Still others felt that Russia had a special claim to the physical territory of Kazakstan and should not relinquish the territory to "nationalists" among the Kazaks who saw independence as an opportunity to reclaim the birthright denied them by "Soviet imperialism."

Although emigration of Russians and other Slavs from Kazakstan back to Russia, Ukraine, and Europe has been reported, it is not nearly on the scale of the emigrations from the other Central Asian states. There are many reasons for this. One surely is that Nazarbaev's government assumed a cosmopolitan posture, which means that it supported moderate nativization while refusing to make concessions to the more ardent supporters of exclusivist policies. Another is that the large cities in northern and western Kazakstan are so heavily populated by Russians and Europeans that the local citizens are not threatened by nativization. They expect that if the situation deteriorates, the Russians to the north will come to their aid.

Although some nationalist political opposition always existed in Kazakstan throughout the Soviet period, the well-organized contemporary nationalist opposition in Kazakstan began in December 1986 with the public demonstrations as a result of the removal of Dinmukhamed Kunaev as the Kazak Communist Party's first secretary. Groups of angry demonstrators paraded through the streets of the capital. Soviet military troops suppressed the demonstrations by force. A leading opposition party, Zheltoksan (December), initially led by Khasan Kozhakmetov, took its name from these events. The popular opposition gave rise to a strong sense of the importance of political activism to promote the Kazak national agenda. Although various government inquiries have inconclusively determined the culpability of public officials in suppressing the demonstrators, in one of his first acts as president Nazarbaev issued a decree that exonerated the demonstrators.[4]

A second major nationalist opposition group was Azat (Freedom), led initially by Sabitkazi Aketai. Azat's objectives were initially similar to those of Zheltoksan. Zheltoksan and Azat organized a joint demonstration in June 1992 that drew nearly 5,000 demonstrators.[5] The demonstrators protested the continuing dominance of the former communist elite over the country, claiming that communists still held 85 of the 360 seats in parliament.

In reality the argument was not about the principles of communism but the personalities of the communists. The transition to independence had put the republic's communists in the position of being an opposition party overnight. Nazarbaev abandoned the party, as did most members of the Kazak intellectual and technical elite. Afterward, the party attempted to reorganize itself as a contending party. It published a new program in February 1992 and held a Congress in March of that year. The party claimed to have 45,000 members. It applied for registration, but the Ministry of Justice denied registration on the grounds that the goals and means of the party were "directed against the constitutional order and independence of the Republic of Kazakstan."[6] A socialist opposition, the Kazak Socialist Party, headed by Yermukhamet Yertyshbaev and Anuar Alimzhanov, was also active as an opposition party during the first days of independence. A smaller opposition party, Edinstvo, drew its support mainly from the Russian population living in the northern sections of the country. A movement representing a coalition of Slavic groups, Lad, actively supported a pro-Russian political agenda.

The nationalist opposition has taken some extreme positions. A leader of Azat, Mikhail Isinaliyev, even argued that Kazakstan should remain in the nuclear club in order to maintain its international standing and prestige. He opposed promises made by Nazarbaev during Nazarbaev's 1992 visit to Washington to ratify the Lisbon Protocol of the START arms control treaty that had been agreed to by the USSR and the United States. A yet more extreme group was the nationalist Alash Orda. The group was initially headed by Aron Atabek Nurushev, who fled to Azerbaijan in August 1992 requesting political asylum.

Political organizations represented more than just Kazak and Russian interests. The most successful political organization outside of the government itself was probably the Semipalatinsk-Nevada organization that emerged in the mid-1980s, constituting a form of "green opposition." The movement warned of the dangers of Moscow's mismanagement of the nuclear materials complex. The Semipalatinsk testing area was permanently closed by a presidential decree in Kazakstan in August 1991 and declared an "ecological disaster area" by a presidential decree in June 1992. (The last nuclear test was conducted on October 17, 1989.) A second test facility, located near the western city of Atyrau, was closed in October

1992. Between 1949 and 1963, at least 266 atmospheric nuclear tests were conducted in Kazakstan. Between 1963 and 1989, probably an equal number of nuclear tests were conducted underground in Kazakstan.

Perhaps the most important aspect of political opposition, however, is the nonofficial press in Kazakstan, which attempts to provide a forum for the expression of responsible but divergent opinion. A variety of newspapers in particular provide competing perspectives on issues of public and social policy.[7] The variety of opinion expressed in the Kazakstan press led many supporters of Nazarbaev's government to urge that the autocratic features of the system be seen in terms of Kazakstan's distinctive culture. Kazakstan's democratic experiment, these proponents urge, may not follow the path of European liberalism but nonetheless represents a form of "Asian liberalism."

KAZAKSTAN: THE ROAD TO A MARKET ECONOMY

Nazarbaev's postindependence development strategy was decidedly different from that outlined in the old socialist dogmas. Nazarbaev spoke out in favor of the establishment of a democratic political order based on Kazakstani traditions. Nazarbaev stressed the importance of the transition to market-economy relations and the country's integration into the world trading community. He encouraged Kazakstan's representation in major international organizations, the international banking community, the diplomatic community, and nongovernmental organizations. In September 1992 Alma-Ata changed its name to Almaty. Almost overnight this sleepy vacation town for Soviet officials was transformed into a regional capital, becoming a nexus for international flights, traveling businesspeople, and circuit-riding diplomats. Restaurants, hotels, car dealerships, and a panoply of service industries opened offices in Almaty, which became the commercial and diplomatic hub of Central Asia.

Kazakstan adopted the most ambitious economic liberalization program in Central Asia, assuming a "Kazakstan means business" attitude. The government signed what was referred to as "the deal of the century" with the oil multinational Chevron. The agreement led to the formation of a joint venture, Tengizchevroil, and committed Chevron to spend about $20 billion over twenty years to develop the Tengiz oil field in western Kazakstan. The field has proven crude reserves of over 6 billion barrels. A Turkish engineering company, Birlesmis Muhendisler Burosu, signed a deal in July 1992, agreeing to invest more than $11 billion in oil fields around the Caspian Sea and to build a gas-fired power station. British Gas and the Italian firm Agip jointly won a competition to negotiate a $7 billion contract to develop an oil-and-gas field on the northwestern border. The prospect of major foreign currency earnings from the state sale of oil rights gave Kazakstan greater latitude in devising a domestic liberalization program than was the case in the other Central Asian countries.

To invigorate his new economic strategy, Nazarbaev added to his policy circle a group of exceptionally bright and forward-looking young Kazak intellectuals. Many members of the Kazak intellectual elite, formerly associated with the universities and research institutes, were drawn into advisory and consultant relationships with the new government. Many of the supporters of Nazarbaev's general course toward liberalization and democracy were technocrats, trained and oriented toward technocratic engineering rather than political solutions.[8] Nazarbaev also attracted a foreign cadre of experienced economic advisers and consultants.

The official liberalization agenda (the "Strategy for the Formation and Development of Kazakstan as a Sovereign State") was announced in May 1992 and envisaged the creation of a multiparty system, an export-led growth strategy with an emphasis on primary commodity exports, and reliance upon Kazakstan's unique geopolitical position. The three-stage destatification plan involved a reduction of the public sector to 30–40 percent of gross national product.[9] The first stage called for liberalization of the consumer market. The second stage called for reconstruction of Kazakstan's economic infrastructure. The third stage contemplated the integration of Kazakstan's new industrial economy into the world market. The 1992 economic reform package was revised in 1994 under the influence of the Kazakstan parliament. It was then again revised and extended in November 1995, this time by the government but in the absence of a parliament, with the adoption of the 1996 budget and a three-year program committed to economic restructuring and macroeconomic stabilization.

A form of limited privatization in agricultural land was introduced in 1992. Vice Premier Boltash Tursumbaev noted in an interview in June that 1,000 farm cooperatives already had been established and some 5,000 farmers had received land for cultivation by April 1992. It was estimated that by the end of the year 1,480 state farms were to be privatized.[10] According to any strict interpretation of the law, however, this land reform—despite having been billed as a privatization reform—did not introduce true private ownership. It relied instead on a leaseholder concept, with title still being held by the state. IMF research-team members who collected data in early 1992 in Kazakstan were told that "private ownership of land is not under consideration for the time being."[11] The IMF team concluded that the changes that were being contemplated were mainly managerial and did not involve the establishment of true private-property institutions.

The IMF team members encouraged a rapid liberalization of energy prices, but Nazarbaev's government objected to this measure on the grounds that this would hobble light industry. Kazak officials were unwilling to commit to what was widely regarded as "shock therapy." They did, however, commit to gradual privatization of both light and heavy industry.

Kazakhstan's probusiness attitude also was reflected in the aggressive trade promotion program that included new policies on communication, transportation, investment, and taxation. In June 1992 Kazakhstan set up the National Agency for Foreign Investments to coordinate and centralize investment from abroad.[12] Also in June 1992, a railway line begun in the 1950s but then abandoned after the deterioration of Sino-Soviet relations following the 20th Congress of the CPSU was reopened. The line links Urumchi, capital of the Xinjiang-Uigur Autonomous Region of China, with Almaty. The line is 3,000 kilometers shorter than the existing northern route located in Russia.

In July 1992 a free economic zone was created in the western area of the republic where the Tengiz and Kenbai oil-and-gas projects are located. But given the country's variable and complex tax laws, even free economic zones were insufficient to attract foreign investment outside of the lucrative energy sector. Depending upon their interpretation, Kazakhstan's tax laws could set tax rates at roughly 45 percent of profits, too high to attract many foreign investors. A new tax code was adopted in the summer of 1995 that brought the tax rate on profits down to 11 percent.

The privatization program in Kazakhstan, known as *Zhekeshelendiru*, was first established by government decree in June 1991 but only got under way in 1994. The program drew upon what is known among privatizers as the Czech model, whose distinguishing feature is the "destination point." Rather than distribute state property to cash-paying conglomerates or foreign investors—which is appealing to the government since it would instantly raise revenue—the Kazakstan program redistributes state property to individuals or firms who trade vouchers or a combination of vouchers and cash for shares in the joint stock companies that hold title to the property. The vouchers are distributed to all citizens on the basis of simple rules. In this kind of program, the "destination point" of the privatization process is the largest and most inclusive group of citizens possible.

There are both governmental and private entities involved in the privatization process. The lead government agency in privatization, the Government Committee on Property (GKI), developed an overall privatization plan. The plan included protocols for voucher sales, joint stock company (JSC) formation, and a list of enterprises to be privatized. As late as 1996, the full list had not been made public. The GKI did, however, announce that the list included over 2,000 enterprises to be privatized before the end of 1995.

According to the program, excluded from privatization were military-industrial facilities (except for those components producing consumer goods), enterprises producing industrial building materials, strategic materials enterprises, and the facilities of the national academies and scientific institutes. Foreign investment is not permitted in the ferrous and nonferrous metallurgy, uranium, precious metals, gold-processing, chemical, and primary petrochemical–processing industries. The list of soon-to-be-privatized facilities was made available only shortly in advance of particular auctions.

By March 1994 the GKI issued "Privatization Investment Coupons" (PICs), or vouchers, to nearly all of Kazakstan's citizens. To avoid speculation Kazakstan decided that PICs would not be freely tradable but could only be invested in government-registered Investment Privatization Funds (IPFs), financial organizations that encourage investment concentration. The IPFs use citizens' vouchers and their own capital for acquiring shares in JSCs, which are formed to manage enterprises. The IPFs may also issue their own stocks, which can be exchanged for PICs. In early 1995, Kazakstan had about 160 registered IPFs. Most of the largest—Astana, Butya, and Raimbek—were very successful. The smaller ones usually represented individual investors. The IPFs are entitled to a share of the profits of the JSCs in which they purchase shares. Both IPFs and JSCs must be registered with the Kazakstan Central Bank. A JSC's equity in a JSC facility is capped at 33 percent, and the government retains 39 percent of the equity. The remaining equity is made available to the public through the Small-Scale Privatization Program.

The process of privatization took place through coupon auctions. The auctions were organized in five "waves," each lasting four months. Twenty of each citizen's 100 allotted coupons can be used in only one of each wave. The first Kazakstan coupon auction was held in March 1994. Auctions have been held every two weeks since then and continued on a regular basis through the autumn of 1996.

Not surprisingly for a government program that intends to redistribute the wealth of an entire society in a short period of time, Kazakstan's privatization program has come under much criticism. One criticism is that there is little public understanding of the process of privatization. The chairman of the parliament's Committee on Economic Reform, Olzhas Sabdenov, announced in an October 1994 parliamentary hearing on privatization that 30 percent of the cases of privatization in 1993 were investigated due to formal complaints. The Prosecutor-General of Kazakstan, Jamil Tuyakbaev, said in the same parliamentary session that in all there were more than 5,000 violations of privatization laws and that there were some 877 appeals then in court. Some criticism also focused on the role of foreign organizations in privatization. Some saw privatization as an elaborate ruse for the outside world to capture control of Kazakstan's resources. Complaining of the establishment of "peripheral capitalism," they claimed that the local economy was becoming dependent upon foreign investment capital.

Kazakstan's privatization program during its first three years succeeded in initiating the process of economic transition by successfully creating private-property institutions and starting the transfer of ownership. But it did not achieve the level of public sector transformation necessary to fully disestablish the former policies and practices of the centrally planned economy.[13]

THE DEMOCRATIC EXPERIMENT IN KYRGYZSTAN

When the August 1991 coup collapsed in Moscow, initial press reports indicated that the members of the coup committee had commandeered a plane for Bishkek, the capital of Kyrgyzstan. Kyrgyz intellectuals are fond of pointing out that these press reports were in error. The Moscow journalists had apparently mistaken the Kyrgyz capital of Bishkek for Belkek, a village in the Crimea. In fact, Kyrgyzstan's newly elected president, Askar Akaev, was among the first to condemn the coup attempt. Bishkek certainly would not have been considered a friendly destination by the coupmembers. Kyrgyzstan declared national independence on August 31, 1991, just days after the outcome of the coup attempt became clear.

After independence, Bishkek quickly became the favorite city of European, North American, and Asian diplomats and development assistance officials. Since the Kyrgyz capital is located close to Almaty, it was an easy stopover for Western diplomats, economic specialists, and businesspeople on their way to and from the capital. Although Bishkek did not have the infrastructure of Almaty, the Kyrgyz commitment to reform impressed everyone. Kyrgyz citizens took pride in asserting that Kyrgyzstan was not an "Islamic-communist-feudal" society of backward Asia, but rather a society seeking to develop European-style democratic institutions and social programs.

Kyrgyzstan was the first Central Asian country to adopt IMF-sponsored liberalization policies with real enthusiasm. But the first years of independence were by no means easy. A mountainous country with enormous but underdeveloped hydroelectric generation potential, Kyrgyzstan has mineral deposits of coal, gold, mercury, and uranium. The country has four major economic zones: the Issyk-kul area, largely devoted to animal husbandry and tourism; the Namangan and Osh areas, mainly agricultural regions populated by native Kyrgyz; and the Chui area, where the bulk of the country's nonnative population is located. Most industry is situated in the city of Bishkek. Past generations of leadership and administrative personnel were dominated by cadres drawn mainly from the Issyk-kul and Chui regions.

Agricultural and industrial energy demands are modest in Kyrgyzstan, yet the republic nevertheless has been an energy importer, producing only negligible amounts of crude oil, coal, and natural gas. Consequently, Kyrgyzstan is potentially rich yet confronted independence with a higher level of trade dependence on the outside world than any of the other Central Asian countries.

During its first year of independence, Kyrgyzstan immediately encountered some of the classic problems of a small and dependent country entering the international marketplace. In addition, Kyrgyzstan suffered a series of natural calamities during 1992. Exceptionally heavy rains and mud slides caused serious economic problems. A major earthquake left as many as 65,000 inhabitants in the areas of Jalalabad and Osh without shelter and disrupted water and power systems. In late April 1992, hail and late frost killed a large portion of the early plantings. Under these difficult circumstances, the fact that Kyrgyzstan held to an ambitious policy of Western-oriented reform can be attributed largely to the leadership of President Akaev.

As a young man Akaev left his native Kyrgyzstan to study in Leningrad (now St. Petersburg). He achieved distinction in the most competitive and prestigious academic discipline in the USSR, physics, eventually earning a doctorate. He was elected president of the Kyrgyz Academy of Sciences before being elected president of Kyrgyzstan in 1990 as a compromise candidate. Since Akaev joined the Communist Party only in 1981, it is reasonable to assume that he did so only under pressures of career advancement and not out of ideological commitment.

Akaev had a sober appreciation of the strengths and achievements of liberal civil societies and economic reform. As the Soviet Union was disintegrating in 1991, policy circles debated the strengths and weaknesses of the market. Opponents of the transition to a market-based economy pointed out that whereas both India and Angola had market economies, this fact alone did not propel those societies toward prosperity. Akaev was reported to have argued in such debates that although it was true that there were both poor countries and rich countries among the market economies, in the socialist world there were only poor countries.

Akaev brought into his administration like-minded enthusiasts for a new Kyrgyzstan. As the coup in Moscow unfolded in August 1991, Akaev's opponents took the opportunity to plot his removal. The top law enforcement official in Kyrgyzstan, Feliks Kulov, is widely credited with saving Akaev's position (and possibly his life) during the transition.

Askar Akaev, independent Kyrgyzstan's first president. A physicist by training and former president of Kyrgyzstan's Academy of Sciences, Akaev is widely regarded as the most intellectual and liberal, if not the most effective of the presidents of Central Asia. Photo by Anvar Ilyasov.

Kulov's special area of expertise was fighting drug trafficking.[14] He was named vice president of Kyrgyzstan on February 27, 1992. In August 1992, Akaev also appointed Kulov to head the Business Council, a new organization charged with drafting measures to develop private enterprise. Another example of Akaev's appointments is Rosa Otunbaeva, a vice premier who was named ambassador to the United States and Canada in May 1992 and later returned to Kyrgyzstan in 1994 to fill the post of foreign minister.

Kyrgyzstan's early efforts at liberalization were distinguished by continual competition between the executive and legislative branches. Kyrgyzstan's initial privatization program began with a presidential decree in November 1991.[15] The presidential liberalization program envisaged a transition to a market economy and included the creation of a so-called land fund that would eventually turn 1.5 million hectares over to private farmers.[16] Because of parliamentary opposition, Akaev vetoed versions of the enabling legislation three times until he was satisfied with a final version.[17] In July 1992, parliament adopted Akaev's comprehensive economic reform package after he threatened to resign if the legislation failed to pass.[18] The eighteen-month program of economic reform was designed to privatize 90 percent of the capital in Kyrgyzstan by the end of 1993.[19] The reform program envisaged closing some 200 state-owned enterprises as well as privatizing 35 to 40 percent of the remaining enterprises, 70 percent of housing, 100 percent of the service industries, and 25 percent of agriculture. Prices on most goods were to be deregulated by January 1993.[20]

The first year of the privatization program in Kyrgyzstan illustrates what can go wrong. An early adherent of the liberalization course, Kyrgyzstan was the first to deregulate prices. Yet this did not lead to increased production as the market model suggested it should have. Instead, it triggered a doubling of prices for many commodities. In the spring of 1992 the Kyrgyz government tried to relieve what it assumed was the temporary pain of shock therapy and increased social expenditures, resulting in a ballooning budget deficit. In August a new plan was announced to improve labor laws to help the 100,000 people in the republic who were jobless.

As late as mid-July 1992 only 3 percent of the Kyrgyz economy was in private hands. Announced as a way to encourage the transition to the market, the plan doubled the amount of state expenditures on jobless benefits.[21] To salvage the situation the government sought during the summer to regulate exports and imports to improve the trade balance. (In early June 1992, Akaev had worked out an agreement with Russian officials to reinflate the Kyrgyz economy by literally importing boxcars filled with Russian rubles.) Akaev announced that the IMF program for reconstruction of the Kyrgyz economy would require $400 million in loans, which Kyrgyzstan sought from the European Bank for Reconstruction and Development (EBRD).

The Kyrgyz economy is primarily agricultural. Agriculture accounts for about 40 percent of the net material product and about one-third of the country's employment. Privatization in Kyrgyzstan did not mean a shift to true private-property arrangements, but only involved a transition from state property to collective forms of local ownership. Thus, Kyrgyz privatization meant that lands were distributed according to assignment rules determined by the state—but the decisions as to who got what were left largely to local officials.[22]

Akaev said in May 1992 that the privatization plan envisaged turning over 20 percent of the land to farmers within five years. He said that only 159,000 hectares, less than 1 percent of the arable land, had been privatized so far, and of that land only 30,000 hectares were irrigated. Akaev went on to explain that in the south, where nationalist feelings were stronger, privatization would be avoided.[23] Just days after this interview appeared Akaev, concerned about the failure of the harvest, announced at a conference of Kyrgyzstan's farmers that there would be a temporary suspension of the land reform until the end of harvesting.[24]

THE DEMOCRATIC EXPERIMENT GOES AWRY

Throughout 1992 the *Jogorku Kenesha*, the new Kyrgyz parliament, debated different versions of the new constitution. Debates centered on relations between executive and legislature, language policies, and privatization, particularly that of land. One version of the constitution—preferred by Akaev—provided for a presidential system with strong executive powers. The other version of the constitution, the one favored by Akaev's opponents, favored a strong legislature. Akaev argued that parliamentary supremacy would spell disaster for the country, because it would lead to a struggle in parliament that would pit the country's clans and tribes against one another. "As a result, the southerners would win because they are in the arithmetic majority. The northerners couldn't accept that, since the capital is in the north."[25]

The parliament became the staging ground for political opposition to Akaev's proreform agenda. Parties and organizations that were not in the least bit democratic took advantage of the opportunities provided by the freedom of legislative activity. Aman Amanbaev, the first secretary of the Kyrgyz Communist Party and a supporter of the August 1991 coup, reemerged from obscurity in June 1992 to be elected a *Mejlis* deputy, vocally opposing Akaev's program of land reform. Opposition parties such as Erkin Kyrgyzstan and Asaba (National Rebirth Party) exploited public dissatisfaction over economic breakdown, the role of the Kyrgyz language, and the distribution of land and apartments. Asaba, for instance, maintained that the Kyrgyz language law had been implemented too slowly and that only ethnic Kyrgyz should be eligible to receive land. A third party, the Kyrgyzstan National Renewal Party, opposed privatization in general, claiming that a disproportionate amount of shares would go to the urban population, a large proportion of which is nonnative. Other nationalist parties had narrow objectives, such as the irredentist movement Free Uigurstan, whose platforms called for the establishment of a separate Turkic-speaking state in the regions of China bordering Central Asia.

Kyrgyzstan's difficulties over nationality flow from the ethnic specialization of the population. The Russian-speaking populations tend to be represented in the technical and skilled trades. The Caucasus nationalities and the Turkic-speaking non-Kyrgyz tend to be involved in service and trade industries. The native Kyrgyz tend to be occupied in agriculture and animal husbandry. Since these economic sectors were affected differently by the economic dislocations produced by liberalization, the standard of living of different nationality groups diverged widely. Those occupied in the service sectors benefited most; those in the primary agricultural sector faced the greatest hardship. Kyrgyz intellectuals tended to attribute interethnic conflict in the republic to these economic differences.[26]

All of these regional, national, ethnic, and economic fractures in the society were reflected in the composition of the parliament. Akaev, buoyed by his international prestige, his reputation among the international lending and banking institutions, and political support from the five key regional hakims (whom he had personally appointed), embarked upon a bold effort to counter the political opposition. Asserting that the communist-era parliament was the chief cause of Kyrgyzstan's inability to push decisively forward in solving economic problems, Akaev departed from his course of making Kyrgyzstan the "democratic showcase of Asia" and embarked upon a new "Asian development path."

Akaev's lurch toward authoritarianism can be traced to a meeting between the heads of state of Kazakstan, Kyrgyzstan, and Uzbekiston that took place in Almaty in July 1994. Pressure from Uzbekiston to agree upon an "Asian development path" apparently persuaded Akaev to abandon his efforts to reach national consensus democratically. Under threat that Akaev and those closely associated with him (mainly family members) would be accused in the autumn parliamentary session of corruption and malfeasance, Akaev decided to strike preemptively at his political opponents. He engineered a quiet revolution in which he disbanded the parliament, forced the resignation of the government, cowed the judiciary, shut down the opposition press, set up a new electoral commission, and announced new parliamentary elections.

In September 1994 a majority faction of the *Jogorku Kenesha*, in league with Akaev and leading regional hakims, coerced members of parliament into boycotting the autumn session. Unable to reach a quorum, a group of parliamentarians under the leadership of M. Sherimkulov, Akaev's leading opponent, met in an extraordinary session and voted to disband the current session—but to continue their benefits and perquisites. Akaev then issued a presidential decree that observed that "since parliament has ceased to function" the government itself was illegitimate. Bowing to pressure from Akaev, the Cabinet of Ministers then issued a mass resignation (with the proviso that the government ministers continue to work and receive their salaries on a temporary basis). Akaev then announced a referendum to change the constitution to permit a bicameral house consisting of thirty-five permanent deputies and seventy regionally selected deputies. Akaev's critics charged that this was simply an instrument to create a docile parliament and to establish one-man rule. The referendum was set for October 27, the new parliamentary elections for December 24, 1994. To ensure his control of the elections Akaev announced that a new electoral commission would be formed.

Akaev's constitutional referendum itself was patently illegal since Kyrgyzstan's constitution only empowered the parliament, not the president, to call referenda. Kyrgyzstan's human rights organizations were torn. They supported Akaev's policies but were obliged to deplore his autocratic tactics. The international community was less divided. Some principled international observers objected. The U.S. ambassador to Kyrgyzstan, Edward Hurwitz, insisted that Kyrgyzstan's government be judged not only by the ends but also the means of leaders.

Some observers pointed out the irony of Akaev's breaking the rules to get his way, particularly since Kyrgyzstan had been vocally embraced by many Western politicians as the showcase of democracy. They felt that Kyrgyzstan should be held to internationally accepted standards of behavior if its leaders were to profit from the rhetoric of democracy. Yet the international assistance community had made a commitment, which would have been embarrassing to abandon. Fearful that public criticism of the expensive democracy-building efforts might lead to embarrassment for Western politicians, the international community colluded to diminish the opposition's objections. Akaev's undemocratic gamble succeeded for reasons wholly unrelated to Kyrgyzstan's politics.

TOJIKISTON: LAND BETWEEN TWO WORLDS

After the failure of the August 1991 coup, Tojikiston was quick to announce its national independence, adopting a declaration on September 8, 1991. But Tojikiston's independence was purely symbolic in light of the scale of discord in the country. Tojikiston was the least prepared of the Central Asian states to embark upon policies of national consolidation. Remote, poor, internally divided, and bordering war-torn Afghanistan, Tojikiston faced a combination of pressures unknown by the other Central Asian states. Independence produced new opportunities for political opposition groups to openly challenge the claim of the former members of the communist apparat to lead the postcommunist government. What happened in Tojikiston—what one Tojik survivor described as "a hurricane that swept into our lives and took over our hearts"—is one of the great tragedies resulting from the disintegration of the USSR.

Great uncertainties beset Tojikiston's society today as the country struggles to overcome the consequences of the economic collapse of the USSR and the psychological and political consequences of the brutal Tojik civil war of 1992–1993. By any standard, Tojikiston's first steps on the road to postcommunist political independence were disastrous. Reflecting on the experiences of Tojikiston in the past five years, many citizens openly question whether Tojikiston can make a transition to a free, democratic, and prosperous society in their lifetime.

The civil war in Tojikiston defined the first few years of independence. It is important, consequently, to identify the various causes, culpabilities, and costs. Why was there war in Tojikiston? The older and wiser of the Tojik population might give a shrug of resignation and testify that "for someone it was useful." Given the limited space, the description that follows is a very general account of the war. But we should remember that the story of war is rarely told adequately by any outsider.

There is a side to this war that does not come across in the books and journal articles: Politics and real-world events aside, it is important to consider that the costs of modern war are borne most directly and cruelly by the civilian population. In Tojikiston these costs simply stagger the imagination. Five years before the Soviet breakup, Dushanbe, the capital, was a beautiful, quiet, mountain-rimmed southern city. It was an exotic and pleasant resort where Russians and other nonnatives from the Soviet Union crowded the broad, tree-lined streets and moved freely among the native population. Then came the Soviet disintegration and the whirlwind.

Tojikiston's Declaration of Sovereignty of August 24, 1990, maintains that the "land, mineral wealth, and other natural resources on the territory of the republic are the exclusive property of the Tojik republic." The Declaration of Independence of September 8, 1991, unambiguously declares Tojikiston an independent country. The government proceeded swiftly to adopt legislation that distinguished Tojikiston from the Soviet system, such as the new land legislation adopted early in 1991 or the language legislation that claimed, "The state language in Tojikiston is Farsi [Tojik] and its knowledge is obligatory for citizens."[27]

It is unclear whether much of this legislation was ever implemented in any formal sense.[28] The capacity of the administration to implement policy dissolved as political confrontation among contending groups produced a dynamic that soon led to armed conflict. For months the government could not act in any decisive way; the privatization program was brought to a standstill by uncertainty and vacillation; private foreign investors were frightened off and foreign adventurers drawn in.

Rakhman Nabiev's government was rhetorically in favor of privatization. In August 1991, the establishment of a Committee on State Property for guiding privatization was announced. The committee reportedly identified 840 enterprises to be privatized.[29] Throughout the subsequent winter and spring a series of declarations and announcements were made. On February 26, 1992, Nabiev issued a decree ordering all unprofitable state-owned farms to be privatized. On April 15 a new land law officially went onto effect, stipulating that landholders could have lifetime possession, that land may be inherited, and that land could be leased. The law also provided for compensation in the event of state confiscation. Despite decrees and rhetoric, however, in realistic terms it is unlikely, given the ongoing political instability, that any state-managed economic reform occurred.

In the midst of the energy crisis of the winter of 1991–1992, some of the power stations in Uzbekiston that supplied Tojikiston cut off electricity to urban and industrial users in Dushanbe, ostensibly because of fuel shortages. The Tojiks compensated by opening the Nurek Dam. Consequently, the water, which is typically saved for use during the spring irrigation season, was drawn down.[30]

The position of nonnative national groups in Tojikiston is illustrated by the draft language law that was considered in July 1992. As noted, the law made Farsi (Tojik) and its knowledge "obligatory" for citizens.[31] The exclusivist tenor of nationalism reflected in this law had alarmed many nonnative Tojik citizens long before the events of 1992. The emigration process started in 1989 and gained momentum in 1990–1991. Most of those that could leave did. Nabiev and other republic officials vocally opposed Russian out-migration, warning of "brain drain," but did little to actually instill confidence among the nonnative population. According to Jamshed Karimov, the first deputy prime minister in August 1992, "Practically the entire Russian population, or at minimum, sixty percent of the Russian population, is doing everything possible to leave the republic."[32]

Tojikiston's agricultural economy consisted of a state sector dominated by cotton production and an informal sector devoted to cash crops and subsistence farming. Tojikiston's substantial hydroelectric potential (18 billion kWh), organized mainly to supply industrial facilities, was also disrupted by the civil disorder. Tojikiston produced only negligible amounts of coal, oil, and natural gas. Prior to 1991, about half of Tojikiston's energy consumption was supplied by imported gas and oil. During 1992 Tojikiston was unable to continue payments to Turkmenistan and Russia for energy supplies. By the end of 1992 Tojikiston's economy had ground to a standstill. The exact number of refugees created by the fighting in 1992 is impossible to state. Tojik authorities in early 1993 referred to 350,000 refugees and 20,000 deaths as a result of the war.

The Tojikiston situation had its origins in the Great Power conflicts of the Afghan War. On December 27, 1980, sixty Soviet special service troops stormed the presidential palace in Kabul, Afghanistan, on a mission to capture the president and establish friendly Soviet control in Afghanistan. In the process, the president, Khafizulla Amin, was killed, and a nine-year war ensued. The Soviet leader at the time, Leonid Brezhnev, explained that the rationale of the occupation was to prevent U.S. penetration to the borders of the USSR. Minister of Defense Dmitrii Ustinov explained that the effort also included an attempt to test contemporary military technology to ensure the Soviets' capacity to counter the threat of midrange missiles being deployed by forces of the North Atlantic Treaty Organization (NATO). U.S. President Jimmy Carter decried the operation as Moscow's attempt to realize a long-standing dream of acquiring a warm-water port.

By the time the war officially ended in 1989, the USSR was transformed by the processes of economic decline and reorganization under perestroika. The influence of the aftermath of the Afghan War on the Tojikiston civil war, however, is not easy to evaluate. The Afghan War brutalized the local Afghan population and produced a generation of trained fighters and mercenaries. The withdrawal of Soviet military forces and the cessation of foreign technical and financial assistance to the mujahideen brought an end to the superpowers' rivalry over the territory, but it certainly did not bring a political solution to Afghanistan's internal contest over power. These internal contests indisputably had an influence on events within Tojikiston during 1992. Revolutionary doctrines, trained military cadres, and military assistance crossed the Afghan-Tojik border and contributed to the civil conflicts in Tojikiston during 1992. However, Tojik officials of virtually all the factions reacted angrily to Western press reports that the Tojik civil conflict was being sponsored by Afghanistan at the encouragement of Afghan strongman Mojahed Gulbeddin Hekmatiar. The evidence is not clear, but it may indeed be that the bulk of the weaponry used in Tojikiston came from the former Soviet garrison in Tojikiston rather than from abroad and that the bulk of the cross-border traffic between Tojikiston and Afghanistan was less involved in gunrunning than in illicit drug trafficking.

TOJIKISTON IN FLAMES

Throughout the USSR the process of democratization dates to Gorbachev's policies of perestroika. In Tojikiston perestroika did lead to initial openness and change, but it also unleashed many of the long-suppressed regional and political tensions in Tojikiston's society. Serious efforts to establish consensus were soon overtaken by increased nationalistic tensions over land and language issues, increased competition for political control of the republic, a mass exodus of nonindigenous nationalities, and political polarization that eventually led to the civil war.

Nationalist passions were inflamed by the events of what became known as Black February. On February 11, 1990, a major disturbance erupted in Dushanbe. Rumors regarding a government intention to distribute apartments to Armenian refugees provoked demonstrations, which soon erupted into riots. The government declared a state of emergency and troops fired on demonstrators in the streets. The events polarized segments of the opposition. By the following April, demonstrations were started by *fedayin*.

Sangak Safarov (center, being interviewed, with other leaders of the winning civil war coalition), the mysterious outlaw chieftain who marshaled an army against Tojikiston's political opposition in late 1992 and early 1993 and retook the Tojikiston capital under arms. Photo by Makhmujon Babajonov.

A new election law was passed by Tojikiston's Supreme Soviet in November 1989. The elections in Tojikiston were held in two stages: Local elections were held in December 1989, followed by national elections to fill the 230 seats on the Supreme Soviet in February 1990. Communists dominated the election process from the campaigning and preelection meetings to the elections themselves, and while the communists won a large (roughly 94 percent) number of the seats, communist domination of the process did not result in strengthened communist control of the country. The communist designates quickly fell into serious disagreement once the electoral process had changed the rules of the game.

The Islamic Revival Party (IRP) appealed to be recognized late in 1990 but the Supreme Soviet declared the IRP illegal. The IRP confronted the government directly with a demonstration that lasted for two weeks. The government lifted the ban. By mid-1991, the communist-backed government found that it was one of a number of competing political organizations—and it was losing the competition.

After the failed August 1991 coup in Moscow, Tojikiston quickly announced national independence, adopting its declaration on September 8.

The political conflicts that emerged soon after independence appeared to represent diverging ideological viewpoints and positions. Judging from formal statements, a coalition of "democrats" and "Islamic revivalists" vied with "former communists" for control of the new state. But in reality the fault lines in the postindependence conflicts were regional rather than ideological. Leaders from the eastern areas of Tojikiston, particularly the Garm Valley, aligned with leaders from the Kurgan-Tiube region in a coalition that sought to unseat the ruling groups from the Kuliab and Leninabod regions. The contest over political power produced paralysis in the republic that eventually deteriorated into armed conflict.

The main divisions within Tojik politics include clans from Hujand in the north, Badakhshan in the east, and the Kuliab region and some displaced intellectuals from the Persian-speaking cities of Uzbekiston. The balance of power among these groups dissolved after the Communist Party elite lost its footing in August 1991. The situation gained even greater complexity from the emergence of an active political agenda associated with the diverse Islamic groups in Tojikiston, ranging from the Afghanistan supporters of revolutionary doctrines to Shiite groups based in eastern Tojikiston. Unlike Iranian Shiites, the Tojik Shiites are mainly Ismailis and tend to be much more secular than the Iranian Shiites or the Sunni groups exerting influence from Uzbekiston and Afghanistan.

After the August 1991 coup attempt, a public debate emerged in Dushanbe over candidates for the presidential election. A slate of candidates went before the public. The candidates included Rakhman Nabiev; Usmon Dovlat, a vocal opponent of Nabiev and chairman of the IRP; Davlat Khudonazarov, the candidate of the Democratic Party; Akbar Turadzonzoda, Tojikiston's highest-ranking Muslim cleric; Takhir Abdujabbor, a leader of Rastokhez; and Shodmon Yusuf, chairman of the Democratic Party. Nabiev and Khudonazarov emerged as the front-runners. Turadzonzoda swung his support behind Khudonazarov and the Democratic Party faction. In the runoff election, Nabiev won 58 percent of the vote to Khudonazarov's 29 percent.

The newly elected Nabiev set out to restore much of the old party hierarchy and, in March 1992, arrested Maksud Ikramov, mayor of Dushanbe, and fired a deputy of the Supreme Soviet on charges of accepting bribes. While mayor of Dushanbe Ikramov had sanctioned the removal of Lenin's statue during anticommunist demonstrations in September 1991. The communists were settling the score. Nabiev circulated a decree announcing the establishment of direct presidential rule. But widespread public protests erupted over Maksud Ikramov's removal, crippling the Nabiev government.

On May 5, 1992, the standoff between the two forces came to a head. Nabiev's supporters, either at his direction or acting independently, dis-

Tojikiston civil war refugees fleeing to Uzbekiston in the spring of 1993. Photo by Maryanna
Schmuki.

tributed automatic weapons to friendly forces. Street fighting erupted
throughout Dushanbe. Initial reports indicated that as many as sixty people were killed during the fighting in the two days before Nabiev fled the
parliament building and opposition groups captured the government.
Control of the city passed to General Said Kyomdin Gozi, who had previously been head of the national army. The opposition party of National
Revival, Shokhidon, demanded that Nabiev resign.

Pressed into compromise, Nabiev signed a decree on May 12, 1992,
forming the National Assembly (*Milli Majlis*). The new assembly was to
act as interim legislature until a new legislature could be elected in the
general elections planned for December 6, 1992. The assembly was to
have eighty members drawn from both the old Supreme Soviet and the
opposition parties, with forty seats reserved for each.

A draft of the proposed Tojikiston Constitution was published in
Dushanbe on June 3, 1992. It defined a government in which the president
was the head of state and of government. The president would be elected
for five years. It provided for a cabinet that included the president, vice

Emomli Rakhmonov (center, amid bodyguards and supporters), the "head of the government" of Tojikiston, elected president in November 1994. Photo by Makhmujon Babjonov.

president, state secretaries for foreign and internal affairs, ministers, and chairmen of government committees. The draft extended citizenship only to Tojiks. The Russians and other non-Tojiks who had earlier pressed claims for the possibility of dual citizenship by this time had left Tojikiston in such large numbers that there were few left to lobby.

Fighting broke out anew in the Kurgan-Tiube region in southern Tojikiston in June 1992. The fighting was particularly intense because heavily armed groups from Afghanistan had been transporting arms and militia into the area. On July 27, 1992, a cease-fire agreement went into effect. The agreement was known as *Khorog* after the capital of Badakhshan Province, in which it was signed. The agreement was signed by representatives of a number of political parties, the Muslim clergy, the military detachments, and the leaders of all the provinces and regions of the country, but it was violated within two hours of its conclusion. No clear count of the number of people wounded in the civil unrest was made, but an executive committee announced 300. As many as 150,000 were reported to have fled the area. Major foreign powers, included the United States, moved their diplomatic staffs out of Tojikiston.

In September 1992 the presidents of Uzbekiston, Kazakstan, Kyrgyzstan, and Russia issued a warning that if the civil war in Tojikiston continued it would present a threat to the CIS and would be grounds for mili-

Abdumalik Abdullajanov (center, amid bodyguards and supporters), the popular Leninabod opponent of the southern Tojikiston coalition. Photo by Makhmujon Babajonov.

tary intervention. War raged on in the south. On September 7, 1992, Nabiev resigned when armed opponents took him into custody at Dushanbe's airport. Nabiev handed over his powers to Supreme Soviet Chairman Akbarsho Iskandarov. By September 10, 1992, approximately 1,000 border troops from Russia had taken up positions along the Tojik-Afghan border. Fighting between pro- and anti-Nabiev forces continued throughout September. Charges that the Russian troops were aiding Nabiev loyalists led to a Russian military decree of October 5, 1992, restricting all Russian military forces to their bases.

In late October, Iskandarov set up the Security Council, consisting of the leadership of parliament and the Cabinet of Ministers, and appointed Davlat Khudonazarov as his chief adviser. On October 24, 1992, Safarali Kenjaev, former speaker of the parliament and a Nabiev supporter who was forced out of office the previous April, descended on Dushanbe with an armed militia to reestablish Nabiev's control. Kenjaev's forces were repulsed two days later after heavy street fighting.[33] Another attack was made against the city, this time led by Sangak Safarov, a sixty-five-year-old former prisoner. Safarov received clandestine military support from Uzbekiston. In the fracas, Akbar Turadzonzoda and Shodmon Yusuf fled Dushanbe. Akbarsho Iskandarov oversaw the installation of Emomli Rakhmonov as the new president of Tojikiston on November 19, 1992.

The civil war period was symbolically closed not by the end of fighting, which went on in the hills and in the larger villages throughout 1993 and early 1994, but by two events. The first was the death under mysterious circumstances of Nabiev in his home in Hujand in May 1993; the second was the death of Sangak and his closest lieutenant in a mysterious shoot-out in his home in May 1993.

The civil war over, Tojikiston struggled through 1993 and 1994 to redefine a strategy for national consolidation. The avoidance of potentially polarizing political deliberations concentrated power in the hands of Rakhmonov, who as chairman of the Supreme Soviet—a legislative branch, remember—continued to issue decrees to the executive branch as "head of the government." By April 1994, however, a new commission was established to develop a postwar constitution for Tojikiston. Members of the commission visited European countries and solicited advice from constitutional experts in North America and Europe. The new constitution was announced in the summer of 1994, and an election was scheduled for November 1994 to vote on the referendum and elect a new president. The constitution described a "presidential" system rather than a Westminster parliamentary system. The two leading presidential candidates were Abdumalik Abdullajanov from the north and Emomli Rakhmonov from the Kuliab region. In an election that did not meet international standards of fairness, Rakhmonov was elected president and the new constitution was adopted.

The situation following the election was tense and complex. Widespread popular feelings that the elections had not been free and fair were coupled with an almost universal fear of renewed hostilities in the country. The sense of resignation among the populace was expressed in the phrase that could be heard again and again in private conversations: "Anything, just as long as there is no more fighting." Throughout the winter of 1994 and 1995, psychological uncertainty and tension were a fixture of everyday life, every bit as real as the breadlines and the lack of heat and hot water. During 1995 more than 700 people perished in border skirmishes, according to the Russian military.[34]

The fifth round of talks between the government and the armed opposition continued during 1995 under the auspices of the UN.[35] The negotiations concerned the exchange of prisoners of war, repatriation of Tojik refugees in Afghanistan, and the extension of the cease-fire. Opposition leader Turadzonzoda represented the opposition while Abdumajed Dostoiev, the first deputy chairman of parliament, headed the government's delegation. Meanwhile, relations between the government in Dushanbe and nearby Tashkent continued to deteriorate. Uzbekiston President Karimov, at the CIS summit in May 1995, urged Rakhmonov to learn how to "share his authority."

Even before the Soviet breakup many of the Russian settlers had left. Others remained, expecting that surely they must have seen the worst. But the worse was yet to come. Words fail to describe the brutality of the war. The physical infrastructure of a modern society was ripped apart. Electricity, heat, public transportation, public sanitation, and health services came to a halt in 1993. The population ceased to receive a salary from the public enterprises that ceased to function. Little investment came from Russia. No foreign investment could be attracted under these circumstances. Gainful employment simply did not exist. Basic standards of civil rights were widely regarded as luxuries. Since the beginning of the civil war in 1992, thirty-six journalists died reporting on events; thirty newspapers and magazines were closed. The former heads of the government television and radio stations had been languishing in jail for more than two years.

The surrounding countries blockaded Tojikiston to contain the "Tojik contagion," so those who had not already left the country, particularly pensioners and those without family back in Russia who could summon them, found themselves virtually prisoners in the country. By the end of 1994, many people had lived for as many as two years without any income, without heat or gas in their homes, with only the food that was distributed by the international relief organizations. Science, education, learning, and civilized life virtually came to a halt. When asked "Why do you bother going to work?" most people would shrug and ask, "Is it better to stay at home? It is a diversion." When Westerners expressed hope that democratization and market reform would revitalize Tojikiston, many citizens replied that what they had seen of democracy and market relations could not provide them with any solace, comfort, or hope.

TURKMENISTAN: A CENTRAL ASIAN SULTANATE

Turkmenistan is the strangest of the Central Asian states. It possesses great potential gas wealth and yet has the lowest level of educational attainment of all the Central Asian states. Although much of the backwardness can be attributed to the influence of Soviet-style socialism, the direction of Turkmen society during the postindependence period does not inspire confidence that Turkmenistan's slow start can be overcome by wealth generated by sales of primary commodities. Given the experience of postindependence Turkmenistan, it is unlikely that the potential gas, oil, and agricultural wealth of the country will lead to anything other than Middle East–style political and economic corruption.

Turkmenistan announced political independence on October 27, 1991, with virtually the same enthusiasm with which it had favored the retention of the union just seven months before. In the March 1991 referendum on retaining union 97 percent of the population voted in favor, yet in the October 1991 referendum on independence 94 percent voted in favor of the declaration of independence.[36] A plausible explanation for such voter ambivalence is that the vote represented less an expression of popular preference than it did an acknowledgment of the supremacy of the political leadership of the country.

Modern Turkmenistan is very much a product of the ruling faction led by President Saparmurad Niyazov, who is popularly known as Turkmenbashi (Head of the Turkmen). Until the Soviet collapse, Niyazov staunchly supported the Soviet Union. As the union began unraveling, Niyazov quickly donned the garb of a Turkmen national champion. At the same time, he played a key role in holding the CIS together. He personally appealed to the other Central Asian presidents in December 1991 to adopt a common stance toward Yeltsin's CIS proposal. If Niyazov had swung his support in favor of a rival Muslim commonwealth at that critical point and refused to sign the Alma-Ata Declaration forming the CIS, it is quite possible that the CIS would not have been adopted by the other Central Asian presidents.

Saparmurad Niyazov was born in 1940. He graduated from St. Petersburg (Leningrad) Polytechnic College in 1967 and worked as an engineer at a hydroelectric station in Turkmenistan until 1970. After entering government work, Niyazov began climbing the administrative ladder until he eventually was appointed the prime minister in 1985. He became the head of the Turkmen Communist Party organization in December 1985. In January 1990 he was elected speaker of parliament, that is, the chairman of the Supreme Soviet. Niyazov was elected president of Turkmenistan for a term of five years by the Supreme Soviet in November 1991. Even before the end of his mandate, however, he ran again to establish himself as president of "independent Turkmenistan." In an uncontested race for the presidency in June 1992, he won a reported 99.5 percent of the vote. Part of his campaign strategy was to offer Turkmenistan citizens a number of inducements, including a promise that after October 27, 1992—the first anniversary of Turkmenistan's independence—electricity, gas, and water would be provided to all Turkmenistan citizens free of charge.

In return for public support President Niyazov announced the "Ten Years to Prosperity" program, claiming that the standard of living in Turkmenistan would soon approach that of Kuwait and that Turkmenistan would pursue a policy of "positive neutrality" in foreign affairs, establishing good relations with all countries. During the autumn of 1992, a number of schools, streets, academies, cooperative farms, and other institutions changed their names to honor Niyazov. Even the famed Lenin Kara Kum Canal became the Niyazov Kara Kum Canal. A new Medal of National Distinction was introduced to honor extraordinary service to the state. Niyazov became the first to receive it.

Turkmenistan moved more swiftly than the other Central Asian countries to accommodate the circumstances of independence. With an air of self-satisfaction, Turkmenistan's government announced that it would adopt a new postindependence constitution, the first of the Soviet successor states to do so. Turkmenistan's new constitution was adopted and went into effect in May 1992. It described a "presidential democracy," paying lip service to a tripartite distinction of executive, legislative, and judicial powers. In reality, however, there was no separation of power. The legislature and judiciary possessed only advisory powers. Virtually all authority was concentrated in the executive branch. The president is both head of state and chief executive. The chairmen of the Supreme Court, the members of the Supreme Economic Court, and the Prosecutor-General serve at the president's pleasure. The president appoints judges at all levels. The president has the power to disband the local governing bodies and the *Mejlis*, the new parliament, in the event that there is a no-confidence vote twice in eighteen months. The concentration of power in the president's hands was defended as a temporary expedient. Niyazov explained that "the new vertical structure of power in the last analysis means that ultimate responsibility is in the hands of the president."[37]

The constitution outlined a legislature unlike any of those in the other Central Asian republics. The *Mejlis* consists of fifty deputies elected from territorially defined districts. The first *Mejlis* elections were held in December 1994. The Central Electoral Commission reported a 99 percent voter turnout. Fifty new *Mejlis* deputies were elected in uncontested, single-candidate districts. Virtually all the candidates were registered members of the Turkmenistan Democratic Party, the party headed by Turkmenbashi. At the same time, a "people's council," the *Halk Maslahaty*, was also created. The *Mejlis* deputies sit on the larger *Maslahaty* along with the president, judges, and local officials.

Turkmenbashi repeatedly pointed out that the constitution was the first legal document to explicitly endorse private property among any of the Central Asian states. The constitution guaranteed citizens the right to capital, land, and other material and intellectual property.[38] However, there were no provisions in the constitution regarding the source of this private land or creating a land fund. Niyazov stated that "until the people have learned to be property owners, the government will hold all resources in its hands and use them in the interests of the entire society."[39] The new constitutional provisions did little to establish a land market.

"Turkmenbashi," Saparmurad Niyazov, the former Turkmenistan Communist Party secretary who became the first president of the Republic of Turkmenistan. During his first year in power, Niyazov heavy-handedly used Turkmenistan's ample natural resources to its advantage, aggressively negotiating with Ukraine and Russia and courting foreign investors. Within Turkmenistan, Niyazov expanded his personal powers in an effort to establish a traditionalistic Central Asian emirate, relying heavily on revenues from natural-gas sales. Photo by Bakhrom Ataev.

Furthermore, in order to dissuade non-Turkmen citizens from selling their assets and migrating to Russia, Turkmenbashi issued a series of decrees that effectively made the sale of apartments illegal.

The former Soviet territorial divisions of oblast and raion have been replaced by the more traditional organizations, the *velayet* and *etrap*, respectively, although no territorial borders were actually changed. The territorial units are ruled by the local hakims and *archin*. The local bodies of government were renamed the *gengesh*. Only ethnic Turkmen could head the *gengesh*.

Turkmenistan's efforts to transform into a market economy have met with little success. Russia's price liberalization in January 1992 forced Turkmenistan either to free prices or to impose restrictions on exports of subsidized goods. Neither option was attractive, since exports were needed to bring rubles into the economy. Free prices, the government reasoned, would result in inflation and perhaps social dislocation. Turkmenistan's solution was to introduce rationing of basic foodstuffs, flour, rice, butter, and sugar at subsidized prices while restricting the export of these commodities. The decision was made to undertake gradual privati-

The manat, Turkmenistan's national currency. Note the Latin alphabet and the photo of Turkmenbashi, the country's president.

zation in most spheres of the economy, with the notable exceptions of energy, transportation, and public utilities such as water. Agriculture was identified as an area of gradual privatization. The State Committee on State Property and Privatization, headed by economist Khudaikuli Kerimov, was established to oversee the transition of state enterprises to private management and ownership.

Two sectors, agriculture and petroleum, dominate Turkmenistan's economy. The organizational changes in the gas sector illustrate the leading tendency in Turkmen pluralism, namely, the reliance upon parastatal trading organizations. Parastatal organizations are firms that appear to be private and independent but in reality are closely tied to the government either through management or financial accountability. An example is Turkmengasprom. This organization, an inheritance of the Soviet period, was redesigned in 1992 to attract large-scale direct foreign investment in the gas industry. A new agricultural equipment corporation was established to compensate for the disruption in the supply of former Soviet agricultural technology. Ostensibly independent firms, these entities appear to act as independent, profit-maximizing firms. In reality, they function as branches of the government.

Turkmenistan is rich in energy reserves. It has 8.1 trillion cubic meters of known gas reserves and 700 million tons of oil reserves.[40] Some petroleum analysts, however, claim that further exploration would reveal that the total reserves could be much larger, perhaps as great as 20 trillion cubic meters of gas. A major oil refinery is located at Turkmenbashi (Krasnovodsk) on Turkmenistan's Caspian coast, a second in the northern city of Chardzhou. In 1992 the Turkmen Oil Production Association announced that it found a new oil deposit in the midst of the Kara Kum Desert near Bakhardok.

At independence, Turkmenistan quickly turned its gas reserves to its advantage. Turkmenistan had been supplying gas under the Soviet distribution system at artificially low prices.[41] After independence, Turkmenistan announced that it would begin to sell gas only at prices that approached market levels. Subsidized supplies of gas to Armenia, Georgia, Ukraine, and Russia were suspended. According to Nazar Suyunov—then a deputy prime minister in Turkmenistan—Kazakstan, Kyrgyzstan, and Tojikiston were all in debt to Turkmenistan for gas sales.[42] A dispute erupted immediately with one of Turkmenistan's largest clients, Ukraine. Ukrainian foreign minister Vitold Fokin charged that Turkmenistan's behavior amounted to "economic blackmail."[43] He then called their methods "uncivilized." Niyazov's response was merely that "business is business."[44] In the end, Turkmenistan won. Ukraine settled for the Turkmen terms.

The value of Turkmenistan's gas, however, is determined in large measure by access to markets. Turkmenistan was integrated into the Soviet energy grid, and its gas was shipped to all regions of the USSR and passed through this "friendship" to markets in western Europe. After the Soviet breakup, Turkmenistan continued to use the Soviet pipeline—until November 1993, when Russia cut Turkmenistan's access to Europe and redirected the gas to areas less able to pay (Ukraine and the Caucasus). Turkmenistan's response was to emphasize a plan to develop an alternative pipeline through Iran to Turkey and then to European markets. The cost of establishing the pipeline is substantial, in the area of $7 billion. The cost in terms of the politics involved may be more substantial. Investors are leery of vulnerable gas supplies crossing long stretches of unprotected areas in unstable countries. The U.S. government and others have quietly exerted influence to delay or scuttle any projects that increase Iran's influence in the region.

Turkmenistan's government maintained control of the service and trading industries related to its gas, oil, and chemical industries. Together these made up about 80 percent of the industrial economy. The architect of the parastatal strategy in the gas industry, Valerii Otchertsov, argued that Turkmenistan's privatization program would stress small businesses in trade, the service sector, and the petroleum and gas refining and processing industries. Otchertsov explained to his fellow citizens that these industries were "within the government sector" in most market economies.[45]

During the first stages of independence the distinction between "privatization" and "nationalization" was obscure in the minds of many Turkmen officials. The Soviet airline Aeroflot was reorganized early in 1992. During the period of Soviet "privatization," Turkmenistan's own government airline, Turkmenavia, was created, the first official flight taking off in March 1992.[46] However, in reality the transition had already taken place: By late 1991 one could take off on Aeroflot in Moscow bound for Ashgabat and find, as soon as the plane entered Turkmenistan airspace, the pilots and crew referring to "Turkmenistan National Airlines."

The long-denied cultural heritage of Turkmenistan was immediately revitalized by the collapse of the USSR. By presidential decree most cities readopted their names from the pre-Soviet era, and new official spelling conventions were adopted in accordance with local Turkmen pronunciation. Ashkhabad became Ashgabat, Tashauz became Dashkouz. Language use in general underwent progressive Turkicization. Inhabitants who were not Turkic-speaking were confronted with the need to learn the indigenous language or face minimal opportunities for career advancement. Interestingly, a large proportion of the Russian-speaking population supported the nationality policy of the Turkmen state, viewing President Niyazov (who, incidentally, was married to a Russian) as a protector of Russian culture and traditions against those who favored more complete and rapid Turkmenicization.

Language policy is the cornerstone of nationality policy. During the early changes of 1990, Turkmenistan's government officially favored bilingualism. In 1991 laws on language and citizenship supported this position, but these laws were superseded in 1992 by a new constitution, which maintained that Turkmenistan "had its own citizenship" and named Turkmen as the state language. In the autumn of 1992, Turkmenbashi decreed that dual citizenship was not in conflict with the constitution and that, although knowledge of the Turkmen language would be required of Turkmenistan citizens, there would be a seven-year grace period for those who were not native Turkmen speakers.

Turkmenbashi was less tolerant of those who viewed the political situation differently. The dissolution of the Turkmenistan Communist Party came later than that of other parties—indeed, not until after the USSR, in a legal sense, had already ceased to exist. The Turkmen party had its last meeting on the morning of December 16, 1991. At that meeting the party faithful agreed to disband the party. The assembled then went to lunch together and reconvened afterward to establish the People's Democratic Party of Turkmenistan. Within months the Democratic Party had a membership of nearly 52,000, of whom 48,000 were former communists.[47] Turkmenbashi became its president.

Small and fragmented opposition parties have emerged from time to time. For instance, a group called Agzybirlik (Solidarity) nominated group leader Nurberdy Nurmamedov as its presidential candidate in 1992, but Nurmamedov was not allowed to register for the election. An alternative Democratic Party, headed by Durdy Murad Khadzhi-Mukhamed, has been tolerated by the government but not allowed to organize as an official opposition party. Clandestine political opposition exists within the existing political structures, however. It can be assumed to play a more important role than does the visible opposition.

According to the information circulated by the Turkmen State News Agency, open political opposition in Turkmenistan is small and not influential. At a meeting between President Niyazov and U.S. Senator Alan Cranston in Turkmenistan in September 1992, Niyazov stated that the government in Turkmenistan "faced no political opposition" and that the United States vainly sought individuals with grievances against the government. Such opponents, Niyazov explained, have no real influence in Turkmenistan. Cranston noted that the two most important steps toward developing relations between the two countries were the creation of a legal basis for opposition parties and the attraction of foreign investment into the country.[48] Cranston asserted that these two were closely connected and that Turkmenistan could not expect success in attracting U.S. investment without demonstrating a commitment to pluralism. An OSCE report also concluded that "Turkmenistan is still a repressive country which ignores the basic human rights commitments of OSCE states."[49]

AUTHORITARIAN POPULISM IN UZBEKISTON

Uzbekiston is the heartland of Central Asia. The relations of the Uzbeks with the other peoples of Central Asia reflect a sense of aristocratic heritage, and they view the Farsi-speaking Tojiks that live among them as a minority, although a talented minority. They perhaps have seen the Turkmen to the south and the Karakalpak to the west as backward. Uzbekiston indeed would seem to be the rightful heir to moral leadership in Central Asia. It is an accident of the Soviet breakup that Uzbekiston finds the path to its restoration of ancient glory obstructed by the rising fortunes of some of its neighbors.

Uzbeks have a distinct style of behavior, very different from, for instance, their Tojik and Kyrgyz cousins. Traditions of tribal democracy and intertribal confederation that were strong among the nomadic peoples of the mountains and the plains did not exist in Uzbekiston. Uzbekiston celebrates traditions of hierarchy and authoritarianism more characteristic of a settled people of river valleys and desert oases. Among the nomadic peoples the act of discussing is considered to be gracious. Among the oases peoples, it is considered gracious to obey, impolite to disagree, treacherous to oppose. As long as people are human beings, of course, different values and goals will exist. But in native Uzbek society, open political contestation is considered foreign.

Uzbekiston's declarations of sovereignty and independence were less far-reaching than those of the other Soviet republics. The documents were intended primarily as instruments of negotiation aimed at Moscow, not as foundational instruments for a new system of governance. But by the early months of independence, it was clear that the existing Uzbek government had resolved to assume the responsibilities of governing.

In Uzbekiston, as in all of the Central Asian republics, the transfer of power from the Soviet elite to the national elite was mainly a matter of changing the names on the office doors. Political opposition did emerge upon independence, but the beneficiaries of the old Soviet system used their power to quickly brush it aside. Uzbekiston embarked upon a course of national consolidation that emphasized the state as the "leading and guiding force" of the society. The government publicly emphasized the symbolism of Central Asian traditions of strong but benign leadership. Meanwhile, in private, the government relied on Soviet-style techniques of manipulation and intimidation.

The government immediately took on a personalistic tone, with the president, former party boss Islam Karimov, at the center. Born in 1938, Karimov was a party worker who had risen through the financial bureaucracies of the republic. He had worked in the party, served as first secretary of the Kashkadaria Oblast committee, and rose through the party bureaucracy. He was not an Uzbek nationalist, but neither was he a socialist cosmopolitan in the mold of Nazarbaev or Akaev.

Although Karimov was known as a staunch supporter of Moscow's authority, he quickly changed his tune after independence, championing the national values he had once scorned during the years of Soviet rule. He was trained in Russian and spent most of his professional life working in the language. But as independence approached he changed quickly. His stumbling speeches in Uzbek in 1990 were soon replaced by a fluent command of the native tongue. Just days after Karimov gained legal authority over all court cases in Uzbekistan, he issued a decree on December 25, 1991, pardoning most of those convicted in the notorious "cotton scandal." The cause of the convictions, as a symbol of foreign intervention, had become a celebrated issue among the working populace. In the nationalist atmosphere of political independence, Karimov proudly exonerated those who a few years before he had roundly condemned.

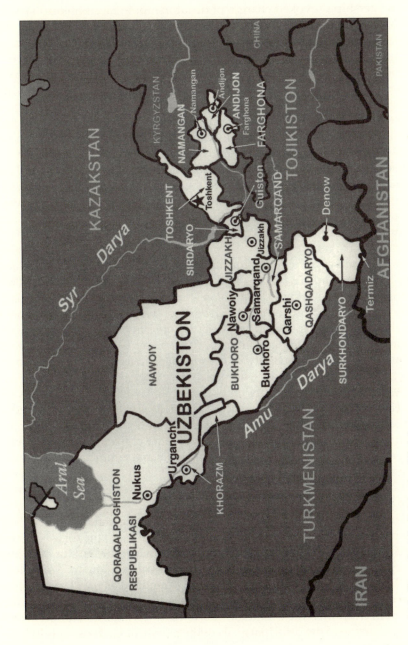

Uzbekiston's Administrative Divisions

Karimov's concentration of power under the general idea of presidential leadership provoked charges of dictatorship. In fact, Shukurulla Mirsaidov, a former first secretary of the Fergana Communist Party and vice president of Uzbekiston between 1990 and November 1991, resigned as deputy of parliament in August 1992, claiming, in a letter to his constituents, that an authoritarian regime was being established in Uzbekiston with the connivance of the parliament.[50] On September 8, 1992, he resigned as vice president, again warning of the emerging dictatorship.

As Karimov amassed power, the legislature continued to function, but a July 1992 parliamentary decree authorized the president to withdraw the immunity of a parliamentarian who was charged with "anticonstitutional actions aimed at undermining the state structure."[51] The president presided over a presidential council, the economic ministries, a new system of regional administration, and the legislature. The KKASSR was brought under the direct supervision of the Uzbekiston government. The chairmen of Karakalpak's Supreme Soviet and its Council of Ministers were forced to resign.

In the summer of 1992, the Consultative Council was established, which included the ministry officials and the new presidentially appointed regional bosses, the hakims. Uzbekiston then proceeded to establish distinct new institutions of government. Uzbekiston's constitution was adopted by the parliament in December 1992. It consists of a preamble and six main divisions, including twenty-six chapters and 128 articles. The divisions concern the sovereignty of the republic, civil rights, the social contract, and the state legislative, administrative, and judicial systems.

According to the constitution, the Supreme Soviet (parliament) was replaced by the *Oliy Majlis* (Supreme Council). The judiciary adopted a three-tiered system consisting of the Constitutional Court, the Supreme Court, and the Arbitration Court. In theory, the judiciary is independent; in practice, however, the capacity of the judiciary to function as an independent branch of government is limited. The government branches are not coequal or balanced; the executive branch is superordinate in virtually all matters.

The constitution describes a secular, democratic state in which "the people are the sole source of state power." According to the rhetoric of the constitution, the highest organ of power is the legislature. But as to the blueprint of government, the constitution describes a unitary "presidential" form of government. The president is identified as the "head of state and executive authority" and there are no meaningful lower tiers of independent authority (i.e., there are no federal divisions). The preamble notes that one of the principal goals of the people of Uzbekiston is to "create a humane and democratic rule of law." The constitution is written in Uzbek with parallel text published in Russian and other languages. It guarantees freedom of speech, assembly, and religion as well as the right to express one's national heritage. What the constitution does not say is also important: The vice president is not mentioned, and no relationship is specified between the president and a political party.

Included among the president's powers is the right to form and head a government and to appoint and dismiss the prime minister and cabinet ministers, appoint and recall diplomats, establish and dissolve ministries, appoint and dismiss the Procurator-General and his deputies, nominate appointees to the Constitutional Court, Supreme Court, and Board of the Central Bank, appoint and dismiss judges of regional, district, city, and arbitration courts, appoint and dismiss hakims for violations of the law, suspend or repeal acts of hakims, sign all laws of the *Oliy Majlis* or return them for reconsideration, declare states of emergency, serve as commander-in-chief of the armed forces, declare war, award orders and medals, rule on matters of citizenship, issue amnesty and pardons, and form and dismiss heads of the national security service. The president is elected by direct secret (but not necessarily competitive) election for a term of five years, serving no more than two terms. After state service, the president becomes a lifetime member of the Constitutional Court.

The *Oliy Majlis* serves as an advisory and legitimating instrument, not as a deliberative body. Following the last parliamentary elections in December 1994, the 150-member parliament convened to formally adopt Uzbekiston's legislation and propel it toward a law-governed society.

The three-tiered judicial system is subordinated to the Ministry of Justice. The court system is funded from the state budget. In order to avoid partisanship, no judge may be a member of any political party. The Procurator's office represents the prosecutorial arm of the justice system. It is responsible for public observance of the laws. Procurators are appointed by the president and are restricted from any political or party activity during their period of service. There are local and neighborhood conflict-resolution committees—the *Mahalla*—which are reported to function effectively at the local level in many areas, particularly rural areas.

The core of Uzbekiston's government is not the legislature or courts but the system of administration that relies upon the twelve *veliatlar* (former oblasts) headed by hakims. Of the hakim appointments announced in March 1994, all were ethnic Uzbeks, all had been previous oblast-level Communist Party committee secretaries, and all were members of the People's Democratic Party of Uzbekiston, the party headed by Islam Karimov. The hakims administer their territories as emissaries of the president.

The political process is carefully monitored and controlled. The Central Electoral Commission (CEC), a fourteen-member board established by parliament on the advice of the president, is responsible for oversight of the nomination process, the campaigning, and the organization of the

Abdurakhim Pulatov (center, at microphone), a leader of the Birlik (Unity) opposition movement in Uzbekiston, April 1990. Photo by Anvar Ilyasov.

election. Campaign financing and publicity is managed by the CEC. According to the election law passed in December 1993, the right to nominate candidates was reserved to registered political parties, the *veliat* legislative councils, and Karakalpak's parliament. Moreover, political parties must also have been registered with the Ministry of Justice no less than six months prior to the election and have collected 50,000 voter signatures supporting the party's participation in the election. These and other restrictions on the nomination process make it possible for the government to exercise a determinative influence on the preselection of candidates.

The most visible opposition movements in early postindependent Uzbekiston were Birlik (Unity) and Erk (Will). Birlik gained its support by spearheading protest efforts, drawing attention to pressing problems, and generally awakening Central Asian citizens from a state of apathy. Birlik's leaders defined the organization's main goals as achieving economic and political sovereignty while restoring the cultural values of the people of Uzbekiston.[52] Birlik started as only a small group of intellectuals but quickly discovered broad popular support. Timur Valiev, a member of the presidium of Birlik's Central Council and one of the founders of the group, once observed that members were surprised by the number of people from all over the republic who approached them asking what Birlik intended to do to help the rural workers.[53]

Established in early 1990, Birlik was allowed by the government to officially register in November 1991 but did not succeed in getting on the bal-

Muhamad Solih, writer, former member of
Uzbekiston's parliament, and chairman of
Erk in 1990. Photo by Anvar Ilyasov.

lot. Erk won formal status on September 11, 1991, having collected the
necessary 40,000 signatures (that number being the threshold under the
old election law). During his trip to the Central Asian states in February
1992, U.S. Secretary of State James Baker III met with Birlik leader Abdurakhim Pulatov to indicate the U.S. government's commitment to the
principle of political pluralism.

Religious political opposition groups also exist in Uzbekiston. The goal
of the Islamic Renaissance Party (IRP), for instance, is to establish an Islamic state in Uzbekiston. But the form of the state that this movement
envisions, according to its chairman, Abdullakh Utaev, more closely resembles the modern state of Pakistan than that of Iran or Saudi Arabia.[54]
According to the Pakistani model, the Muslim style of life would be preserved by law. Such practices as drinking, drug use, and prostitution
would be illegal, and the official Islamic clergy that was allowed to operate under the Soviet regime—considered by the IRP to have compro-
mised itself—would be replaced. But within the broad outlines of an Islamic state the government would observe international standards of

Muhamad Sadyk Muhamad Yusuf, former mufti of the Muslims of Central Asia and Kazakstan, removed from his position by the Uzbek government. Photo by Anvar Ilyasov.

human rights, including the freedom of speech and of religion as a matter of individual choice.

In addition to the nationalist and religious opposition, there is some opposition based on policy differences. For instance, Faisulla Ishakov, chairman of the Organizing Committee of the Uzbek Social Progress Party, opposed the government on the grounds that it continued to pursue the policies of the Soviet government. Ishakov favored a new agricultural policy that included handing over land to peasants. But even Ishakov, reflecting widespread fears that land privatization would result in racial stratification, claimed that there should be no right to resell the land for twenty years. Otechestva, a party bearing a Russian name meaning "fatherland," claimed to be modeled after Western liberal-democratic parties. The goal of the party, according to its general secretary, Uzman Azim, was to achieve economic and spiritual independence in Uzbekiston.[55]

Official and unofficial harassment of the opposition parties took a variety of forms during 1992. The newspapers *Halk Suzi* and *Narodnoe Slovo*

Islam Karimov, former finance minister and party secretary who became the first president of the Republic of Uzbekiston. During the first years of independence, Karimov stressed an "Uzbek path to development," emphasizing a cautious blend of state-engineered economic reforms and traditional government. Karimov, an intelligent but sometimes ruthless leader, dealt harshly with political opposition, insisting that avoiding the "Tojik variant" was the government's number-one priority. Photo by Anvar Ilyasov.

were closed down in early 1992. President Karimov was harshly criticized by Russian and other foreign observers for attempting to silence political opposition and for allowing opposition leaders to be isolated and even beaten. Karimov defended his policy as the only means to avoid what he termed the "Tojik variant." He stated publicly that his model of leadership would be Indonesia's president, Suharto. Suharto, Karimov claimed, may have brooked little political opposition but he would be revered in history for setting his country on the road to economic modernization.[56]

Karimov insistently pushed the message that economic development, not European-style civil rights, was the true benefit of national independence. But the road to prosperity was not an easy one for Uzbekiston. Russia's decision to free retail prices on many goods and services in January 1992 forced Uzbekiston to do one of two things: either free prices or impose restrictions on exports to prevent subsidized goods from flowing out of the republic. Uzbekiston opted to do both simultaneously. Restrictions were immediately placed upon exports, and prices for many goods and services moved upward, although not as swiftly as in Russia. At the same time, the government gave the green light to the formation of parastatals (as in Turkmenistan, these are essentially government-run enterprises that are nominally private). The Ministry of Trade was transformed into a State Stock Association called Savdo. The presidential gave the local hakims the right to run the branches of Savdo on a regional basis. At the same time, the State Committee on State Property and Privatization, headed by economist Shukhrat Gafurov, was established to oversee the transition of state enterprises to private management and ownership.

Uzbekiston adopted a probusiness posture. The government moved to boost foreign trade through a number of mechanisms. A presidential decree in May 1992 provided that agricultural enterprises would be relieved of the value-added tax. A decree designed to attract direct foreign investment came into effect on a few months later. According to the decree, enterprises that included a specified amount of foreign investment would be exempt from income tax during their first five years of operation.[57] A major law on foreign investment was signed in May 1994, designed to create confidence among foreign investors that profits could be withdrawn from the country.[58]

The economy was more diversified than the economies of the other Central Asian states. It included agriculture, light industry, heavy industry, and important branches in primary commodities. The primary commodities industries were buoyed in the first years of independence by two important developments. In February 1992 oil prospectors in Uzbekiston's Fergana Valley struck oil near Namangan. The gusher erupted with such force that it took more than a month to cap. The area was renamed Ming-Bulak (Thousand Springs). At about the same time, the managers of the Muruntau gold quarry, one of the largest gold-bearing deposits in the world, signed an agreement with the U.S.-based Newmont Mining Company to process the area's gold deposits. With Soviet technology, it was necessary to process between one and two tons of ore to extract two grams of gold. The technology that Newmont introduced made the mine profitable to operate. Both the mining and petroleum industries stayed under the direct control of the government.

The largest sector of Uzbekiston's economy is agriculture. Uzbekiston established a state agricultural trust in 1992. Agriculture had been dominated in the past by large government-managed operations. For instance, in 1990 Uzbekiston had some 940 kolkhozes and 1,108 sovkhozes.[59] The IMF team that collected data in the Central Asian states during site visits in the spring of 1992 reported that in 1990 and 1991 about 500,000 hectares of arable land were distributed to families for use as private farms or as personal plots.[60] But this land came largely in two categories:

The main office building of the Milii Havsizlik Hizmati (State Security Service) in downtown Tashkent. Photo by Gregory Gleason, 1995.

It was either of marginal quality or it was located in the immediate vicinity of large urban areas.

Foreign trade, however, has been stymied by the lack of access to foreign markets. Uzbekiston has no natural ports, no developed foreign trade infrastructure, and little foreign trade expertise. Moreover, political relations with bordering countries forced Uzbekiston into a reflexive withdrawn posture. For instance, as conflict broke into the open in the northern regions of Tojikiston during the spring of 1992, Uzbekiston acted to establish border controls. In August 1992 the Dushanbe-Tashkent railway line was closed to prevent political refugees from entering Uzbekiston. A short time afterward, Uzbek officials attempted to close the entire border between Tojikiston and Uzbekiston. The border with the northern Tojikiston province of Leninabod remained open for a period but then also was closed, cutting off Tojikiston from the outside world almost entirely. Customs and duty stations sprouted at every border checkpoint, giving the newly independent Uzbekiston the character of a "closed society."

In the few very brief years since independence, the nationality question has assumed an entirely new character. Karimov's policy since independence has been to encourage the groundswell of popular support for the celebration of national identity. The decree on Uzbekiston citizenship adopted in July 1992 granted citizenship to all persons living in the territory regardless of national origin, social status, race, sex, education, language, or political view. It excluded, however, dual citizenship, a demand that many Russians and many in the Russian government continued to press.[61] In late 1995 a presidential decree maintained that pensions and other social services would only be provided to those individuals who presented an Uzbeki passport.

The use of the Uzbek language is an even more important example of the narrowing nationality focus of the Karimov government. Uzbek, it is sometimes argued, is not one language but a family of related languages. The literary language—the Fergana dialect—is the language of the media but is not comprehensible to all Uzbeks. The new government emphasis on Uzbek, however, is designed to impose a single linguistic convention on the country in a short time. In September 1992 the general director of the Uzbek National Information Agency announced that the agency would soon produce information only in Uzbek.[62] Russian-language street signs have virtually disappeared in Uzbekiston. Although a few of these signs remain in Tashkent and other areas with larger Russian-speaking populations, they have been entirely replaced by Uzbek-language signs in the rural areas. The difficult situation of the Russian-speaking population was underscored late in 1989 with the passage of the new official-language law that calls for a transition from Russian to Turkic by 1997.[63]

Non-Uzbeks fear the future, particularly the futures of their children, convincing many to leave.[64] The year 1990 was one of debate among many Russians whether the time had come for a return to the "Russian homeland."[65] In most cases, those who could return to Russia did so, sometime at great expense to Uzbekiston. As one observer warned in 1990, if the trend toward out-migration was not reversed, in two to three years the technologically advanced production sectors in Central Asia would experience a "catastrophic shortage of technological specialists," ultimately leading to "Angolicization" of the Central Asian economy.[66] But such catastrophic consequences have not occurred, perhaps because there are many ethnic Russians and other non-Uzbeks who have resigned themselves to staying in "stable" Uzbekiston rather than risk relocation to their homelands.

TIDES OF UZBEK HEGEMONY

Uzbekiston's transition to national independence was clearly a case of revolution "from above." Virtually the entire political and economic leadership is a carryover from the Soviet period. Uzbekiston's national independence did not "restore" autonomy and national self-determination,

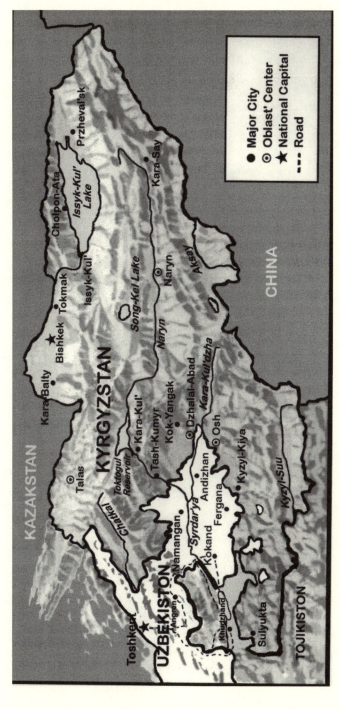

Fergana Valley Border Complexity

for Uzbekiston never existed as an independent political unit prior to its annexation in the late nineteenth century by Russia. Furthermore, after independence Uzbekiston did not achieve "splendid isolation" and complete autonomy, for its infrastructure was tightly meshed with that of the former USSR in such a way that immediate disentanglement would have been suicidal and impossible.

If the politics of independence in a country as proud, self-confident, and richly rooted in tradition as Uzbekiston teaches us any lesson about national independence at all, it is that autonomy in the modern period is limited and constrained. Globalization, economic interdependence, and instant communication have limited the scope of independence. Traditional nation-state conflicts seen in economic nationalism and security competition have further constrained the meaning of independence. It is clear that Uzbekiston is linked to the other countries of the CIS in ways that will continue to dominate Uzbekiston's political agenda for many years to come.

Within Central Asia, particularly among the Tojiks and Kyrgyz but also among the Karakalpaks, Turkmens, and Kazaks, there are historical grounds to fear that Uzbekiston will seek to establish a dominant role in Central Asia in the post-Soviet period. The complicated border arrangement in the Fergana Valley creates incessant problems of border maintenance. Uzbekiston proper has only one road that links the capital and the bulk of the country with the Fergana Valley. Ninety percent of the road traffic must travel through Tojik territory to get back and forth from these sections of Uzbekiston.

Many of these fears of "Uzbek hegemony" probably would have stayed in the background if it had not been for the outbreak of hostilities in Tojikiston. At independence, Tojikiston was a remote, poor, internally divided country bordering Afghanistan. The Afghan War created conditions that produced extreme pressures during the first year of the post-communist transition. Political independence produced new opportunities for powerful regional cliques to emerge both as opposition movements and political parties. But rather than stimulating compromise and agreement, this new pluralism produced only polarization and civil war. In the eyes of extremists and moderates alike, the war served as a pretext in Tojikiston and Uzbekiston for policies ranging from domestic political crackdowns to aggressive foreign adventures. Leaders throughout the region, particularly in Uzbekiston, warned that the Tojik situation was a potential precursor of the "Yugoslavia syndrome" (the tendency of countries to break into warring factions).

By mid-1992, the Tojik civil war became the defining element in the Central Asian security regime. On September 3, 1992, the presidents of Uzbekiston, Kazakstan, Kyrgyzstan, and Russia issued a warning that if civil war in Tojikiston continued it would present a threat to the CIS and would be grounds for military intervention. Finally, in November 1992, Uzbekiston—with Russian military assistance—led the Central Asian states in reestablishing the Hojent-Kuliab coalition to power.[67] It was this coalition that wrested back control of the government and maintained power throughout 1993. The restoration of the Hojent government in Tojikiston was possible only by assistance from outside.

The effort to reestablish the "procommunist," that is, "conservative" coalition in Tojikiston is more than an isolated attempt to restore and prop up what was regarded as a friendly government. It is the signal event in a much broader change in regional power relationships. Under pressure from the Tojik conflict, Uzbekiston drew a very old conclusion of realist international politics: *Si vis pacem para bellum* ("If you seek peace, prepare for war"). Uzbekiston began arming itself, developing alliances, and seeking to extend its political influence into its neighboring states, particularly in those areas of Kyrgyzstan and Tojikiston surrounding the Fergana Valley.

For the most part, Uzbekiston's efforts have escaped the notice of Western observers. Unfortunately, the whole story cannot be told, because no one was watching closely enough to record the events as they happened. But a few examples may illustrate the trend. For one thing, Uzbekiston established itself as the guarantor of stability in the entire region of the Fergana Valley, including those sections physically located within the territorial borders of Kyrgyzstan. In the spring of 1993, Uzbekiston conducted military exercises on adjacent territory in Kyrgyzstan without even requesting permission from the Kyrgyz government. Similarly, by early 1993 Uzbekiston had moved to essentially annex Leninabod, the northern province of Tojikiston. Uzbekiston President Karimov even reportedly took control over the appointment of Leninabod's hakim. Karimov became the protector, the *Aka* of northern Tojikiston.

Uzbekiston also took advantage of the challenge presented by the Tojik civil war to seek outside assistance. Karimov's appeals to the United Nations for peacekeeping forces, although unsuccessful in eliciting any response, nonetheless established him as the champion of political stability in the region. The Tojik events also furnished a rationale for a continued close political and military alliance with Russia. Russian politicians were pleased to see the "burden" of administering Central Asia removed from their shoulders while finding that the southern border of the USSR—the old "Curzon Line"—remained the boundary of Russia's sphere of influence in the south.

Most important, the Tojik civil war stirred to life ancient memories of the Uzbeks as leaders in Central Asia. Uzbekiston saw the Tojik civil war as an irrefutable argument for Uzbekiston's assumption of the role of guarantor of regional stability in Central Asia. In the autumn of 1995 President Karimov publicly embraced the idea of the unity of Central Asian peoples, announcing, "Our homeland—Turkestan—is one big home, one great household, one great family."[68]

The Uzbeks have historically seen themselves as moral and political leaders in Central Asia. Uzbek politicians eagerly contemplate the prospect of reestablishing that role. They assert that it is only an accident of history that the collapse of the USSR left nuclear weapons on the territory of their northern neighbors, the Kazaks, thereby catapulting them into the arena of international attention. The rightful claim to the position of authority within Central Asia, many Uzbeks feel, is based on historical, cultural, and geopolitical factors and not on military capability. Uzbeks explain that Soviet power was calculated in terms of decades. Central Asian history, in contrast, must be reckoned in terms of millennia. The tides of Central Asian history, they assert, favor a return to prominence of the Uzbeks.

NOTES

1. These semantic conventions acquired much more than symbolic meaning. In many cases the Central Asian societies returned to place-names that were in widespread use prior to the Soviet period. In some cases, the Russianized forms of place-names in many cases were changed slightly but sufficiently to "de-Russify" pronunciation. This was often interpreted by the nonindigenous, Russian-speaking population as an intentional slight. Even the Western world found the renaming process problematic. The U.S. government, for instance, after much bureaucratic wrangling over the meaning of the changes, adopted "Kazakhstan" as the official name for Kazakstan, avoiding the seemingly quixotic "Qazaqstan." However, the *kh* in the middle of the word is clearly a Russianism. Somewhat later, the U.S. government followed Kazakstan's practice in dropping the *kh* sound in favor of the native *k*, yielding Kazakstan.

2. Dmitrii Valovoi, *Kremlevskki tupik i Nazarbaev* (Moscow: Moladaia gvardiia, 1993), p. 60.

3. This should be understood in light of the fact that Nazarbaev ran unopposed in this election.

4. *Izvestiia* (18 December 1991): 1.

5. On 18 June 1992, police cleared away the tent camp the demonstrators had established and cordoned off the area, although the demonstrators were allowed to remain.

6. *Izvestiia* (2 April 1992): 1.

7. These include: *Egemen Kazakstan* (a government newspaper); *Kazakstanskaya Pravda* (a government newspaper); *Halyk Kenesi* (the legislature's newspaper); *Zhas Alash* (an independent newspaper); *Ekspress K* (independent); *Karavan* (independent); *Panorama* (indpendent); *Azia* (independent); *Kazakhstan* (a Russian-language newspaper produced by the Ministry of Foreign Affairs); *Gorizont* (a paper distributed by the Ministry of Culture); *Stolitsa* (independent); as well as others.

8. As an example of the technocratic approach, see P. Svoik and E. Lan'ko, *Sud'ba Kazakhstana kak Gosudarstvo: Pervye shagi ot propoasti* (Almaty: Evrazia, 1994).

9. *Kazakhstanskaia Pravda* (16 May 1992): 3–6.

10. INTERFAX report of 17 June 1992, FBIS-SOV-92-118 (18 June 1992): 60.

11. International Monetary Fund, *Economic Review: Kazakhstan* (Washington, D.C.: IMF, May 1992), p. 8.

12. Abdullaev was reportedly relieved of this job on 20 July 1992 in connection with a transfer to other duties.

13. The process of privatization in Kazakstan is, unfortunately, not well documented in open sources. The references to the hearings are from the author's own notes from participation in the parliamentary session. Discussions of capitalism in terms of the role of primary commodity suppliers are now taking place in some of the most advanced economic and political scholarship in Kazakstan. An example is Nurlan Amrekulov and Nurbulat Masanov, *Kazakhstan mezhdu proshlym i budushchim* (Almaty: Beren, 1994).

14. Shortly after independence, the Kyrgyz government legalized opium cultivation for medicinal purposes for a brief period but, reacting to Western pressure, suspended the law in January 1992.

15. "Zakon Kirgizskoi SSR o zemle," *Sovetskaia Kirgiziia* (30 June 1990).

16. *Izvestiia* (13 November 1991): 2.

17. Ostankino television interview of 24 May 1992, FBIS-SOV-92-104 (29 May 1992): 63.

18. INTERFAX report of 4 July 1992, FBIS-SOV-92-133 (10 July 1992): 81.

19. FBIS-SOV-92-131 (8 July 1992): 70.

20. INTERFAX report of 3 July 1992, FBIS-SOV-92-131 (8 July 1992): 69.

21. Kyrgyztag report by Al'bert Bogdanov (21 August 1992).

22. International Monetary Fund, *Economic Review: Kyrghyzstan* (Washington, D.C.: IMF, May 1992), p. 45.

23. INTERFAX report of 1 June 1991, FBIS-SOV-92-108 (4 June 1992): 88.

24. Interview by Otto Latsis, *Izvestiia* (28 May 1992): 2.

25. K. Baialinov, "V interesakh svoego naroda inogda prikhoditsia kogo-to obnimat' . . . ," *Komsomol'skaia Pravda* (19 October 1992): 2.

26. Pavel Seregin, "Rozhdenie natsii," *Vek* 20, no. 2 (1992): 24–31.

27. FBIS-SOV-92-142 (23 July 1992): 56.

28. "Zemel'nyi kodeks Tadzhikskoi SSR," *Kommunist Tadzhikistana* (23 January 1991).

29. International Monetary Fund, *Economic Review: Kazakhstan*, p. 7.

30. *Izvestiia* (6 March 1992): 2.

31. FBIS-SOV-92-142 (23 July 1992): 56.

32. *Komsomol'skaia Pravda* (21 August 1992): 1.

33. Kenjaev's account of the war was printed in two volumes in Uzbekiston by the official press as Safarali Kenjaev, *Tabadduloti Tojikiston* (Tashkent: Uzbekiston, 1994).

34. The figure was provided by the commander of the Russian border forces, General Pavel Tarasenko, at a 28 November 1995 news conference.

35. An account of the initial round of negotiations between the government and the opposition may be found in Arkadi Dubnov, "The Elusive Negotiations," *Uncaptive Minds* no. 26 (Summer 1994).

36. *Trud* (29 October 1991): 1. A total of 97.4 percent of the eligible voters participated in the referendum.

37. Vitalii Portnikov, "Ritm reform my dolshny opredeliat' sami," *Nezavisimaia gazeta* (20 October 1992): 1.

38. *Turkmenskaia Iskra* (19 May 1992): 2.

39. Portnikov, "Ritm reform my dolshny opredeliat' sami," 1.

40. International Monetary Fund, *Economic Review: Turkmenistan* (Washington, D.C.: IMF, May 1992), p. 1.

41. For instance, in 1991 Georgia received 2,088 million m^3 of natural gas costing 2.979 billion rubles (at a rate of 1,426 rubles, 29 kopeks per 1,000 cubic meters of gas and a 28 percent tax and transport fee). FBIS-SOV-92-094 (14 May 1992): 59.

42. *Nezavisimaia gazeta* (8 May 1992): 1.

43. *Izvestiia* (5 March 1992): 1.

44. V. Kuleshov, "Turkmenistan gotov prodat' svoi gaz Ukraine po tsenam, priblizhennym k mirovym," *Izvestiia* (6 March 1992): 1.

45. INTERFAX report of 15 June 1992, FBIS-SOV-92-116 (16 June 1992): 56.

46. *Turkmenskaia Iskra* (31 March 1992): 1.

47. INTERFAX report of 27 February 1992, FBIS-SOV-92-045 (6 March 1992): 56.

48. INTERFAX (8 September 1992).

49. "Report on the Parliamentary Election in Turkmenistan, December 11, 1994," Commission on Security and Cooperation in Europe, Washington, D.C., February 1995, p. 16.

50. Radio Rossii broadcast of August 21, 1992, FBIS-SOV-92 (24 August 1992): 50.

51. INTERFAX (30 July 1992).

52. I. Mikhailova, "Nachalo," *Zvezda Vostoka* no. 4 (1990): 73–81.

53. Mikhailova, "Nachalo," pp. 74–81.

54. See Utaev's remarks in the interview with Robin Wright, "Report from Turkestan," *New Yorker* (6 April 1992): 53.

55. Ostankino television (5 August 1992).

56. Semen Novoprudskii, "Prezident Karimov gotov vstat' na koleni," *Nezavisimaia gazeta* (9 July 1992): 3.

57. Moscow radio report of 2 August 1992, FBIS-SOV-92-149 (3 August 1992): 39.

58. "Law on Foreign Investments and Guarantee of Foreign Investors' Activities" (5 May 1995). Texts of laws are available in the Uzbek government's regularly published compendium *Uzbekiston Respublikasi Konun va Farmonlar* (Uzbekiston Republic Laws and Decrees) and in translation in *Business Laws Uzbekistan*, published routinely by the Asian Business Agency, Tashkent.

59. *Narodnoe khoziaistvo Uzbekskoi SSR v 1990* (Tashkent: Uzbekiston, 1991), p. 225.

60. International Monetary Fund, *Economic Review: Uzbekistan* (Washington, D.C.: IMF, May 1992), p. 6.

61. FBIS-SOV-92-146 (29 July 1992): 42.

62. Moscow Radio Mayak (26 September 1992).

63. Not everyone thinks that the transition to a native language standard will be damaging to the position of the Russians. As one commentator noted, when

the local groups have returned to their native languages they will tend to separate from one another. "The Russian-speaking population will strengthen their position because the means of communication between different speaking republics naturally will be Russian." Alisher Il'khamov, "Vozmozhno li 'Uzbekskoe chudo' ili Rynochnaia ekonomika s vostochnym litsom," *Zhizn i ekonomika* (Tashkent) no. 11 (1990): 7.

64. Sergei Tatur, "Vmeste podnimat' Uzbekistan," *Zvezda Vostoka* no. 1 (January 1991): 3–17.

65. "Bezhentsy v Rossii: Chto dal'she?" *Pravda Vostoka* (28 November 1991): 3.

66. Timur Pulatov, "Dogonim i peregonim Angolu!" *Moskovskie novosti* no. 14 (October 1990): 7.

67. Uzbekiston's Karimov supplied a large amount of military assistance to the Hojent faction. He also repeatedly requested military assistance from the CIS. Nazarbaev agreed to send troops in January 1993, but it was not until April that the Kazakstan parliament gave its consent. *Egemendy Qazaqstan* (April 10, 1993): 1.

68. ITAR-TASS (21 November 1995).

FIVE

Central Asia and the World

Central Asia was considered the heartland of the ancient Asian world. Its pivotal geographical position allowed it to play a key role in the relations among the tribes and peoples of Eurasia. Central Asia's importance was symbolized in the ancient idea of the "Gordian Knot"—the power that controlled Central Asia also controlled the passageways to the riches of the East and to the markets of the West. Many khans, conquerors, chieftains, and warriors found the Gordian Knot to be their undoing. Boundaries of empires and khanates shifted like the Central Asian desert sands. At one point, Central Asia formed the northern frontier of the Persian empire. At another time it formed the southeastern frontier of the Mongol khanates. In the Middle Ages, it was the land bridge linking China with Europe. In the modern world, Central Asia's importance grew from its role as a sphere of contestation among the Great Powers, particularly England and Russia.

With the expansion of the European colonial empires in the nineteenth century, Central Asia was transformed into a buffer zone of the European powers. British expansion into India and Persia coincided with Russian expansion into the steppes of southwestern Siberia and then, further south, into all of Central Asia. The competition between the Great Powers for control of Central Asia was motivated primarily by their desire to expand their spheres of influence, not by a desire to bring these areas under direct colonial control. Spheres of influence provided buffer zones for security purposes and provided raw materials and commodities for commercial purposes. This contest became known as the "Great Game."[1]

THE "GREAT GAME" REVISITED

The competition of the Great Game was more a cold war than a hot one. Only rarely did the competition between the Great Powers involve direct confrontation. The preferred style of competition was the kind of activity described in Rudyard Kipling's novel *Kim*—intelligence intrigues between the British and the Russians over the Afghanistan border. The dividing line between the spheres of influence of the two empires, proposed by the British diplomat Lord George Curzon and known afterward simply as the "Curzon Line," demarcated the southern boundary of Russian imperial control in the nineteenth century. This boundary lived on in the twentieth century as the southern frontier of the USSR.

As the USSR began to collapse in 1991, a sense of alarm swept through the foreign chancelleries of governments around the world. Many diplomats feared that the Soviet collapse could only mean a renewed competition among the Great Powers for regional influence in Central Asia. Diplomats and analysts struggled to define the situation and identify vital interests at stake in this new Great Game.

The modern Great Game differs from the nineteenth-century competition in many respects. First, the distinction between Great Powers and the lesser powers is less well defined today than it was a century ago. To be sure, differences in national capabilities are as great as they ever were, perhaps even more so. But economic interdependence, instantaneous global communication, and the importance of world public opinion has given smaller states greater latitude than they had in the realpolitik of a century ago. Second, the Great Powers of a century ago established spheres of political influence. The goal of this effort was to remove the arena of potential conflict from one's borders and to ensure that hostilities, should they take place, occurred on a neighbor's territory rather than on one's own. Competition, therefore, tended to take place at the interstices, between the spheres of influence in remote regions such as Afghanistan. In the modern world, spheres of influence are overlapping and interspersed. States have a variety of greater interests and, accordingly, less focused objectives. Modern means of mass destruction have made it less certain that hostilities can be successfully confined to remote lands.

But the defining aspect of the contemporary competition is the collapse of the ideological paradigm of communism. With the declining salience of ideological conflict following the collapse of communist doctrine, the contemporary Great Powers do not have clear adversaries and allies in the region. The Cold War indisputably helped define the lines of competition by making it easy to distinguish allies from adversaries. In the post–Cold War period, these definitions have become much more ad hoc and pragmatic. In Tojikiston's civil war, for instance, European diplomats were at a loss to decide which side to support in the conflict. Should they support the former communists who were championing law and order, or the Islamic Revival Party, who clearly represented the more democratic elements but nonetheless appeared to have links to foreign Islamic revolutionary movements? Puzzled by the chaos of the situation, diplomats turned their attention to other, more tractable matters.

The features of the new Great Game and the post–Cold War order in Central Asia suggest that there are two tiers of influence in the region. The first-tier countries have vital interests, that is, interests that directly affect the well-being of their citizens or present great opportunities or, perhaps, threats to their country's domestic security. The second-tier states are those whose interests in the region are principally derivative, that is, they flow from long-term considerations of balances of power, ideological or moral concerns, or a single, specific issue such as the importance of oil or the control of nuclear technology.

According to these definitions, the first-tier countries include all the states immediately adjacent to the Central Asian countries.[2] These states have direct and vital interests in the region. Listed roughly in their order of importance, they are Russia, China, Turkey, Iran, Afghanistan, and Pakistan.

RUSSIA AND CENTRAL ASIA

Russia is the most important neighbor of all the Central Asian countries. Russian interests in Central Asia flow from the fact that Russia has domestic political concerns that permanently and profoundly affect its foreign policies toward the countries of the region. For one thing, large numbers of Russians live in Central Asia. Although some have returned to Russia for fear of becoming displaced colonials in the new "Muslim states," many Russians in the Central Asian states have resigned themselves to remaining. In late 1994 and early 1995, Foreign Minister Andrei Kozyrev reiterated that Russia would be prepared even to intervene militarily in the "near abroad"—those republics that the Soviet collapse turned into "foreign countries"—to protect the interests of Russians.[3]

The events in Central Asia during the first year of independence had a significant influence on domestic Russian political debates. During the summer and fall of 1992, Boris Yeltsin's government was reeling from criticism that its foreign policy toward the near abroad was a national disgrace. The criticism came close to challenging the authority of Yeltsin himself and did result in a substantial change of course in domestic Russian policy in December 1992. Radical nationalists in Russia made the "abandonment" of Russians living in the near abroad a cause célèbre in their campaigns against Yeltsin and the reformers.

Leading political figures in Russia used the defense of the civil rights of Russians and other Slavs living in the near abroad as an instrument in Russia's complex political gambit to maintain a Central Asian sphere of influence. During the campaign leading to the December 17, 1995, parliamentary elections in Russia, Aleksandr Lebed, a leading nationalist politician, proposed extending the Russian sphere of influence in an effort to protect ethnic Russians stranded in the near abroad by the Soviet collapse. Lebed said that Russia should solve the problem of ethnic Russians living "outside the borders of their historic homeland" with "any available means, including military."[4]

The former Soviet Union continues to be heavily dependent upon raw materials and supplies from some of the Central Asian states. Disengagement from Central Asia, therefore, is not economically desirable. Yet many Russians seem psychologically incapable of accepting a change in the status of the Curzon line. They continue to see policing their southern external frontiers as a responsibility of Russia. And it must be noted that Russian influence was not rejected by many Central Asians themselves. All of the Central Asian presidents spoke out forcefully and unambiguously in favor of retaining good foreign relations with Moscow.

At independence, Russia quickly recognized the new Central Asian states as independent countries. Russia appointed ambassadors to all the Central Asian republics. Reciprocating, all of the Central Asian states made it clear that maintaining good relations with Russia was their principal foreign policy objective. Kyrgyzstan's Askar Akaev, for instance, said, "No matter what new ties we establish in the West and East, no matter how great our urge to merge into the eastern, western, or worldwide economic community, our ties with Russia and our friendship and cooperation with the Russian people will always be special. We will give this priority."[5] Kazakhstan's Nursultan Nazarbaev said, "We attach the highest significance to ties with Russia. And this is understandable. For many years we lived side by side. We have many common tasks which we have to solve."[6] Nazar Suyunov, Turkmenistan's deputy prime minister, told a *Nezavisimaia Gazeta* reporter that "Russia has been and will be our republic's main economic partner."[7] Upon his appointment as the new foreign minister of Turkmenistan, Khalykberdy Ataev noted, "I believe that Turkmenistan must maintain special relations with Russia."[8]

Contrary to expectations that upon real independence the Central Asian countries would denounce their former imperial overlords and reject any entreaties for postcolonial cooperation, Central Asians willingly accepted the proposition that the Russians per se were not responsible for their hardships but rather the flawed doctrines of Soviet Bolshevism were to blame. It was in fact Russia—not the Central Asian countries—that seemed most to withdraw into internal affairs upon the breakup of the USSR. During the first three months of the CIS, Yeltsin struggled to reverse the tide of devolution to which he himself had contributed mightily with his insistent efforts to break up the USSR. Yeltsin declared that although he was in favor of ending the Soviet Union and of further decentralization, he could not accept the further breakup of Russia. By March 1992 Yeltsin had negotiated an end to the devolutionary trend. The Treaty of Russian Federation was signed and, although some areas continued to press for greater decentralization, the bulk of Russia's concerns turned again to outside affairs. The war in Chechnya in 1994 and 1995, started by Russia in an effort to draw the line against further devolution, illustrates the Yeltsin government's macabre commitment to the principle of maintaining a unified Russia.

As the new Central Asian states began to develop along independent lines, they increasingly ran into problems of policy coordination with Russia. One problem was the exercise of military authority in the CIS forces and, after the dissolution of the single CIS military command, the interoperability of the new national militaries. Another issue was the currency arrangements and the maintenance of the ruble zone. Yet another issue was the question of human and civil rights, particularly the issue of citizenship and the treatment of the Russian-speaking populations in Central Asia. There was the troubling problem of dividing the Soviet physical infrastructure of transportation and communication. Then there was the difficult issue of dividing the foreign debt of the USSR.

The problems encountered in maintaining the ruble zone illustrate the close linkage of the fates of all the countries. None of the successor states was in a position at independence to rapidly introduce its own currency, yet none of the countries wanted to be dependent upon monetary decisions taken by Russian authorities. The Central Asian states' aversion to dependence on Russia increased as the Russian Central Bank flooded the ruble zone with cheap currency, allowing the ruble rate to depreciate with respect to the U.S. dollar from 30:1 in 1991 to 5,500:1 in 1994.

Each of the Central Asian states considered introducing separate currencies during the first months of independence. Early in 1992 officials in Uzbekiston publicly debated the wisdom of introducing a new currency but later announced that any plans to introduce a native currency would be postponed until the end of 1993. Throughout 1992 all of the Central Asian countries stayed in the ruble zone. When the Estonian kroon was introduced in late June 1992, both Turkmenistan and Kazakstan immediately announced that the kroon would not be accepted at any rate except that which was established by Russian authorities. Russia announced that it would make the ruble a fully convertible currency by July 1, 1992, then changed the date to August 1, 1992. After the ruble floated on the international market as a tradable currency, it plunged in value, falling quickly from 130:1 to more than 450:1 against the U.S. dollar. The Central Asian states and the other states in the ruble zone were passive victims in this currency devaluation. The experience steeled the resolve of each of these states to introduce their own currencies in 1993.

RUSSIA AND OIL

The Central Asian countries are confronted by issues related to the area's tightly interconnected energy supplies. Russia plays a pivotal role in Central Asian regional issues through its control of existing trade routes. The Russian role of virtually controlling transportation in the Caspian Sea region has created one of the region's most serious political issues. The Caspian Sea, the world's largest inland body of water, has long been dominated by Russia. The region's rich oil and gas reserves are located primarily in Azerbaijan, Kazakstan, and Turkmenistan. Uzbekiston was buoyed by recent oil discoveries in the Fergana Valley, but Uzbekiston intends to use most of its oil for domestic purposes. Oil industry analysts expect that the entire Central Asian region could be exporting as much as 2 million barrels per day by 2010.

Even before the collapse of the USSR, government officials in Kazakstan began negotiating what the country's press referred to at the time as the "the deal of the century"—developing Kazakstan's Tengiz oil fields. Kazakstan's government joined the large multinational oil firm Chevron to form a joint venture, Tengizchevroil. The agreement committed Chevron to spend about $20 billion over twenty years to develop the Tengiz field's 6 billion barrels of proven reserves. Other firms, including Birlesmis Muhendisler Burosu, British Gas, and Agip also have invested in the country's oil fields.

Turkmenistan is potentially a very rich country. It has 8.1 trillion cubic meters of known gas reserves and 700 million tons of oil reserves.[9] Petroleum analysts claim that further exploration will reveal that the total reserves could be much larger, perhaps as great as 20 trillion cubic meters of gas. Turkmenistan has its own refinery capacity, with a major unit located at Turkmenbashi (Krasnovodsk) on Turkmenistan's Caspian coast and another located in Chardzhou. In 1992 the government announced the discovery of major new gas deposits in the Kara Kum Desert near Bakhardok.

Russia's geographical position and the physical and political realities of Asia and the Middle East leave access to markets, and therefore much control, in the hands of the Russians. As the Soviet Union broke up, the question immediately arose regarding how to finance and move the energy riches to outside markets. Equally important, much of the potential oil riches of the region lie in the Caspian littoral area. No agreement on equitable apportionment of these common property resources existed when the Soviet Union broke up.

Firefighters at the oil field in Ming-Bulak, Uzbekiston. The economies of the Central Asian countries were organized and maintained by Soviet authorities as suppliers of raw materials to industry located in the Soviet heartland. Political independence imposed upon the Central Asian countries impelled the necessity to quickly develop manufacturing capacity to break out of the cycle of economic dependence. Kyrgyzstan was the most vulnerable country, having virtually no usable industrial potential. Turkmenistan's position was the most favorable. Virtually limitless reserves of natural gas offered this country a simple development strategy. The discovery of large oil fields in Kazakstan suggested a development strategy that relied heavily on foreign investment and international trade. Uzbekiston's position was mixed. Photo by Anatoly Rakhimbaev.

Russia first sought to impose hefty taxes and surcharges on the movement of gas and oil and then, in order to block economic development that might run contrary to the interests of Russian energy firms, sought to blockade its southern neighbors by cutting off access to foreign markets entirely. Negotiation and posturing dragged on for almost two years. Chevron's returns from the Tengizchevroil joint venture, falling far short of expectations because of bureaucratic red tape, were threatened by Russia's intransigence. As late as October 1995 the Tengiz field was producing only 50,000 barrels per day, about half of its pumping capacity. When the Tengizchevroil agreement was first reached, it was anticipated that eventually Kazakstan would be exporting as much as 700,000 barrels per day. Chevron and Kazakstan's government began seeking to enlarge the players in the Central Asian energy market to increase political pressure

The discovery of a large oil field at Ming-Bulak (Thousand Springs) in the Fergana Valley captured Uzbekiston's imagination, particularly since the new find erupted into one of the largest oil-field fires in history. The photograph shows Albert Khasanov, the fire brigade leader, and other firefighters wrestling in March 1992 to bring the large fire under control. Photo by Anatoly Rakhimbaev.

on Russia. In November 1995, Russia's largest oil company, Lukoil, joined Tengizchevroil. Lukoil acquired a 10 percent share each from Kazakstan and Chevron. In exchange, Lukoil agreed to give Tengizchevroil a part of its oil export quota from Russia or make concessions to Chevron in the context of the Caspian Pipeline Consortium (CPC). About the same time, the Russian state-owned gas conglomerate, Gazprom, entered into an agreement with Turkmenistan's Oil and Gas Ministry, forming a joint venture, Turkmenrosgaz. Turkmenrosgaz, according to the agreement, would be responsible for all of Turkmenistan's gas exports to former Soviet countries.

The southern-tier countries began discussing ways to bring energy supplies to market without having to pass through Russian territory. Under the auspices of the Economic Cooperation Organization (ECO), the Central Asian countries discussed four major pipeline projects: Baku-Ceyhan (Turkey); Kazakstan-Turkmenistan-Afghanistan-Pakistan to the Indian Ocean; Turkmenistan-Iran-Turkey toward Europe; and the supply of Uzbekiston's and Turkmenistan's gas to Pakistan through Afghanistan.

Russian government officials, alarmed by the discussions to circumvent them, threatened to take unilateral action in retaliation. Russians accused Azerbaijan and Kazakstan of acting independently to exploit nat-

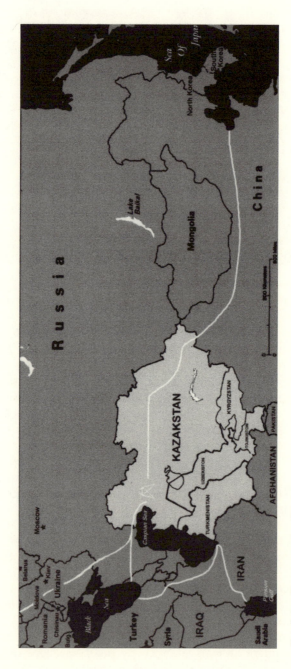

Kazakstan Transportation Routes

ural resources in the Caspian Basin, asserting that the oil resources belonged to all the littoral states. The disagreement forced negotiators to the table to develop an overall regional development strategy. These negotiations resulted in the signing of the Caspian Littoral Agreement. Parties to the agreement included Azerbaijan, Iran, Kazakstan, Russia, and Turkmenistan. The agreement was designed to coordinate trade routes, regulate access to natural and mineral resources, and unite efforts at environmental protection. The agreement also established the Caspian Council, consisting of a secretariat and four specialists' committees. The council would be politically controlled by an intergovernmental council representing the littoral states.

The CPC was founded by Russia, Kazakstan, and Oman in 1995. The original goal of the consortium was to deliver oil from the Tengiz field in Kazakstan to a Russian port on the Black Sea for transshipment to Western markets. The consortium is made up of eleven companies (Amoco, Pennzoil, Unocal, Exxon, McDermott International, and British Gas as well as smaller companies from Britain, Norway, Russia, Saudi Arabia, and Turkey). The consortium agreed to supply the Western markets through an existing pipeline into the existing Russian system and by building a pipeline through Chechnya and another, more expensive pipeline through Georgia. A proposed natural gas pipeline would run through Turkmenistan, Uzbekiston, China, and the Korean Peninsula. Construction is to begin in the year 2000. The project, expected to cost nearly $10 billion, is expected to move 18 million cubic meters (m^3) of gas per year.

CENTRAL ASIA'S NEIGHBORS

The second most important foreign country in Central Asian regional affairs is China. During the first year of Central Asian independence, China championed a development strategy for the new Central Asian countries, emphasizing domestic political stability and export-led economic growth programs. Central Asian leaders, particularly Uzbekiston's Islam Karimov and Turkmenistan's Saparmurad Niyazov, often cited the "Chinese model" as a rationale for their view that political stability was a precondition of economic growth.

China's long-term interests in Central Asia lie primarily in four categories: strategic interests, commercial interests, transboundary issues, and ethnic issues. China's strategic interests flow from the fact that Central Asia forms a buffer to Russia. China would be an important staging area in any conflict with Afghanistan, Iran, Pakistan, or India. China's commercial interests flow first from the fact that the Central Asian countries are resource-rich; second, they present a market for Chinese-made consumer durables. China also offers a long but dependable trade route for Central Asian primary commodities. Transboundary resources have not been a sore point of Sino-Soviet relations in the past, but new economic development plans for the western reaches of China place a premium on Xinjiang's transboundary resources. Eighty percent of the water in Kazakstan's Ili Valley originates inside China. International law is not clear on the extent to which China would be able to make future claims on this resource, but it is unlikely that China would be satisfied with any international transboundary agreement that legally entitled China to less than 50 percent of the water.

Cultural links between China and the countries of the Pamir, particularly Kyrgyzstan, are ancient. They are based in the cultural and linguistic kinship between the Central Asian populations and the large Turkophone Uigur population in China. Soviet policy in its Central Asian republics did little to permanently reorient these populations away from their ancient, common heritage. To the contrary, Soviet official policy often had the effect of preserving individual ethnic and religious identities in Central Asia even as it absorbed and transformed the native elites.[10] Parallel interests between Central Asians of the former Soviet Union and the groups in Inner Mongolia and Turkic Xinjiang continue to provoke discussions of cultural and even political unity. Although a formal political union of these groups has never existed and is not likely to emerge, there have been attempts to establish a more conscious and deliberately focused community of interests in the area. For example, Free Uigurstan held its first meeting in July 1992 in Bishkek, Kyrgyzstan.[11]

Whereas China looms large as the future's most important regional power in Central Asia, Turkey's contemporary influence in Central Asia is second in importance only to Russia's. Turkey's entrance into the Central Asian region was sudden and dramatic. Long aligned in foreign policy with the countries of NATO, Turkey was systematically excluded from diplomatic and cultural contacts with elements inside the old USSR. A delegation of Turkish diplomats led by Turkey's president, Suleyman Demirel, descended in large numbers on the Central Asian states in early 1992 to find a fraternal culture whose language and traditions they recognized as their own. The ecstatic first moments of contact resulted in anticipations of sweeping cultural, economic, and even political integration. Turkey's Minister of Foreign Affairs, Khikmet Chetin, proclaimed, "There will come a day when we [Turkey and Uzbekiston] will sit together in the same parliament."[12]

Turkey almost immediately proposed foreign aid, offering educational scholarships for a large number of Central Asian students. Turkey's goal was to help Central Asia but also to ensure that the next generation of Central Asian leaders would be trained in Turkey rather than in

Moscow.[13] Direct airline service from Turkey was opened to the Central Asian capitals. In early March 1992, Uzbekiston's Karimov, probably motivated by cost considerations, asked Turkey to represent Uzbekiston's interests in international organizations on a temporary basis. Turkish national television began broadcasting to the Central Asian states in May 1992.

Turkish diplomats and officials saw a natural affinity in the Central Asian countries, an affinity that was presumed to have implications for commerce as well as culture. A Turkish delegation under the leadership of Government Minister Ikram Dzhaikhun visited Uzbekiston in mid-April 1992. Dzhaikhun expressed his sense of pan-Turanian commonality, noting:

> Uzbekiston is an area that is rich in every respect. If the possibilities are properly and rationally used, there is no doubt that Uzbekiston will become one of the developed countries of the world. . . . The greatness of soul and the hospitality of the Uzbeks flows from the nature of the Turkic peoples. Their roots are intertwined from ancient times. There is no alternative to the strengthening of our friendship and cooperation.[14]

The conclusion that the Turks drew from this affinity was that the Turkish development model was the clear solution to the development problems in the Central Asian states. In a similar vein, Uzbekiston's prime minister, Abdulkhoshim Mutalov, stated:

> Until Uzbekiston can enter the world market with finished products, it will be very difficult to make a fundamental turn in an economy that has developed over decades. For this reason, the example of Turkey and its model of market relations can lead this country out of the economic crisis. The form of privatization of government enterprises pursued in Turkey can be of real, practical help in solving Uzbekiston's vitally important problems.[15]

Askar Akaev, at the close of his visit with Turkey's president, Turgut Ozal, in July 1992, claimed that "Turkey is the locomotive of development for the countries of the Black Sea region."[16] With the passage of time, however, some aspects of the "Turkish miracle" appeared to many Central Asians as less appropriate than the Turks first supposed. A certain measure of paternalism in the tone of many Turkish representatives soon became identified with Great Power pretensions. Some Central Asians began to think of Turkey as only a partner, not a model.

Another major influence in the region is Iran. Iran has key geostrategic interests in the states north of its border. With the close of the Iran-Iraq War and the destruction of much of the Iraqi war machine in the expulsion of Iraq from Kuwait, Iran reemerged as the most important regional power in West Asia. Iran concentrated its foreign relations efforts in Azerbaijan, in part because of the large Azerbaijanian population located in northern Iran. Shortly after Central Asian independence, Iran, according to one source, offered assistance totaling $130 million to Central Asia, most of it to Azerbaijan.[17]

Iran also established active diplomatic and trade ties with the other Central Asian states, beginning in early 1992. In March of that year Iran reportedly offered Turkmenistan a credit line of $50 million.[18] Just six months after Central Asia's independence, Iran began implementing provisions of an agreement with Turkmenistan to facilitate trade and cultural exchange. The Iran-Turkmenistan border was opened to automobile traffic at eight points. A simplified customs inspection procedure was also established at some points on the border, including the Badjigeran-Gaudan Road near Ashgabat and the Pasgakhepol-Gidriolum Road in western Turkmenistan. Citizens of both countries could purchase bus tickets on a daily route between Meshhed and Ashgabat. A Tedjen-Meshhed railway line was opened and plans were drawn up to build a Turkmenistan-Iran-Turkey-Europe gas pipeline. Direct phone service was established between Meshhed and Ashgabat. The first Turkmenistan National Airlines flight on the Ashgabat-Tehran route went into service in the summer of 1992.

Central Asia's other neighbors to the south—Saudi Arabia, Kuwait, the United Arab Emirates, Qatar, Bahrain, and Oman—also quickly recognized the independence of the Central Asian states. Among these countries, Saudi Arabia was a leader in drawing the new states into firm diplomatic relationships. The government of Saudi Arabia had already embarked upon a major assistance program to the region before independence was a fait accompli. In October 1991, Prince Bandar bin Sultan, the Saudi Arabian ambassador to the United States, announced that Saudi Arabia was providing Central Asia with millions of dollars in emergency aid.[19] The Saudi government's efforts in Central Asia had already included widely publicized programs for providing copies of the Qur'an to Central Asian Muslims and for aiding in the rehabilitation of the region's mosques and holy shrines.

The Saudi government extended diplomatic recognition to Uzbekiston in February 1992.[20] Uzbekiston's Karimov was the first Central Asian leader to visit Saudi Arabia. After a meeting with Fakhda Ben Abdul Aziz, the king of Saudi Arabia, a communiqué was issued in which the leaders agreed upon efforts to assist in economic development in the Muslim world, to improve "fraternal relations," and to eschew the use of force between governments and people.[21] By the summer of 1992, all the presidents of the Central Asian states had personally visited Saudi Arabia.

India is a country with a great variety of interests in Central Asia. Indian consumer goods, with prices and quality sometimes below international standards, find a ready market in the cash-starved but large and undiscriminating markets in Central Asia. The Indian government was anxious to encourage bilateral contacts, hosting a succession of Central Asian leaders and diplomatic delegations during the spring of 1992.

Pakistan was loath to be outdone in the race for influence in Central Asia. Pakistan was among the first countries to announce its intent to establish direct economic links with the Central Asian republics and to open consulates in the region.[22] The speed with which Pakistan welcomed independence in the Central Asian countries reflects Pakistan's assessment that Central Asia was originally part of West Asia and only artificially separated by the machinations of foreign Great Powers.

Along with Turkey and Iran, Pakistan actively encouraged participation of the Central Asian states in the ECO regional trade organization and in other regional organizations. In October 1991 Turkmenistan and Kyrgyzstan announced their intent to join the Organization of Islamic Countries.[23] All of the Central Asian states sent missions to this organization's meeting in Tehran in 1992.

In July 1992, Pakistan reportedly offered Tojikiston a $500 million agreement to help construct a hydroelectric dam inside Tojikiston that would supply electricity to northern Pakistan. A commission was set up to study the construction of a highway that would link Pakistan with the city of Badakhshan in Turkmenistan. Both of these efforts were potentially contentious in the respect that Pakistan is not contiguous with Tojikiston. Any transfer of electricity or road construction would require access across the narrow Wakhan Corridor in northeastern Afghanistan. It is clear that Pakistan's interests in Central Asia are not only commercial; they are derived from Pakistan's security interests in stabilizing friendly relations with Afghanistan.

The chaotic politics of postwar Afghanistan does not lend itself to unconditional support for any particular faction, ideology, or leading group. Afghanistan's mujahideen groups are divided along primarily regional and ethnic lines. The Hizb-i Islami group, one of the more radical factions, was predominantly Pushtun. The Jami'at-i Islami group, led by Akhmad Shakh Masud, was more moderate and largely controlled by ethnic Tojiks living in the northeastern part of Afghanistan. Although these groups are often described as "Islamic fundamentalists," there is good reason to believe that much of the cross-border traffic in guns and drugs was commercially motivated rather than ideologically inspired.

An agreement between India and Russia for the supply of Soviet ballistic missile technology in the spring of 1992 unsettled Islamabad and provoked strident objections from Washington and other capitals. The Russians countered that the agreement was negotiated by the former Soviet government and that Russia, under international law, was bound to abide by Soviet treaties and agreements. For their part, the Indians insisted that the technology was not weapons-related. The Indians tested a surface-to-surface short-range missile on May 5, 1992.[24] India announced that it was unwilling to sign the nuclear nonproliferation treaty (NPT) until it had received assurances from China and Kazakstan that they would sign it also. To make matters worse, India's Secretary Minister of Foreign Affairs, D.N. Diksit, clarified the Indian position by saying that India was unwilling to sign the NPT as long as Kazakstan possessed nuclear arms (Kazakstan later agreed to give them up).[25]

Japan and South Korea have been particularly active in commercial relations with the new Central Asian states. Their security interests in the region seem minimal. Early in 1992 Japan announced that it had reached an agreement whereby its ambassador to Russia would also represent Japan's interests in Kazakstan, Kyrgyzstan, and Turkmenistan. The Japanese were particularly active in Kazakstan, where they negotiated contracts for the construction of airports, railways, and highways. Already in 1992 a plant opened in Karaganda, Kazakstan, that produced refrigerators with the help of Japan's Marubeni Corporation. The Honda Motor Company announced that it was considering an auto assembly plant in Ust-Kamenogorsk, Kazakstan.

THE UNITED STATES AND CENTRAL ASIA

As the USSR began to unravel in 1991, the U.S. government supported Mikhail Gorbachev's administration as the legitimate government of the USSR. After the Russian declaration of independence and the August 1991 coup, the legal status of the USSR according to international law was sufficiently opaque that the United States was essentially free to make independent judgments regarding who legally represented the peoples of the Soviet republics. The United States chose a cautious course. In a practical sense the United States began to recognize the authenticity of the republics' declarations of independence, but in a legal sense the United States continued to require the Soviet government to abide by the terms of international agreements and to provide for an orderly devolution of authority.

One week after the Minsk Declaration of December 8, 1991, U.S. Secretary of State James Baker III quickly scheduled a meeting and flew to Bishkek and Alma-Ata to meet with the leaders of Kyrgyzstan and Kazakstan. When these leaders attended the Alma-Ata meeting of December 21, the meeting which formally declared an end to the USSR, they were freshly apprised of U.S. intentions and capabilities regarding the breakup of the USSR. In mid-February 1992, Baker toured the collapsing USSR, stopping in Moscow, Tashkent, and Cheliabinsk (where the major Soviet nuclear weapons engineering lab was located) as well as Moldova, Azerbaijan, and Armenia.

Baker then sent the Central Asian presidents a letter that articulated key diplomatic points: The letter linked U.S. diplomatic recognition to the observance of human rights, the adoption of market-oriented economic reforms, and the establishment of democratic institutions. Shortly thereafter, the U.S. government was quick to officially recognize Kazakstan and Kyrgyzstan as separate, post-Soviet governments. A U.S. representation was established in Alma-Ata on February 3, 1992, followed, a short time later, by a United States embassy.

But the United States acceded to requests to recognize the countries swiftly. This was a result of several factors. For one, the United States responded to complaints from the other Central Asian states that they were singled out for special negative treatment. For another, the United States acted out of compassion for the Russian-speaking populations that appeared to be trapped in the new countries. Yet another important factor was that the United States perhaps exaggerated the threat of Iranian and Pakistani designs on the Central Asian countries. By mid-spring 1992 the United States had consulates in each of the countries and was rapidly moving toward the establishment of embassies. A U.S. diplomatic representation opened in Tashkent on March 16, 1992. The office shortly thereafter became a U.S. embassy. All of the Central Asian embassies were opened by U.S. foreign service officers who carried their offices in briefcases, opening for business in the only vacant locations they could find— former Communist Party hotels.

Soon U.S. concerns shifted from ideological and moral considerations to security considerations. There were four reasons for this. First, the presence of nuclear weapons, ballistic missiles, and strategic bombers in Kazakstan and nuclear weapons technology in some of the other countries of Central Asia presented a clear threat to U.S. vital security interests. Second, the states of Central Asia (or independent actors located within these states) were seen to present a danger of transshipment of weapons or weapons-related technology to third parties. Third, given the political, ethnic, or religious affinities with neighboring states in the Middle East and West Asia, the Central Asian states (or independent actors within the states) might possibly broker weapons technology or knowhow. Fourth, the states of Central Asia were viewed as potentially spreading revolutionary doctrines and ideas, inspired by terrorist organizations in the Middle East or by state sponsors of terrorism such as Libya or Iraq.

The best example of this was Kazakstan's decision to relinquish possession of the nuclear explosives on its territory. The United States was anxious to convince Kazakstan, which emerged from the breakup of the USSR as the inheritor of the world's fourth largest stockpile of nuclear arms, to voluntarily give up the weapons. The United States offered development assistance if Kazakstan complied.

Despite some reservations by government officials in Kazakstan who felt that if it relinquished these weapons it would no longer command the attention of the West, Kazakstan accepted the offer. In one of the most dramatic and least widely acknowledged foreign policy successes of the United States, the U.S. ambassador to Kazakstan, William Courtney, engineered an agreement by which Kazakstan voluntarily relinquished its weapons and weapons-grade material and became a nonnuclear state in March 1995.[26]

FOREIGN ASSISTANCE TO CENTRAL ASIA

The outside world became engaged in the domestic affairs of the Central Asian countries in three ways: through the establishment of direct diplomatic relations, through multilateral institutions, and through foreign aid agencies. Diplomatic efforts began immediately upon the collapse of the USSR. The multilateral agencies established relations somewhat more slowly, and the foreign aid agencies followed a short time later.

As early as January 1992 most of the large intergovernmental international institutions such as the United Nations, World Bank, IMF, EBRD, the Asian Development Bank, and OSCE had already conducted assessment trips to Central Asia and begun preparations for the establishment of permanent presences. Regional multinational agencies, such as the European Union's (EU) program of Technical Assistance to the Commonwealth of Independent States, were also established.

Bilateral cooperation was based in national foreign aid agencies such as the U.S. Agency for International Development (USAID), Japanese Overseas Development Assistance, and the Canadian International Development Agency. Private foundations and philanthropies such as the Soros Foundation and Human Rights Watch/Helsinki also established field programs.

USAID was one of the first foreign organizations to establish a permanent office in Central Asia. In September 1992, the first permanent USAID field officer in Central Asia, Paula Feeney, opened an office in a hotel in Almaty, Kazakstan. The office was later expanded to become the USAID Mission for Central Asia with responsibility for programs in all of the five Central Asian countries. The mission's first director, Craig Buck, oversaw the establishment of offices for field representatives in each of the other four Central Asian countries. These offices were first situated in the U.S.

embassies and later were moved to separate facilities. The United States also established an office of the U.S. Information Agency in Almaty, Kazakstan.

In most developing countries, foreign assistance usually comes in four categories: humanitarian assistance, such as food or medical supplies; security assistance, such as military equipment; capital development projects, such as dams and power systems; and technical assistance, such as training or information about how to conduct government or business. In the case of Central Asia, USAID undertook no capital projects. Most humanitarian assistance was directed to Tojikiston and the areas hardest hit by the desiccation of the Aral Sea. Because of the USSR's human rights record, USAID refrained from extending any security assistance in Central Asia to modernize the police or military, restricting all security assistance exclusively to Kazakstan for weapons conversion and dismantling.[27]

Initially, most U.S. aid was in the form of technical assistance, providing expatriate consultants as advisers for various governmental and nongovernmental organizations in Central Asia. A large number of U.S. government–financed nongovernmental organizations began working under contract to carry out projects designed by USAID.[28] The EU provided substantial sums for technical studies and technical assistance programs, less in the form of direct aid. The EU was not well positioned to play a direct role in Central Asia, however, because of the nature of coalition decisionmaking within the EU. Europe's focus stayed in the West due to intense concern with the outcome of the Russian transition, the burden of German reunification, the efforts to assist the transformation of the former communist states of Eastern Europe, and the ongoing conflict in the Balkans.

Although Germany was preoccupied with reunification questions, the Germans nonetheless had a particular interest in Kazakstan. A substantial number of Germans were forcibly resettled in Kazakstan after World War II. Throughout the postwar period, West Germany sought the repatriation of German citizens displaced by the war. But with the burden of reunification Germany grew more reticent about repatriation. The German government's response to the question of repatriation of former German citizens living in Kazakstan therefore became somewhat delicate. The German government (wanting to slow repatriation) established a German-Kazak commission to address cultural problems, established a direct phone link with Germany, and established German radio and television programming in the country. All of these efforts had the not-too-well-concealed goal of encouraging many ethnic German citizens living in Kazakstan to stay put rather than seeking repatriation to Germany. The measures were to little avail, however. Most Germans who could leave did so.

The EU was particularly active in Kyrgyzstan. The EU had already provided technical assistance in privatization, tax reform, project assistance with the Naryn Dam project, new road construction, and the establishment of small commercial enterprises. Now the EU pledged $40 million in aid for economic development programs in Kyrgyzstan (in 1992). Two years later this figure had increased fivefold as the EU identified Kyrgyzstan as the most needy and most deserving of the former Soviet countries.

What is the overall extent of assistance provided to the Central Asian countries? The United States spent about $17 billion for foreign affairs in 1994, up slightly over annual averages during the previous decade.[29] In the 1990s, overall annual expenditures for humanitarian and development assistance (that is, foreign aid excluding security assistance and other forms of aid) totaled $8.9 billion in 1993, $8.72 billion in 1994, and $8.739 billion in 1995; President Bill Clinton's budget proposal for fiscal year 1996 projected $9.146 billion.[30] Actual figures for the amount of assistance received are often misleading composites, such as those provided in the politically motivated report of the European Commission on Foreign Assistance in February 1996. The report asserted that in the first four years of independence the international community provided $127.4 billion to the countries of the former USSR. According to the report, the United States contributed about 14 percent of overall assistance.[31] Some critics of the U.S. assistance effort estimate that the Central Asian states received only about 10 percent of all the aid directed toward the former Soviet states.[32]

Despite the impressive overall figures, the total amount of technical assistance actually received by a country is much less than what the dollar figures suggest. Much foreign aid is "tied aid," or connected to conditions that require expenditures to be made within the donor country. The impact of foreign technical assistance is yet an entirely different issue. Any briefcase-toting attorney and accountant on assignment from foreign capitals to help transform the Central Asian infrastructure will likely recognize an element of truth in the wisdom of British diplomats from Lord Curzon's time: "The sands of Central Asia are littered with the bones of Westerners in a hurry."

The provision of assistance to Central Asia is closely related to the value that the outside world attaches to Central Asia and, of course, to the degree to which assistance can be expected to build long-term relationships that are valuable to the donor. The outside world clearly has interests in the rich lands of Central Asia. But in the past few years the question has been hotly debated as to what extent countries of the developed world have "vital" interests in Central Asia. This question gives rise to a great deal of grandstanding on the part of Western academics and policy analysts. Many are inclined to see the agricultural and mineral deposits of the area as untapped sources of wealth, sources that should influence the policies of Western countries. Others tend to see Central Asia as the staging ground for the geopolitical, ideological, and even theological contests of the next century. They see the region as the front line between Christendom and Islam.

A more sober assessment is that it is difficult to identify any clear long-term interests of the United States or any of the other major powers for that matter. U.S. commercial interests in the area are negligible, with the exception of oil and a few other primary commodities, and to the extent that any potential market for goods or services does exist it is likely to be captured by Turkish, Israeli, Pakistani, or Iranian business concerns. In terms of an objective ranking of U.S. foreign policy priorities then, it is fair to say that the individual states of Central Asia must be ranked somewhere in the vicinity of Venezuela.

Even if much of the developed world's commercial and geopolitical interests are limited in this region, it may still be contended that there are key environmental values at stake in Central Asian development. According to this view, the problems of the Aral Sea, regional desertification, and environmental pollution should at least command the attention of the outside world.

AGRICULTURE, LAND, WATER, AND THE ENVIRONMENT

The agricultural specialization of the economies of all the Central Asian countries links them closely to one another in many ways. The close linkage between agriculture, land use, and water use makes agricultural specialization a key element in the emerging disputes among the republics over transboundary natural resources. In terms of potential market opportunities, the existing patterns of agricultural specialization also make the countries, as economists put it, trade competitors rather than complementors; that is, they are more likely to offer the same goods and services for sale to one another than to offer goods and services that differ.

The importance of agriculture in Central Asia is underscored by the desiccation of the Aral Sea. The problem is not one of water scarcity but of water management. Central Asia has an adequate amount of water, but it is simply in the wrong places and is being used irrationally. The resulting water crisis has great implications for the trade strategies of the countries. A water crisis imposes constraints upon farm incomes, rural employment, and agricultural export opportunities. Water disputes thus frequently act as a constraint upon states' development strategies. In the absence of economic asymmetries that make possible complementary trade exchanges, uncoordinated and conflicting development strategies can easily lead competing states into overt conflict with one another over transboundary resources.

Central Asia's water crisis is a result of the excessive development of an agriculturally based economy in a semiarid region. Decades ago, the leading political and government organizations committed themselves to the goal of the "industrialization of Central Asian agriculture."[33] Soviet leaders reflected on the experience of such Western countries as the United States, where the introduction of mechanical cotton harvesters virtually eliminated the need for cotton pickers in the space of fifteen years. Soviet leaders reasoned on the basis of such examples that the introduction of mechanized methods of agriculture, the adoption of industrial forms of labor organization on the farm, and the diffusion of new agricultural technologies promised a technological breakthrough of even greater proportions for socialist agriculture. They anticipated a socialist counterpart of the so-called Green Revolution, which transformed traditional agricultural practices in many parts of the Third World.[34]

Policies aimed at a breakthrough in Central Asian agriculture began with great expectations. As early as 1957, the Soviet central government announced targets of 80 percent for mechanized cotton harvesting. During the 1960s and 1970s, large numbers of mechanical cotton harvesters were produced in new and expensive factories constructed specifically for this purpose. An elaborate administrative system was established to employ the most advanced scientific methods in managing cotton production, micromanaging everything from the selection of seeds to the setting of itineraries for trucks to carry cotton to ginning stations. A vast irrigation network was constructed on the semiarid Asian alluvial plains. Scientific agronomic institutes were established to conduct research and act as agricultural extension services. In the eyes of both Moscow and native Central Asian officials, the republics of the southern tier were poised for a technological revolution.

The 1950s did indeed witness a vast expansion in sown area throughout the regions of the USSR east of the Urals, particularly in Kazakstan and Central Asia. Cotton production in Central Asia more than doubled during this period. Although the USSR often led the world in production throughout the 1970s, it fell behind China as the foremost producer by the 1980s, alternating with the United States for second place.[35] But the USSR continued to be a major exporter, particularly to the member countries of the former Council for Mutual Economic Assistance. The USSR annually exported an average of 30 percent of its cotton crop. Cotton production was described by a team of specialists from the U.S. Department of Agriculture as the "success story" of Soviet agriculture.[36] Both Soviet and non-Soviet scholars alike considered the cotton complex to be a model of development for the underdeveloped world.[37]

Children swimming in a village irrigation ditch in the Fergana Valley, 1992. Photo by Gregory Gleason.

But by the late 1980s, the practice of extreme specialization in cotton—a practice that for so long had been heralded as the "patriotic duty" of the Asian republics—came to be identified as the cause of disastrous social and economic conditions in the Asian republics. In the words of Rafik Nishanov, cotton monoculture was carried "to monstrous proportions."[38] Speakers at the USSR Congress of People's Deputies in 1989 presented a litany of complaints claiming that cotton monoculture had saddled the Asian republics with declining production, farm inefficiency, economic corruption, mass unemployment, and environmental decay. From a high point of 9.9 million tons of raw cotton in 1980, cotton production—and the associated cotton revenues—fell by 20 percent toward the end of the decade. Economic corruption spread throughout the cotton industry, affecting an entire stratum of the managerial elite and eventually reaching the heights of power in Moscow.[39] Soil exhaustion, salination, and the accumulation of residue from agricultural by-products, pesticides, herbicides, and defoliants damaged the region's ecology and precipitated a public health crisis.[40]

Mass unemployment in the rural areas coupled with popular resentment, leading to waves of interethnic strife and violent antiparty and antigovernment protests. Reflecting popular antagonism toward the "cotton obligation," leaders of opposition groups bitterly attacked the area's cotton specialization, proclaiming that the "Uzbeks are not cotton slaves, but a nation."[41]

Uzbekiston was at the center of the cotton enterprise. Roughly 60 percent of its total national income was reportedly generated by the cotton complex. The economic importance of cotton to Central Asia was summed up in the words of a former head of the republic's party organization: "There is not one person in the republic of Uzbekiston who is not anxious about the price of cotton." The price of cotton "determines literally everything," from the fiscal solvency of the farms to the "social well-being of millions of people."[42] The social structure of Central Asian agricultural societies was heavily distorted by such practices as relying on manual labor, particularly women and children, during the harvest season.[43]

Central Asian officials responded by announcing that they would reduce emphasis on cotton and create a "regulated" market to advance sovereignty in the republics. Land under cotton cultivation, it was claimed, would be sharply curtailed. The high of 2.1 million hectares sown to cotton in Uzbekiston was reduced to 1.95 million. The "evils of monoculture" brought forth a new emphasis on crop diversification.[44]

By the time of independence, the political leadership in the Central Asian states was rhetorically committed to a market economy on the basis of "national sovereignty." In reality this meant that the 10 billion ruble annual return from cotton would be at the disposal of the new states rather than at the disposal of Moscow. In addition, the Central Asians began actively seeking to acquire secondary processing capacity for cotton. In the words of one proponent of local processing, "We do not have any doubt that precisely in such a processing industry is the key to the transformation of Uzbekiston from a economy based on a primary commodity to one based on a self-sufficient industry. With this will come the solution to many of the problems of our republic, unemployment among them."[45]

The textiles industries in the north began bracing for these changes as well. Russian textile mills began seeking new kinds of contracts with Uzbekiston producers to develop "a more correct policy of rational output for cotton products."[46] By the summer of 1992, many of the cotton mills of the European regions were at a virtual standstill. On May 26, 1992, hundreds of textile workers from the Ivanovo textile factories picketed government buildings in downtown Moscow, protesting the interruption of deliveries of raw cotton, which had put them out of work.

The 1992 growing season was one of the most difficult on record. In Khorezm *Veliat* (Oblast), heavy and continuous rains combined with below-average temperatures in May and June, making it necessary to replant fields sometimes three times over. Cotton wilt also took its toll. Desperate to bring in the 1992 cotton crop, the new Central Asian countries fell back on old instruments of the command economy, such as preannounced production targets and reliance on handpicked cotton. Turkmenistan's farmers were directed at the beginning of the harvest season to bring in a crop of 1.288 million tons.[47] Half of the 1992 crop was brought in by hand rather than by machine.[48]

In independent Central Asia, as in many open agricultural economies of the underdeveloped world, the cotton question today can be reduced to two issues: crop diversification and technical diffusion. In practical terms, crop diversification is not a technically difficult issue. Diversification can take place in a single growing season. What holds the crop structure in place is not agronomic resistance, but rather economic resistance.

During the first year of independence, political leaders in all five states of Central Asia committed themselves to liberalization programs. All of these states produced detailed privatization plans and adopted enabling legislation. In all of these states, the cautious, state-engineered privatization that began in the service sector spread to the industrial sector. At the same time, the leaders of all these states announced intentions of instituting agricultural land reform. But as late as 1996, no detailed programs on agricultural land privatization were announced. No legislation that would enable true and comprehensive land reform was adopted. There was no serious parliamentary discussion of the timetable for land reform.

Central Asians explain the reluctance to press forward with decollectivization by pointing to a number of factors. First, they assert that privatization is not consistent with traditional Central Asian culture. Second, they say that privatization would lead to exploitive use of farmland by settler farmers who would exhaust the land, sell or abandon it, and then move on. Third, they say that privatization would undercut the existing farm networks and violate the interests of collective and state farm managers.

If pressed further on the sources of the hesitation to privatize farm land, many Central Asian officials add another reason. They say that privatization, however it might be accomplished, would leave the best lands in the hands of the most powerful ethnic groups and would leave the least desirable land in the hands of the least powerful. The view of Kyrgyzstan's president, Askar Akaev, is representative of those of many Central Asian political figures. In response to the question, "Do you think there should be privatization of land?" Akaev responded, "I support that idea. I see the mood of the peasant favors it. The leaders, particularly in the middle level, are skeptical and suspicious of land reform."[49] Akaev then went on to explain his personal assessment by adding, "If you start to turn over the land [to the peasants] the national question arises. It has already appeared here. At one time the Kyrgyz were crowded out of irrigated land."[50] Land reform invariably involves the redistribution of land

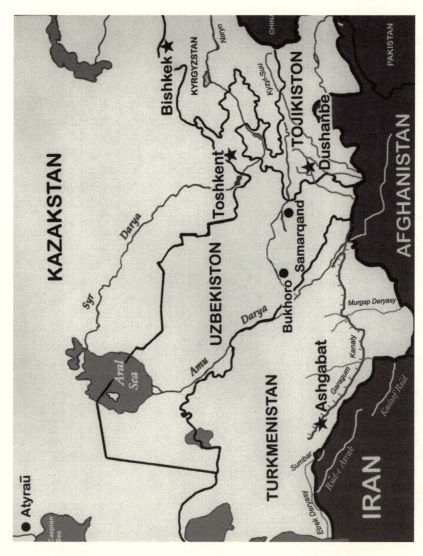

Aral Sea Basin Water Resources

from one social group to another. Land reform therefore involves reassignment of property rights, a procedure that inevitably involves the state as a pivotal actor.

In Central Asia's arid agricultural landscape, irrigation accounts for about 84 percent of water usage. The most visible consequence of the water crisis is the impending desiccation of the Aral Sea. In general, as water is consumed by the irrigation process and by evapotranspiration, the concentrations of salts and other dissolved solids remaining in the water increase. Thus, as a general principle, the greater the water use upstream, the lower the water quality downstream. Water added through irrigation percolates to groundwater and, even in semiarid areas, can raise the water table to the point where it may damage crops by depriving roots of oxygen.

Central Asia's two main river systems, the Syr and the Amu, are responsible for irrigating roughly 75 percent of Central Asia's agriculture. Each of these rivers flows through four of the five Central Asian states. As recently as three decades ago, about forty-five cubic kilometers (km^3) of water reached the Aral Sea annually from these rivers. But the ambitious agricultural expansion programs started in the 1950s resulted in the creation of an extensive, regionwide irrigation system. The withdrawals of this irrigation system put increasing demands upon the region's water resources throughout the 1970s. By 1982 the annual inflow to the Aral Sea fell to nearly zero.

The water crisis in Central Asia is not a crisis of quantity but a crisis of distribution. An annual aggregate total of about 117 km^3 flows through the Central Asian water system. In 1987, the flow, at 125.3 km^3, was greater than normal. Of the total water available in the Aral Basin, about 87 percent is used in rural areas, 10 percent is dedicated to industrial use, and about 3 percent is consumed in municipal uses. For a long period, criticism of the damage being done by water mismanagement was held in check by Soviet authorities and by the expectation that diversion of water from north-flowing Siberian rivers would replenish the Aral Sea. Only months after Gorbachev's administration came to power, however, the Siberian river-diversion projects stalled, and a short time later the plans to construct a "trans-Siberian canal" were abandoned altogether. Central Asia's water problems acquired a renewed urgency.

The goal of achieving sustainable development in Central Asia may not entail the restoration of the Aral Sea to a pristine condition. If the withdrawal of water for irrigation purposes could be reduced to zero for the next twenty-five years—an unlikely policy objective given the importance of agriculture to the economy of the region and the generally short time horizons of the national actors—the Aral Sea might be restored. Since this is an implausible assumption, however, the restoration of the Aral Sea is not a policy objective of Central Asian officials despite what they might say to foreign visitors anxious to save the Aral Sea. However, they are committed to mitigating the region's environmental degradation.

How can this be brought about? The fact that there are different user groups with different interests suggests the possibility of asymmetry and thus complementarity of interest. That is, the fact that interests differ among certain groups means that preferences may differ, which suggests that there may be mutually beneficial trade-offs among the groups. What are these trade-offs? With respect to the problems of water quantity, user groups upstream and downstream have complementary interests. Kyrgyzstan, after all, cannot keep the water (although it could divert substantial flows to Kazakstan to the detriment of Uzbekiston). The trade-offs suggest the importance of tying economic benefits associated with hydroelectric power to the interests of agriculture. The upstream users would thus have an interest in optimally managing water flow for agricultural purposes. Such an association would diminish state sovereignty.

With respect to the problems of water quality, upstream-downstream differences between head users and tail users are not key. Differences between midstream users and tail users are extremely important, however, since downstream-downstream differences are the most likely ones to lead to overt conflict among the states. Since most midstream differences involve conflicts within individual states, the greatest potential for interstate conflict is among Kazakstan, Uzbekiston, and Turkmenistan. With respect to the competing users (municipal, agricultural, industrial), the most important conflicts are within individual states.

Then there is the problem of the emergence of five separate watermasters where once there was one. If negotiated interstate compacts can be reached regarding the volume, quantity, and timing of interstate water transfers, the internal management of the system can be operated more efficiently by five watermasters than by only one. But the optimal arrangement would be to divide the water management system into two separate water districts, each associated with one major basin. This would have the effect of linking upstream and downstream users in mutually advantageous relationships as well as avoiding conflictual, zero-sum confrontations among the three downstream countries.

The fundamental principle of the international law of transboundary resources is the "doctrine of equitable apportionment." This doctrine holds that each coriparian is entitled to an equitable share of the uses of water of a river system. In practice, the principle often has a number of corollaries: First, no single party is entitled to all of the waters of a transboundary river system; second, a transboundary river system must be equitably shared by all coriparians; and third, no single party can unilaterally determine its share. A companion principle often recognized in international law is the doctrine of prescription. In English common law, "prescription" holds that long possession may operate to confirm the existence of title, even if the origin of title cannot be shown.

Neither the doctrine of equitable apportionment nor the doctrine of prescription can mechanically be used to derive the ideal division of the waters among the new states of Central Asia. This will have to be done in a process of negotiation, a process that outside actors have the opportunity—and perhaps the obligation—to influence. If presumed inequities in interregional distribution are adopted as a cause célèbre and if local leaders transform the water scarcity issue into a matter of "national survival," the water crisis could easily become a pretext for divisive and potentially violent political change in Central Asia. The states would very likely look for "miracle" solutions, charismatic leadership, or scapegoats.

Only concerted action on the part of all the Central Asian states can solve the problems of air and water pollution in Central Asia. Yet for reasons familiar to the outside world, the urgency of joint action on environmental problems does not necessarily imply that states will actually cooperate. All of the states share some of the problems, but all have unique environmental considerations. Kazakstan has the largest share of industrial pollution. Moreover, Kazakstan will be forced to deal with the consequences of four decades of nuclear weapons contamination. Turkmenistan faces severe desertification. Uzbekiston finds itself faced with a trade-off between agricultural expansion and responsible water use. Kyrgyzstan and Tojikiston, both reliant upon extractive industries, can find few economic benefits—and thus few incentives—for environmentally sustainable and responsible extraction.

The environmental problem that all of the countries share is the link between agriculture and water use. Long and agonized discussions in Central Asia over crop diversification and cotton monoculture have now disappeared with the collapse of the Soviet "metropole." Today it is clear that the "cotton question" is much simpler than it appeared for several decades. Now that the Central Asian situation may be compared with the agricultural sector in developing countries, it is clear that diversification of the crop structure is a chimera. The experience of many developing countries demonstrates that the difficult aspect of crop diversification is not an agronomic problem but an economic one. The difficult part of crop diversification under Central Asian circumstances will be to sustain a demand-driven, export-led agriculture even while market forces tend to drive farm prices down. In the first year of independence, all of the states subsidized basic foodstuffs to maintain political stability. If demand is artificially suppressed over a long period of time, only state pressure in the form of large farm subsidies or direct agricultural management is likely to sustain diversification.

However the water problem is addressed, the outcome of the development of sustainable environmental policies in Central Asia is not likely to be determined by public education, a new ethic of conservationism, or even technical assistance from the World Bank. It is likely to be a function of the development strategies the countries assume. The countries have not been well positioned historically to develop service economies. The tendency in each of the countries is to continue to rely upon agriculture, extractive industries, and light fabrication and processing. If the countries succeed in adopting rapid reindustrialization programs based upon modernization of such complexes as Shymkent's chemical facilities in Kazakstan or the Angren Basin's coal facility in Uzbekiston, Central Asia can expect a protracted period of increasingly severe environmental stress.

NOTES

1. A colorful interpretation of the rivalry among the Great Powers for control and influence in Central Asia may be found in Peter Hopkirk, *The Great Game: The Struggle for Empire in Central Asia* (London: Kodansha International, 1994).

2. For a different perspective on these definitions, see James Critchlow, "What Is the U.S. Interest in Central Asia's Future?" *Central Asia Monitor* no. 5 (1992): 27–29.

3. The expression "near abroad" is a translation from the Russian. It is a euphemism to denote those regions that were previously included in the former USSR but are now independent.

4. Broadcast on Radio Mayak (7 November 1995).

5. Ostankino television interview of 24 May 1992, FBIS-SOV-92-104 (29 May 1992): 60.

6. Interview with Aleksandr Gagua, "Idei i liudi," *Nezavisimaia gazeta* (6 May 1992): 5.

7. *Nezavisimaia gazeta* (8 May 1992): 1.

8. INTERFAX report by A. Pershin et al. (10 August 1992).

9. International Monetary Fund, *Economic Review: Turkmenistan* (Washington, D.C.: IMF, May 1992), p. 1.

10. Daniel C. Matuszewski, "Empire, Nationalities, Borders," in S. Enders Wimbush, *Soviet Nationalities in Strategic Perspective* (New York: St. Martin's Press, 1985), p. 95.

11. *Nezavisimaia gazeta* (29 July 1992): 3.

12. *Izvestiia* (5 March 1992): 5.

13. In April 1992 Uzbekiston's Prime Minister, Abdulkhoshim Mutalov, announced that 2,000 Uzbek students would be studying in Turkey. *Pravda Vostoka* (18 April 1992): 1.

14. Ikram Dzhaikhun, *Pravda Vostoka* (18 April 1992): 1.

15. Abdulkhoshim Mutalov, as cited by B. Abdullaev and U. Mirzaiarov, "Kogda vstrechaiutsia brat'ia," *Pravda Vostoka* (18 April 1992): 1.

16. ITAR-TASS report of Sergei Feoktistov (2 July 1992).

17. "Idei Islamskogo Fundamentalizma na sovetskie respubliki," TASS radio report by Mikhail Kochetkov (3 October 1991), transcribed in *Soviet Media News and Features Digest*, compiled by Radio Free Europe/Radio Liberty Research Institute (3 October 1991).

18. *Izvestiia* (9 March 1992): 1.

19. Patrick E. Tyler, "Saudis Promise Soviet Union $1 Billion in Emergency Aid," *New York Times* (9 October 1991): A4.

20. Youssef M. Ibrahim, "To Counter Iran, Saudis Seek Ties with Ex-Soviet Islamic Republics," *New York Times* (22 February 1992): A4.

21. *Pravda Vostoka* (18 April 1992): 1.

22. *USSR Today: Soviet Media News and Features Digest*, RFE/RL Research Institute (20 October 1991).

23. *Al-Akhbar* (Cairo) (25 October 1991).

24. Sanjoy Hazarika, "Moscow Affirms It Will Deliver Key Rocket Technology to India," *New York Times* (7 May 1992): A4.

25. Nikolai Paklin, "Indiia protiv bez'iadernoi zony," *Izvestiia* (13 March 1992): 6.

26. For background see Richard A. Falkenrath, "The HEU Deal," in Graham T. Allison, Owen R. Cote Jr., Richard A. Falkenrath, and Steven E. Miller, *Avoiding Nuclear Anarchy: Containing the Threat of Loose Russian Nuclear Weapons and Fissile Material* (Cambridge: MIT Press, 1996), pp. 229–292.

27. As of early 1995, the U.S. government offered Kazakstan roughly $133 million for purposes of strategic arms elimination and defense conversion. At the same time, only about 8 percent of the offered assistance had been obligated (spent) by the U.S. government. See "U.S. Security Assistance to the Former Soviet Union," *Arms Control Today* (April 1995): 24–25.

28. These projects included technical assistance in privatization and legal reform by private firms such as Carana Corporation, Chemonics International, Deloitte and Touche, Price Waterhouse, Ernst and Young, and Burston Marsteller and activities by nongovernmental organizations such as the International Research and Exchanges Board, the American Bar Association, the Academy of Educational Development, Agricultural Cooperative Development International, the American Collegiate Consortium, Mercy Corps International, the National Democratic Institute, the International Republican Institute, the International Executive Service Corps, Volunteers in Overseas Cooperative Assistance, and Winrock International.

29. Robert Greenberger, "As Congress Sharpens Knives to Cut Foreign Aid, Critics Warn of Damage to U.S. Policy-Making," *Wall Street Journal* (18 May 1995): A20.

30. *The United States Budget, 1996* (Washington, D.C.: Government Printing Office, 1995).

31. U.S. State Department figures courtesy of the Business Information Service for the Newly Independent States (BISNIS).

32. Nancy Lubin, "Ethnic Conflict Resolution and U.S. Assistance," in Roald Z. Sagdeev and Susan Eisenhower, *Central Asia: Conflict, Resolution, and Change* (Chevy Chase, Md.: CPSS Press, 1996), pp. 321–332.

33. The transfer of proletarian forms of labor organization, and ultimately proletarian political consciousness, to the peasantry was a prominent theme in the thinking of the early Bolsheviks. It was reasserted in the efforts of the 1950s and 1960s to find formulas for agricultural transformation. Khrushchev frequently cited the Leninist teaching that "there can be but one material basis of socialism— heavy machine industry—and it is capable of reorganizing even agriculture." See his speech to the September (1953) Plenum, reprinted in N.S. Khrushchev, *Stroitel'stvo kommunizma v SSSR i razvitie sel'skogo khoziaistva*, vol. 1 (Moscow: Gosudarstvennoe izdatel'stvo politicheskoi literatury, 1962), p. 7.

34. For a discussion of the management structures of Uzbekiston cotton production, see Gregory Gleason, "The Pakhta Programme: The Politics of Sowing Cotton in Central Asia," *Central Asian Survey* 2, no. 2 (1983): 109–120 (translated into Turkish as "Pahta Programi Ozbeistan'da Pamuk ekimi Politikas," in *Papers of the Orta Dogu Taknik Universitesi* no. 17 [Ankara, Turkey, 1985]).

35. In recent years, China has emphasized cotton production for domestic and export purposes. The area sown to cotton in China increased from 1.3 million hectares in 1952 to 5.36 million hectares in 1989. See Frederick W. Cook, "Trends in China's Crop Area: A Historical Perspective," in U.S. Department of Agriculture, Centrally Planned Economies Branch, *CPE Agriculture Report* 3, no. 1 (January-February 1990): 18.

36. "U.S. Team Reports on Soviet Cotton Production and Trade," U.S.D.A. Report FAS-M-277, Foreign Agriculture Service (June 1977): 1.

37. Alec Nove and J.A. Newth, *The Soviet Middle East: A Communist Model for Development* (London: Allen and Unwin, 1967); Ann Sheehy, "Some Aspects of Regional Development in Soviet Central Asia," *Slavic Review* 31, no. 3 (September 1972): 555–563.

38. See R.N. Nishanov, *Pravda Vostoka* (2 June 1989): 2.

39. See Gregory Gleason, "Nationalism or Organized Crime: The Case of the 'Cotton Scandal' in the USSR," *Corruption and Reform* 5, no. 2 (1990): 87–108.

40. In 1989, the USSR average mortality rate for the first year of life was 22.6 per thousand. The advanced republics had rates similar to the countries of western Europe, e.g., Belorussia, 11.7; Lithuania, 10.7; Latvia, 11.2. The Central Asian republics had rates comparable to those of underdeveloped areas of Africa, e.g., Uzbekiston, 37.8; Kyrgyzstan, 32.6; Tojikiston, 43.4; Turkmenistan, 54.6. Aleksandr Baranov, "Ham neobkhodim zakon o detstve," *Sem'ia* no. 22 (1990): 7.

41. This statement was made by Abdurakhim Pulatov, one of the leaders of the informal Birlik (Unity) movement. See I. Mikhailova, "Nachalo," *Zvezda Vostoka* no. 4 (1990): 73–81. The expression "cotton slaves" is loaded with political and racist connotations. See Bess Brown, "Uzbekistan's Feud with *Ogonek*," *Report on the USSR* (20 January 1989): 9–10.

42. I.A. Karimov, "Orientiry obnovleniia," *Pravda Vostoka* (27 September 1989): 1.

43. "The Use and Abuse of Child Labor in Central Asia," *Radio Liberty Research Bulletin* 322/82 (12 August 1982).

44. For instance, I. Iskanderov has noted that "cotton employs thirty times the workers of grain, six times the workers of melons, four times as many as potato farming, twice as many as grapes." With the current underemployment situation

in Central Asia, this is likely to be a major consideration. I. Iskanderov, "Ekonomika splachivaet natsii," *Pravda Vostoka* (28 January 1989): 3.

45. Nikolai Korolevskii and Sergei Braginskii, "Bezrabotitsa: Real'nost' nashikh dnei," *Komsomolets Uzbekistana* (18 May 1990): 2.

46. Moscow TV channel 1, 13 August 1990, as reported in *USSR Today: Soviet Media and Features Digest*, compiled by RFE/RL (13 August 1990).

47. INTERFAX (17 September 1992).

48. In Turkmenistan, for instance, 1,100,601 tons of cotton lint were collected by early November. This included 504,589 tons that were machine-picked. *Turkmenskaia Iiskra* (30 October 1992): 1.

49. Interview by Otto Latsis, *Izvestiia* (28 May 1992): 2.

50. Interview by Otto Latsis, *Izvestiia* (28 May 1992): 2.

· SIX ·

Transition in Asia

The most interesting part of any Central Asian city is the bazaar. The bazaar is the most elemental of all Central Asian institutions. It represents the essence of Central Asian society. In the bazaars of Central Asia one gets a concrete sense of the daily contact of modernity with tradition. Here one sees how Central Asia's history comes into line with aspirations for the future. In Central Asia, just as in much of the developing world, the contrast between the present and the past is vivid. In the bazaar the merchants smile at the strolling shoppers as they offer fruits, nuts, rugs, and fur hats—the same goods their predecessors offered with the same smiles to similar shoppers centuries ago. Yet today along the lanes of the crowded bazaar, beside the traditional goods one can also find modern electronics from the Orient, candy bars and magazines from Europe, soft drinks and beer from North America.

In the bazaar the contrast between the traditional and the modern is most stark—but the contrast can be found everywhere in Central Asia. One can see a grizzled grandfather driving an oxcart through the automobile traffic near Leninabod's "Sixth Kombinat," the site previously used for uranium processing in Tojikiston. One can hear the students in Ashgabat's Agricultural Academy proudly explain that their agronomic studies are now taught in their native Turkmen, but they add with embarrassment that since there are no curriculum materials in their language the studies are exclusively oral, that is, today's students study essentially the same way students learned the subject in Turkmenistan a thousand years ago. One can watch nomads roam over Kazakstan's central great plains, herding their sheep the same way their ancestors did centuries ago, before nuclear explosions left broad and essentially uncharted swaths of radioactive contamination on the plains. One can view the environmental destruction at the mining operations of Kazakstan's Ekibastuz or Uzbekiston's Angren Basin, sites that fueled the rusting and decaying factories and foundries of the former Soviet war machine.

Tied to the past, and leaning toward an uncertain future, the countries of Central Asia confront a spectrum of daunting problems. They confront problems of regional security, regional development, economic reform, and integration into the international community. They are also contending with domestic problems of development and cultural change. Independence brought the ability to make independent choices, but it did so at a time when all the countries of Central Asia are grappling with poverty, backwardness, and inequality in today's ruthlessly competitive international economy. The new countries find that they must spur economic efficiency and industrial development while protecting an environment crippled by the wasteful excesses of decades of Soviet socialism. They find that they must restore commitment to the absolute value of human dignity in a time when the ideological premises of Marxist idealism are seemingly being replaced by a crude, self-interested, and self-serving consumerist materialism imported from the West. They find that they must create an entirely different basis for the social contract of the new societies they are attempting to create. The grandiose promises of Soviet socialism—most prominently, the hope and expectation that the "exploitation of man by man" would be eliminated—are now being replaced not so much by uplifting doctrines of individualist determination and self-reliance as by a sense of resignation that economic exploitation is part of the nature of things.

The countries of Central Asia are more experienced as a result of the seventy years of Soviet-style socialism. But are they wiser? Wisdom does not mean freedom from poor judgment and miscalculation; it only means that there is a capacity to learn from past mistakes and correct errors. The process of "discovering independence" referred to in the title of this book calls attention to the fact that the countries of Central Asia are involved in a *process*, one of consciously directed change. The transition in Central Asia to independence, self-government, and participation in the international community is probably better seen as "invention" than "rediscovery." The decisions these new states are making are not bringing them into the future—they are creating the future.

If international experience is any indicator, choices made during the first ten years of independence will have ramifications for generations to come. In this period of profound change, Central Asians find themselves confronting the defining questions of Central Asia's future on a daily basis: What are the sources that will build Central Asia's confidence, promote cooperation among Central Asia's disparate groups, and strengthen public will and resolve to endure the trials of transition? Are these sources to be found in Central Asian traditional authoritarianism? Are they to be found in rapid modernization and Westernization? Are they to be found in a restoration of native Central Asian values and traditions? On the surface, Central Asia's public policies—the development of national economic strategies, the establishment of intraregional cooperation, the conduct of destatification and economic reform—should determine the outcome of transition. But, on a deeper level, there is a more fundamental question, the question of the source of Central Asia's values.

THE GATHERING AUTHORITY OF ISLAM

The defining feature of human experience is not wealth or politics, it is the heart and soul. Islam is the mind, heart, and soul of indigenous Central Asian society. It is the defining feature of the native societies of Central Asia. It is impossible to find a genuine Central Asian native who does not profess to be a *Muselman*, a Muslim. If a person's genetic heritage in Central Asia is linked to the native peoples of Central Asia, he or she will invariably identify himself or herself as Muslim.

According to many Muslims, Islam is not just a creed or a system of theological beliefs but a way of life. Islam, they say, is a perfect religion that touches every aspect of human life. It prescribes a general canon of behavior for the social, the political, the economic, the cultural, the private and public, the foreign and domestic. But Islam is not a religion that exists only in the hearts of the believers—it is in the fabric of the civilization as well. These observations raise important questions: If Islamic values are so pervasive and if Islam determines the current cultural values of Central Asia, will Islam not also determine the future of the societies of Central Asia? And, where cultural Islam is pervasive, can political Islam be far behind?

For those outside of Central Asia seeking to interpret its past, its contemporary life, and the direction of its future, the values of Islam as they operate in Central Asian society are surely key.[1] But here again, when we look closely we find not one Central Asia, but many. In the agricultural valleys of Central Asia, the call of Islamic heritage is the strongest. In the canyons of Tojikiston's great mountains, Islam is "reviving" to a level at which it never existed before. In the large urban areas and cities Islam is a shared commitment to the past, to right living, and to a common future. In the villages of Kazakstan's plains, Islam is tradition and heritage, a code of life rather than a set of laws.

In the areas where it is strong as well as in the areas where it is weak, Islam is manifested above all in the fabric of society, the family structure, and the accepted canons of interpersonal behavior. This is cultural Islam, not political Islam. Central Asia is basically conservative. The appeal of revolutionary doctrines, whether of the Islamic variety, the Marxist vari-

ety, or any other variety, is not strong in Central Asia. The fighting that
has taken place, as, for example, in Tojikiston, was a result of blood-feuds
between valleys, not of ideological divisions. In the cases in which political Islam has gained ground in Central Asia, it has been in the context of
existing regional, economic, and territorial disputes. The political agenda
of the mujahideen is not a cultural one, and it has few Central Asian supporters whose loyalty actually stems from the profession of faith.

Western approaches to Soviet Central Asia were premised on the assumption that cultural Islam would become political Islam. According to
these interpretations, Central Asia was particularly susceptible to the rise
in Islamic fundamentalist doctrines similar to those that brought the
downfall of the Shah of Iran in 1978. The prevailing interpretation of the
tragic Soviet decision to invade Afghanistan was that Moscow feared the
contagion effect of Iran's revolution.[2] As the currents of nationalism rose
in the mid-1980s in central Europe, many observers assumed that Central
Asian nationalism, inspired by a fundamentalist fervor and Muslim fellow-feeling, could not be far behind. However, anticipations of widespread nationalist and fundamentalist movements did not materialize in
Central Asia. As we saw earlier, the Central Asian presidents were among
the last supporters of Mikhail Gorbachev's efforts to hold the Soviet
Union together.

Observers in the West were not the only ones who held this view. For
years the leaders of the Soviet Union also subscribed to the fear that Islamic sentiment would imperil the communist project of creating a uni-
form, proletarian, "Homo Soveticus," cosmopolitan approach that supported no territorial, ethnic, or religious values apart from those of the
official Soviet ideology. The Soviet government actively sought to dis-
place Islam as an intellectual tradition in Central Asia.

The Soviet campaign against Islam went through stages. For a time the
Soviet government tried to eradicate Islam completely. Failing in that enterprise, the Soviet government sought to co-opt and thus neutralize the
intellectual and spiritual influence of Islam. During the period of "cultural assault" during the 1920s and 1930s, Islam's claim to the hearts and
minds in Central Asia was directly challenged by the militarist values of
the Stalinist state. The position of Islam improved substantially during
World War II, when Soviet leaders needed the compliance and support of
Central Asian neighbors. After the war, however, Soviet leaders renewed
the anti-Islam offensive. The Soviet government actively pursued a policy
of destruction of Central Asia's religious institutions. The number of prac-
ticing mosques and *medresses* (religious schools) was intentionally limited
by the government during the Soviet period. Those religious monuments
that were not physically destroyed became poorly maintained tourist at-
tractions. Some areas, such as Ashgabat, Turkmenistan's capital, had no

functioning mosques for many years. After a major earthquake in 1948 destroyed much of Ashgabat, the city's many older mosques were never rebuilt.

During the Brezhnev era, however, Moscow officials preferred to make deals rather than engage in confrontation. In Uzbekiston during the rule of Sharaf Rashidov, for instance, local authorities were assured that they could rule virtually as they pleased provided they curtailed any threatening anti-Soviet disturbances. Increasingly in the 1980s, Central Asian cultural practices attracted little attention from Moscow.

Why did Islamic cultural values endure despite the years of repression? One explanation for the resilience of Islam during the Soviet period is that the Soviet regime sought to assimilate aspects of Islam by bringing them into the official doctrines of the state. This prompted a division between official and unofficial Islamic practice. As a consequence, some Islamic institutions were forced underground as "parallel Islam."[3] At the same time, "official Islam," represented by the four Muslim Spiritual Directorates of the USSR, kept the fires burning.

The most visible proponents of Islamic faith in Central Asia during the late 1980s continued to be representatives of "official" Islam. On a political plane, the influence of official Islam in Central Asia was decidedly conservative, that is, status quo–oriented. For instance, Muhammad Sadiq Yusupov, the mufti of Tashkent, took part in Soviet politics as a supporter of the regime. He was elected in 1989 to the USSR Congress of People's Deputies. He also played a role in restoring calm in Fergana after the ethnic riots of 1990. Another example is Kazi Zakhidzhan, the deputy director of the Spiritual Directorate of Muslims of Central Asia and Kazakstan who argued that Soviet patriotism was not in conflict with Islamic practice.[4] During the March 1991 referendum campaign, the Directorate publicly endorsed the retention of the Soviet Union.[5]

The early 1990s witnessed a renaissance of Islam in Central Asia. The first openly permitted *Navruz* celebration in Central Asia in many years took place in Uzbekiston in 1990. A group of 500 pilgrims left on *haj* to Mecca in June 1990 with official sponsorship of Uzbekiston's government. Perhaps as many as 1,500 people in all made the pilgrimage from Uzbekiston alone. The Spiritual Directorate of Central Asia and Kazakstan received 1 million copies of the Qur'an as a gift from King Fakhda Ben Abdul Aziz of Saudi Arabia. Construction was begun on hundreds of *medresses* throughout Central Asia, financed in part by local resources and in part by such patrons as the royal family of Saudi Arabia. Islamic proselytizing reappeared on the streets of Central Asia. By 1991 *Navruz* was restored in Uzbekiston as an official state holiday.[6] Turkic-language translations of the Qur'an appeared.

Navruz celebration in Tashkent, 1993. The Persian spring holiday has been embraced in Uzbekiston as a national festival, celebrating the unity of the Uzbek state and Halklar dostligi (the friendship of peoples). Photo by Gregory Gleason.

As the currents of cultural renewal swelled, the neonationalist political leadership of the new states began to fear the unifying power of Islam almost as much as they did the Soviet regime. Those Islamic organizations that edged into active politics by advocating political change were quickly isolated by political authorities. The All-Union Islamic Party of Renewal, which according to its leaders urged restraint and the avoidance of violence in disputes involving national differences, was allowed to register as a party in Moscow.[7] At the same time, its branches in Tojikiston and Uzbekiston were declared illegal and their meetings were banned.[8] Another party, the Islamic Party of Rebirth, was not allowed to register even in Russia. According to a spokesman for the organization in Moscow, the reason that Russian authorities denied the organization's application was opposition from Saudi Arabia.[9]

The political implications of revolutionary Islamic unity in Central Asia were perhaps best represented by the recent appeals that have circulated throughout Central Asia for the creation of "Islamistan." This concept is related to the mythical community of a Greater Turkestan. Although a Greater Turkestan has never existed in reality, for at least a century the idea of creating a pan-Turanian fraternity of nations has inspired political

A moment of prayer in Tashkent. Photo by Gregory Gleason.

revolutionaries in all of the Turkophone regions of Asia and Asia Minor. As a political concept, the idea of a Greater Turkestan was encouraged by the post–World War I Turkish nationalist leader Kemal Ataturk (literally "Kemal"—the Father of the Turks) who engineered the creation of the modern Turkish state following the collapse of the Ottoman empire. In the modern period, the idea of a Greater Turkestan has been bound up with the anticipation of some form of Middle Asian Islamic cultural, and perhaps political confederation.

The idea of Central Asian unity is tempered by the balance of power among the countries of Central Asia. In military, economic, and ideological terms, none of the Central Asian countries is capable of leading the others, and none is prepared to follow any other. During his tour of the Central Asian countries in April 1992 shortly after independence, the Turkish president, Demirel, pointed out Turkey's cultural rather than political goals, noting, "Our objective is not pan-Turkism. But [Central Asia] . . . is our fatherland. Both our history and culture begin here."[10]

During the first years of independence, all of the Central Asian presidents stressed their support for the separation of church and state in Central Asia and spoke against the practicality of an all–Central Asian political union. As Kyrgyzstan's Askar Akaev expressed at a press conference in Delhi in March 1992, "The probability of the formation of a federation of Islamic governments among the Central Asian republics of the CIS is close to zero. Such a union of governments is impossible both in the form of a federation and in the form of a confederation. The republics of Central Asia are very different. Our paths are very different."[11] Even Turkmenistan's Niyazov, generally regarded as the most reflexively "Soviet" leader of Central Asia, argued strongly in favor of the nation-state principle rather than the Turkic-unity principle: "We want to live in friendship with all neighboring and non-neighboring countries—whether they be Islamic, Slavic, or anything else. Turkmenistan will never become an Islamic government. The larger part of the population believes in Islam, but nevertheless the course of the government of Turkmenistan is the creation of a secular government."[12]

In Central Asia today, contemporary political leaders—both those in power and those in opposition—find as little attractive in the ideas of Islamic political unity as they find admirable in the ideas of Islamic and pan-Turanian cultural unity. The real support for the nationalist doctrine of pan-Turanian unity comes from political activists and commentators outside Central Asia, particularly those influenced by European concepts of nationalism and nation-building. The support for cultural unity within the societies of Central Asia is abiding and pervasive. It is this elemental and widespread unanimity of feeling—"cultural Islam" and not "political Islam"—that is destined to play a determining role in Central Asia's future.

GOOD GOVERNMENT AND THE RULE OF LAW

Central Asian society has reason to be proud of its past. There is a quality of civility inherited from ancient Central Asian tradition, a quality that is unmatched in many of the world's more prosperous societies. Asian traditions of civility are part of the fabric of interpersonal relations in Central Asia, particularly in its southern, more Islamic regions. The practice at introductions and farewells of gently bowing and touching one's hand to one's heart in a gesture of respect and honesty expresses a ceremonial aspect of Central Asian life. That gesture alone says more about society and conditions of governance in a Central Asian country than one is likely to find in volumes of civil codes. It expresses a condition of pure equality in the relations between human beings.

But one does not have to look far in Central Asian society to find that such "pure equality" is highly conditional and dependent on subtle distinctions of station and circumstance. In personal interactions, civility is part of the code of good behavior. However, in all impersonal, bureaucratic, and governmental interactions one finds that subordination and superordination—not equality—are the rule. Throughout the entire social structure of Central Asian society, there is a rigid insistence on a recognition of status, position, and hierarchy. In some places, notably Uzbekistan, the insistence on regard for station and status is most inflexible, but this phenomenon can be found everywhere in Central Asia.

Visitors may easily find the authoritarian and hierarchical aspects of Central Asian culture inimical to Western ideas of democracy such as popular sovereignty, political accountability, voluntary exchange relations, and human and civil rights. Central Asian states have been accused of being the least free, open, and progressive of former Soviet communities. Practices of all the Central Asian governments have invited criticism. The Central Asian governments routinely fare poorly in internationally accepted reviews of human rights practices conducted by such organizations as Amnesty International, Human Rights Watch/Helsinki, and the U.S. State Department's annual global human rights survey.

The criticism of Central Asian governments is leveled most frequently at human rights abuses, but it is often meant and understood in broader terms. In some respects, criticism of violations of civil and human rights in these countries often may be read as a criticism of the entire system of government. Central Asian government leaders repeatedly underscore their commitment to democracy and market economics, but there are suspicions that these rhetorical statements do not represent intent. Many observers view such statements as mainly instrumental, meant to assuage European and U.S. criticism rather than to serve as guidelines for reforming the institutions and practices of the past. The skepticism of many observers has its roots in the view that the Central Asian governments have not taken seriously the scope of the problems inherent to democratic change. Some critics feel, in the words of the distinguished scholar of democracy V.O. Key, "The superimposition over a people habituated to tyranny of a leadership imbued with democratic ideals probably would not create a viable democratic order."[13]

The Central Asian governments have been under scrutiny from North American and European governments to conform to standards of "good government" that are accepted in the West. In terms of conventional definitions, good government prescribes pragmatism rather than ideology, urges the rule of law and public accountability rather than personalistic and arbitrary rule, and emphasizes transparency and openness rather than secrecy and insider politics. Western approaches to good government stress the *procedures* and *institutions* of democratic government. The institutions of good government are typically understood to include constitutionally limited, representative government with separate functions carried out by independent legislative, judicial, and executive branches. The procedures of good government stress the rule of law and an independent judiciary.

The experience of many countries and cultures around the world is taken to confirm the view that democracy and market economics are the most reliable mechanisms for protecting individual and group rights, promoting human happiness and prosperity at home, and promoting peace, security, and a stable international order.[14] A basic principle of good government is that government's proper role is to defend the public interest, not to define it.

The rule of law means that all components of society, including the public bureaucracy, operate under the same legal constraints and with the same legal rights to enable peaceful and predictable political and economic participation.[15] The rule of law rests heavily on the observance of basic property rights, that is, the right of both natural and juridical individuals to own, enjoy, and exchange property.[16] The law of secured transactions provides a framework for stable expectations in the marketplace. Civil and commercial codes provide a well defined and easily understood framework for entry and exit into and out of the marketplace and for sanctity of contracts and remedy in the event of the failure of performance. The rule of law requires that the legal system exist not only on paper but also in practice. Written laws must also be implemented, enforced, understood, accepted, and used. This requires a clear legal framework, mechanisms for the enforceability of agreements, transparency in dispute resolution, and the possibility of recourse against arbitrary acts.

When measured against these standards, critics claim, Central Asian practices seem to be based not on a separation of powers or on representative constitutionalism, but on an unquestioning respect for elders, deference to authority, intolerance for dissent, subjugation of women, and a reflexive return to mythic principles of the past. Central Asia's critics say that such cultural standards make the observance of basic principles of governance and human rights virtually impossible in Central Asia's lower tier (Tojikiston, Turkmenistan, and Uzbekiston) and problematic in Kazakstan and Kyrgyzstan as well.[17]

In response, many Central Asian officials and intellectuals contend that European and U.S. conceptions of human and civil rights proceed from the rights of the individual, not from the rights of the collective; that outside observers presume their definitions of human rights are universal but fail to see how closely connected they are to their own cultural values and standards; that Central Asian political institutions and processes are based in the cultures of Central Asia and the interests of groups rather than individuals. These institutions are given content and meaning in the traditions of *hurmat* (see Chapter 2) and by the conventions of communal property, deference to personalized authority rather than externalized and impersonal legal structures, the preeminence of the family, the importance of the individual's obligation to the group, and the weight of many centuries of established tradition.

Neither side in this dispute can muster much empirical evidence to support its claims. Although Europeans and North Americans may profoundly believe that democracy is both an instrumental and an absolute good in developed societies, the appropriateness of democracy for transitional societies is viewed by many in the developing world to be an article of faith rather than an empirical fact. The record of "transplanted" European political institutions is mixed at best. In some countries political parties, free elections, and independent judiciaries have led to a democratic breakthrough. But for every successful case there is an unsuccessful one, where adopted political institutions have resulted only in further conflict and political decay.[18]

The idea of establishing limited, publicly accountable, constitutionally constrained and responsive government has not won many adherents among those in power in postindependence Central Asia. The presidents in all the countries have concluded that their greatest peril does not arise from the lack of accountability of government, but from the weakness of the executive branch. Central Asians claim that as transitional societies they are dealing with problems that limit democratic choice. They say that the defining problem of the transition is not the inability of the government to satisfy people's wishes, but the necessity of the government to avoid the danger of widespread social disorder.

The civil war in Tojikiston left ruin, fear, and resignation in its wake. Tojikiston's Emomli Rakhmonov, while serving as speaker of parliament, began referring to himself as "head of the government," a post that he eventually won after the November 1994 elections. The elections were so obviously rigged that major international organizations including the CSCE (now OSCE) refused to send official election observers for fear of legitimizing the process. Yet popular sentiment favored stability at any cost. As one vice president of the Tojikiston Academy of Sciences told a group of visiting legal specialists in 1994 who were proposing cooperative work in building democratic institutions, "If your democracy is anything like what we saw in my country last year, we do not want it."[19]

Using the threat of disorder as a pretext for maintaining his power, Turkmenistan's Saparmurad Niyazov established a dictatorship through an elaborately orchestrated popular referendum. Using the most advanced Soviet election techniques, Niyazov succeeded in having his term extended an additional ten years. Uzbekiston's Islam Karimov followed suit, holding elections in February 1995 that, not surprisingly, handed him a landslide victory and an extension of his tenure through the year 2000. Even Kyrgyzstan's Akaev, revered in the first year of independence by European and U.S. officials as the one true democrat of Central Asia, abandoned proceduralism in 1994, dismissing the parliament, firing the Cabinet of Ministers, reorganizing the Central Electoral Commission, and amending the constitution to see to it that a new parliament was elected. He won reelection in December 1995. Kazakstan's Nursultan Nazarbaev braved Western criticism when he too followed suit in March 1995, dismissing parliament and then calling for a popular referendum to extend his personal rule.

Some Central Asians claim there is another, even more important constraint on the adoption of Western political institutions in Central Asia than the power of the executives: It is unlikely that the newly adopted political institutions of legislatures and independent judiciaries will be anything other than superficial, these critics say, unless fundamental changes take place in Central Asia's "fourth branch of government"—the tradition of personalistic rule. During the period of Soviet colonial rule, powerful and resilient mechanisms of public decisionmaking—informal authority structures—developed that were virtually invisible to the outside eye.[20] Unless these subterranean political institutions are taken into account, new political institutions run the risk of either becoming irrelevant or corrupted.

One might agree with these critics as to the limited applicability of Western norms to Central Asian reality but for the fact that domestic Central Asian institutions seem to be incapable of responding to the growing violations of human rights in Central Asia. Given the meager protection afforded individual rights in the patriarchal, paternalistic, and collectivist cultures of Central Asia, the Soviet collapse created immediate problems for nonindigenous peoples living in Central Asia. In particular, ethnic Slavs living in the Central Asian diaspora found that they were transformed overnight into second-class citizens. Without property rights to protect their position in society, they had only their skills and experience to protect them. In most cases, however, skill and experience come in a distant second to nationality, kinship, and family friends.

Slavic individuals who had lived their whole lives as Soviet citizens found themselves faced with a choice: abandon their apartments and friends or become citizens of a republic ruled by a nationalist elite determined to install an official language they did not understand and chart a course as a "secular Islamic state" they could not approve. Each of the Central Asian states adopted a constitution that provided for national citizenship. To protect the rights of Russians in the "near abroad" and to maintain a sphere of influence in Central Asia, Russia pressured each of the countries for provisions that implicitly or explicitly allowed dual citizenship. During 1994, press services in Kazakstan and Uzbekistan repeatedly announced that a forthcoming visit by President Boris Yeltsin of Russia would conclude an agreement on the citizenship issue. Yet the meeting never took place because the negotiators could not reach a compromise. Only Turkmenistan adopted the Russian proposal, granting dual citizenship to its citizens in an effort to prevent its best-trained specialists from abandoning the country.

Since independence came to Central Asia, most Russians and Slavs in Kazakstan, Uzbekiston, and Tojikiston have been unsure about their rights or about the procedures necessary to acquire Russian citizenship. Russia, acting unilaterally, offered citizens of Kazakstan and Uzbekiston the right to declare Russian citizenship in absentia. The northern cities of Kazakstan—particularly such industrial towns as Uralsk, Petropavlovsk, and Pavlodar—tilted toward the north because of their close ethnic and cultural ties with Russia. This challenged Kazak ethnic claims for control of the republic and prompted President Nazarbaev to advocate moving the capital to Akmola to provide better ballast for the government, virtually controlled by Kazaks. When the new constitution was adopted in the summer of 1995 it recognized only Kazakstani citizenship, prohibiting dual citizenship for the ethnic Russian population.

The most routine and severe violations of human rights in the societies of Central Asia concern the position of women. In Central Asia the discussion of the role of women tends to take place in the context of the asserted "protectiveness" of Islamic tradition. In reality, there is simply no justification for many aspects of the treatment of women in Central Asia. The tendencies to regard women as chattel and constrict their role to that of domestic slave are particularly strong in the rural and more remote areas of Central Asia. After the Soviet breakup, unmarried women of Slavic ethnic descent in Central Asia found themselves in an extraordinarily difficult situation, particularly if they lived outside of the large provincial capitals, such as those in Uzbekiston's Fergana Valley or the southern districts of Kazakstan. Unmarried women avoided even going into the streets for fear that they would be kidnapped and sold into domestic slavery. Statistics on the actual danger of such kidnapping are wholly unreliable, but the fears of such a fate were quite real and widespread.

The international community has reached consensus on the importance of human rights as a cornerstone of good governance. Human rights activists, intellectuals, and world political leaders alike affirm a commitment to the core values of respect for life, liberty, justice and equity, mutual respect, caring, and integrity.[21] In such instruments as the Charter of the United Nations and the Helsinki Conference's "Final Act," human rights are defined as universal, inalienable, and self-evident. They include freedoms of speech, thought, religion, choice, and freedom from torture. They include the right of individuals to participate in the process of public choice through free and fair elections, the right of the accused to a trial by an independent judicial proceeding, and the freedom from arbitrary exercise of executive power.

People who hold similar views often disagree as to the means for achieving them. In such cases, conflict can be avoided or managed through skillful leadership. But when fundamentally different values are held, demands tend to be absolute and nonnegotiable. The differences between the international standards articulated above and the values held by many Central Asians may be described as fundamental differences. If conflict with the outside world is to be avoided, consequently, Central Asian leaders and the leaders of the international community must press jointly for a more informed dialogue emphasizing not the particular institutions of democratic change but the protection of human rights in the process of change.

CENTRAL ASIA TODAY AND TOMORROW

In its opening pages this book observes that the states of Central Asia started from a common point within the Soviet Union, yet with the coming of independence they quickly took very different paths. Kyrgyzstan set out with great enthusiasm and commitment on a course of liberalization. Kazakstan adopted a "Western" development model, embracing democracy, a market economy, the rule of law, and civil rights as a road map for the future. Uzbekiston assumed a quite different posture, emphasizing traditionalism, strong leadership and state, collective rights, and national consolidation. Turkmenistan quickly evolved into an Oriental despotism based upon anticipations of economic self-reliance. Tojikiston slid into internal strife. These different experiences would suggest that independence acted as a gyre, magnifying small differences among the cultures of Central Asia and propelling the new states in different directions. Yet despite all the differences among these societies, their common cultural background and historical experience continue to exercise a powerful role. The seeming inability of the new states to proceed along the lines of democratic development may testify to the strength of Central Asian traditions and the power of the past.

One indication of the influence of the past may be the extent to which the transition to independence, although played out differently in each of the states, did not alter the fundamental relationship between the citizen and the state. By the autumn of 1995 all of the states had adopted new, post-Soviet constitutions. But all of these so-called presidential constitutions provided for almost dictatorial rule through top-heavy executive branches. None of the countries has sustained anything resembling Western due process of law. None of the countries has received approval for meeting international standards of election processes. None of the countries has a functioning deliberative assembly protected by a true separation of powers. None of the countries has a legislature that was independently capable of establishing national budget priorities. None of the countries has an independent judiciary. Only Kazakstan has a free press, and that is probably only because Kazakstan's proximity to Russia made it impossible for the government to control the press.

The expectation that independence implies freedom should never have been interpreted by Central Asians or by the outside world to mean freedom from the past, freedom from established habits of thought and practice, and freedom from the compromises of competing interest groups—some of whom are tied to the power and privileges of the past. A large part of Central Asia's current travail is attributable to what might be called a "small-state sovereignty syndrome." These new states find that they are linked in a common endeavor in pursuit of common goals in such a way that the more energetically and enthusiastically they pursue those goals, the more likely they are to come into conflict with one another. This syndrome is a product of the countervailing and almost paradoxical influence of attaining national independence in a tightly interdependent world.

Flags of national independence of each of the Central Asian republics symbolically fly alongside 180 others at the United Nations headquarters in New York. These are symbols of national sovereignty, autonomy, and independence. But in fact the ability of the Central Asian leaders to determine the futures of their countries in the international community is narrowly circumscribed. The crowded and intensely competitive international community constrains small states at every turn.

Throughout the world, the temptation of leaders in small states is to counter their impotence abroad by reinforcing their coerciveness at home. Rather than seek consensus, they attempt to impose it. To increase their international effectiveness they take steps to exert control at home. Yet the more they seek to impose an order that gives them control over local affairs, the more they find that globalization is pressuring them again in the opposite direction, urging them to lower their borders to goods and services, to increase the accessibility of mass media, to improve the transparency of their legislation, and to conform to international standards of civil and human rights. Political leaders in these circumstances easily misinterpret their capacity to shape change.

The outside world too can misinterpret the significance of the emergence of these new states. Many people applauded Central Asian independence as the Soviet Union disintegrated. Freedom, they felt, had finally come to a land so long oppressed. Many Turkophiles were euphoric at the transition and applauded the prospects for a cultural renaissance in Central Asia. Many European and U.S. scholars, mixing ambition and expectation, foresaw new professional implications in the emergence of a newly open area of the world.[22] Many business leaders and entrepreneurs waxed enthusiastic over the prospects of the newly emerging Central Asian market. Many strategic theorists thought they saw geopolitical implications and world historical significance in the renewal of "the Great Game."

Many of these anticipations, however, obscure the real significance of the transition at the heart of Asia. In reality, Central Asia is not about to become the pivot of Asia. Central Asia's fortunes will not determine the economics, politics, or the shape of cultural change taking place in the lands of the former USSR. Central Asian markets are not likely to have an effect, for instance, on European or U.S. producers. The contest over control of Central Asia's oil-and-gas transportation routes has grown more intense, but it is not a contest that will be determined by Central Asian actions. World market demand for oil will determine the outcome of this drama, not Central Asian objectives.

If it is globalization that is transforming the international community, perhaps it is no longer true that "geography is destiny." Central Asia was called the geopolitical "pivot" of Asia, and its position as a crucial trade juncture between East and West may no longer empower it—as it may have done during the nineteenth century—but rather constrain it, in the twenty-first century. Central Asia is lodged between the powerful states of China and Russia, or as some Central Asians colorfully put it, between the Dragon and the Bear. The unwillingness of the United Nations to commit "blue helmet" peacekeeping troops to stop the bloodshed in Tojikiston in 1993 illustrates that European and North American security interests in Central Asia are not likely to be substantial enough to result in any significant engagement in the region. Yet both Russia and China, for varying reasons, are likely to look toward Central Asia when they think in terms of annexation.

The Central Asian states are likely to continue to be subjects rather than actors. Compared to their neighbors in terms of economic, environmental, and political importance, the Central Asian states do not stand out as decisive by any measure. Turkey and Iran each have populations of more than 60 million people, more than the total of the Central Asian states combined. In market potential alone Pakistan, with over 120 million people, is more than five times the size of the largest single Central Asian market, Uzbekiston. In terms of potential environmental impacts, Kazakstan's slipshod industrialization practices should indeed provoke international concern. But when measured against the basically unregulated economy of China—with an annual economic growth rate of more than 10 percent and a population nearly 700 times larger than that of Kazakstan—it is unlikely that Central Asia will or should rank high on the pri-

184 ■ TRANSITION IN ASIA

orities of the international community when considering adverse environmental impacts.

These are reasons why the enduring significance of the transition in Central Asia is not to be found in Central Asia's influence on the world stage. But it is also for these reasons that the enduring significance of the transition in Central Asia is to be found *within* Central Asia rather than in Central Asia's impact on other countries.

Chapter 1 discusses the extent to which Central Asia's traditional social, economic, and political forms of organization were shaped historically by the physical features of Central Asia's geography. The succeeding chapters detailed how the new institutions are increasingly shaped by a combination of the external pressures of the international community and by the internal resourcefulness of Central Asian cultures. As powerful as external forces and actors may be, they can only impose choices and constraints, not determine the course of Central Asian affairs. The Central Asian states are discovering independence by exploring how Central Asian commonalities of culture, language, perspective, and ideas can influence their participation in the international community. The broad constraints of the transition to independence have come from without, but the meaning of independence can come only from within.

NOTES

1. A comprehensive, informed, and sensitive treatment of Islam in Central Asia may be found in Mehrdad Haghaeyeghi, *Islam and Politics in Central Asia* (New York: St. Martin's Press, 1995).

2. Alexandre Bennigsen, "Muslims, Mullahs, and Mujahidin," *Problems of Communism* (November-December 1984): 28–44.

3. Alexandre Bennigsen, "Muslim Religious Conservatism and Dissent in the USSR," *Religion in Communist Lands* 6, no. 3 (1978): 153–161.

4. S. Bagdasarov, "My—za armiiu. Byli I budem!" *Krasnaia zvezda* (10 April 1991): 3.

5. A conference of the representatives of the Spiritual Directorate of the Republics of Central Asia and Kazakstan issued a communiqué calling for citizens to support the preservation of a single renewed union of sovereign republics. *USSR Today: Soviet Media News and Information Digest*, compiled by RFE/RL (26 February 1991).

6. See James Critchlow, "The Crisis Deepens," *Report on the USSR* 3, no. 1 (1991): 40.

7. Vladimir Kazakov, "Gotovy k dialogu," *Literaturnaia Rossiia* (8 March 1991): 10. Also see *Moskovskie novosti* no. 10 (10 March 1991): 2.

8. See "Zaiavlenie," *Komsomolets Tajikistana* (2 December 1990): 3.

9. Elena Deriabina, "Islamskii faktor ili spetssluzhby Saudovskoi Aravii v Miniuste RF?" *Stolitsa* no. 32 (August 1992): 4.

10. FBIS-SOV-92 (30 April 1992): 56.

11. Nikolai Paklin, "Kyrgyzstan predlagaet uran na eksport," *Izvestiia* (19 March 1992): 1.

12. Vladimir Kuleshov, "Turkmenistan I Rossiia gotovy sotrudnichat'," *Izvestiia* (17 March 1992): 2.

13. V.O. Key Jr., *Public Opinion and Democratic Politics* (New York: Knopf, 1961), p. 537.

14. More than two centuries ago, in an essay entitled "Perpetual Peace," Immanuel Kant observed that the road to international peace was in the expansion of the republican form of democratic government. In recent years political leaders and scholars have noted that democracy is a superior form of government because whereas authoritarian governments often fight one another and fight against democratic governments, democratic governments rarely go to war against one another. In the celebrated words of one analyst of international relations, this regularity is "as close as anything we have to an empirical law in international relations." J.S. Levy, "The Causes of War: A Review of Theories and Evidence," in Philip E. Tetlock, J.L. Husbands, R. Jervis, P.S. Sterns, and C. Tilly, eds., *Behavior, Society, and Nuclear War*, vol. 1 (New York: Oxford University Press, 1993), pp. 209–333, at 270.

15. See Friedrich A. Hayek, *The Road to Serfdom* (Chicago: University of Chicago Press, 1944), p. 72.

16. See James W. Ely Jr., *The Guardian of Every Other Right* (New York: Oxford University Press, 1992).

17. On traditions of deference to authority, see Gregory Gleason, "Fealty and Loyalty: Informal Authority Structures in Soviet Asia," *Soviet Studies* 43, no. 4 (1991): 613–628.

18. As one analyst concluded: "The promise of democracy is not that of automatic improvement in areas of life that are not narrowly connected with political freedoms; it is the creation of a window of opportunity, a political framework where groups struggling for development and human rights have better possibilities than before for organizing and expressing their demands. Democracy offers the opportunities; it does not offer guarantees of success." Georg Sorensen, *Democracy and Democratization: Processes and Prospects in a Changing World* (Boulder: Westview Press, 1993), p. 88.

19. A USAID-sponsored technical assistance team in 1994 repeatedly sought to encourage officials in Tojikiston to familiarize themselves with international standards of the democratic process. As a member of that team I found the politics of institutional change was almost solely determined by the consequences of the civil war and the fear of a resurgence of the fighting.

20. For an investigation into some of the bases and implications of informal authority structures, see Gregory Gleason, "Fealty and Loyalty," pp. 613–628.

21. An eloquent statement of the role of these principles in the contemporary international community may be found in Commission on Global Governance, *Our Global Neighborhood: The Report of the Commission on Global Governance* (Oxford: Oxford University Press, 1995), pp. 48–54.

22. Central Asia is not likely to become the "hot" area for a new generation of area specialists. Area-study specializations in general have become problematic as

many academic institutions press for greater emphasis on context-free, general disciplinary approaches. For instance, professional positions in most Western research and academic institutions continue to be filled along disciplinary lines rather than area lines. For an explanation for why this continues to be the case, see Gregory Gleason, "The 'National Factor' and the Logic of Sovietology," in Alexander J. Motyl, ed., *The Post-Soviet Nations: Perspectives on the Demise of the USSR* (New York: Columbia University Press, 1992), pp. 1–29.

▪ Chronology of Events in ▪ Modern Central Asia: November 1917– December 1995

The various Soviet republics underwent numerous mutations and name changes during the Soviet period. For the sake of clarity we will use the acronyms SSR and ASSR in this Chronology even though "Socialist" may or may not have been part of a particular republic's official name.

1917

November 7	Lenin, at the 2nd Congress of Soviets, urges establishment of a government including a Congress of Soviets, a Central Executive Committee, and a Council of People's Commissars.

1918

January 20	The Central Executive Committee decrees dissolution of the Constituent Assembly in St. Petersburg.
January 28	The Declaration on the Federal Institutions of the Russian Republic is issued by the 3rd Congress of Soviets.
April	Turkestan Autonomous Soviet Republic is formed in Central Asia.

1920

April	The Khorezm People's Soviet Republic is formed after the fall of the Khan of Khiva.
August	Kyrgyz and Kazak Autonomous Soviet Socialist Republics decreed.
October	The Bukhara People's Soviet Republic is formed after the fall of the Emir of Bukhara.

1922

December	The 1st All-Union Congress of Soviets adopts the Union Treaty.

1923

October — The Khorezm People's Soviet Republic becomes the Khorezm People's Soviet Socialist Republic.

1924

January — 2nd All-Union Congress of Soviets adopts the 1924 USSR Constitution. The USSR now comprises the RFSSR, the Ukrainian SSR, the Byelorussian SSR, and the Transcaucasian FSSR.

September — Bukhara People's Soviet Republic becomes Bukhara People's Soviet Socialist Republic and enters the USSR.

October — A plan for redistricting Central Asia is announced. The Uzbek SSR and the Turkmen SSR are formed from the Bukhara People's Soviet Socialist Republic, the Khorezm People's Soviet Socialist Republic, and the Turkestan Autonomous Soviet Socialist Republic. The Kara-Kyrgyz Autonomous Oblast is added to the RFSSR.

1925

The Gorno-Badakhshan Autonomous Oblast is formed in Tojikiston. The Karakalpak Autonomous Oblast is formed in the Uzbek SSR. The Kyrgyz Autonomous Oblast becomes the Kyrgyz Autonomous Republic.

1926

February — The Kyrgyz Autonomous Republic becomes the Kyrgyz Autonomous Soviet Socialist Republic.

1929

June — The Tojik Autonomous Soviet Socialist Republic is renamed the Tojik Soviet Socialist Republic.

June — Hujand Oblast (later to be known as Leninabod Oblast) is transferred to the Tojik SSR.

1932

The Karakalpak Autonomous Soviet Socialist Oblast becomes the Karakalpak Autonomous Soviet Socialist Republic and is subordinated to the RFSSR.

1936

The Karakalpak Autonomous Soviet Socialist Republic is subordinated to the Uzbek SSR.

The Kazak ASSR and the Kyrgyz ASSR become the Kazak SSR and the Kyrgyz SSR.

The Transcaucasian Federation is dissolved; in its place three union republics are formed: the Armenian SSR, the Azerbaijanian SSR, and the Georgian SSR.

The 1936 (Stalin) Constitution is adopted. It describes eleven union republics: the RFSSR and the Ukrainian, Byelorussian, Georgian, Armenian, Azerbaijanian, Kazak, Uzbek, Turkmen, Tojik, and Kyrgyz republics.

1940

Bukovina is taken from Romania. Carpathia is taken from Czechoslovakia. The Baltic states of Estonia, Latvia, and Lithuania are joined to the USSR as Soviet socialist republics. The Karelo-Finnish SSR is formed.

June   The Moldavia SSR is formed from Bukovina and Bessarabia, bringing the total number of SSRs to sixteen.

1963

June   The area known as the Jizaq is ceded from the Kazak SSR to the Uzbek SSR.

1977

October 7   A new Soviet Constitution (the so-called Brezhnev Constitution) is adopted by the USSR Supreme Soviet.

1985

March 12   Mikhail S. Gorbachev is named CPSU General Secretary.

1986

December 17   Kazak leader Dinmukhamed Kunaev is replaced by Gennadii Kolbin as leader of Kazakstan's party organization.
December 19   Students in the Kazak capital of Alma-Ata protest Kunaev's removal. The protest forms the basis of Zheltoksan (the "December Movement").

1988

June 28   In a speech to the 19th Conference of the CPSU, Gorbachev announces a major political reform.
November 16   The Supreme Council of the Estonian SSR issues a declaration, "On the Sovereignty of Estonian SSR"; Soviet federal devolution begins.
December 1   Two key reform bills are passed in the USSR Supreme Soviet— the law on elections and the law on constitutional amendment.

1989

April 9   Militia fire on demonstrators in the Georgian SSR; thirty-six are killed.
April 14   Draft of a law declaring Tojik the official language of the Tojik SSR is published in Tojikiston.
May 18   The Supreme Council of the Lithuanian SSR issues a declaration, "On State Sovereignty of Lithuania." The republic asserts veto power over legislation passed in Moscow.
May 18   Lithuanian Supreme Soviet abrogates the Molotov-Ribbentrop Agreement of 1939.

July 22	Supreme Soviet of the Tojik SSR passes law declaring Tojik to be the official language of the republic.
August 24	Draft of a law declaring Kyrgyz to be the official language of the Kyrgyz SSR is published in Kyrgyzstan.
September 20	The Nationality Policy Platform is adopted by the CPSU Plenum.
September 23	Supreme Soviet of the Kyrgyz SSR passes law declaring Kyrgyz the official language of the republic.
October 21	Supreme Soviet of the Uzbek SSR passes law declaring Uzbek to be the official language of the republic.
October 28	The Communist Party of Lithuania publishes a draft platform declaring the party to be an independent organization.

1990

February	Government troops fire on demonstrators in Dushanbe, Tojikiston.
February	Article 6 of the Soviet Constitution, the clause naming the CPSU as the "leading and guiding force" of Soviet society, is removed. Competing political parties become legal.
March 12	USSR Congress of People's Deputies, the first popularly elected deliberative assembly since 1918, is convened in Moscow.
March	Gorbachev is elected by the Soviet parliament to fill the newly created executive presidency.
May 28	Boris Yeltsin is elected chairman of the Supreme Soviet of the RFSSR.
June 11	The Supreme Soviet of the RFSSR declares Russian state sovereignty.
June 20	The Supreme Soviet of the Uzbek SSR declares state sovereignty.
June 23	Leaders of the Central Asian republics, meeting in Frunze (now Bishkek), issue an appeal on social responsibility and sign the Agreement on Economic, Scientific-Technical, and Cultural Cooperation among Central Asian republics. Moscow is not a signatory to the agreement.
August 22	The Supreme Soviet of the Turkmen SSR declares state sovereignty.
August 25	The Supreme Soviet of the Tojik SSR declares state sovereignty.
October 25	The Supreme Soviet of the Kazak SSR declares state sovereignty.
December 15	The Supreme Soviet of the Kyrgyz SSR declares state sovereignty.

1991

January 13	Soviet OMON special forces troops storm Lithuania's radio-television center in Vilnius, killing fourteen.
June	Boris Yeltsin is elected president of the RFSSR by popular vote.

July 23	Provisional agreement on Gorbachev's "Novo-Ogarevo" version of a new Union Treaty is reached. The official signing ceremony is set for August 20, 1991.
August 19	An attempted coup by eight members of CPSU Politburo and high government officials fails. Gorbachev returns from vacation in Crimea. Boris Yeltsin emerges as heroic leader of "democratic opposition."
August 31	Kyrgyzstan's Supreme Soviet declares political independence of Kyrgyzstan.
August 31	Uzbekiston's Supreme Soviet declares political independence of Uzbekiston.
September 2	A postcoup meeting of republican "High Leaders" is followed by an announcement by Gorbachev of a plan to form a Union of Sovereign States.
September 8	Tojikiston's Supreme Soviet declares national political independence.
October 2	Negotiations on the formal provision of an "economic association" begin in Alma-Ata, Kazakstan.
October 12	Askar Akaev is popularly elected to a five-year term as president of Kyrgyzstan.
October 18	A new Treaty of Economic Association is signed on October 18, 1991. Signatories included Kazakstan, Kyrgyzstan, Tojikiston, Turkmenistan, and Uzbekiston.
October 27	Saparmurad Niyazov is elected by Turkmenistan's Supreme Soviet as president of Turkmenistan.
October 27	Turkmenistan's President Niyazov declares political independence of Turkmenistan.
November 24	Rakhman Nabiev elected by Tojikiston's Supreme Soviet as president of Tojikiston.
November 25	Gorbachev announces that the provisions of a new political union—the Union of Sovereign States—are "accepted in principle."
December 1	Leonid Kravchuk is popularly elected president of Ukraine.
December 8	Leaders of Russia, Ukraine, and Belarus, meeting in Minsk, resolve to create a Commonwealth of Independent States and declare that the USSR ceases to exist.
December 11	Members of the Islamic Rebirth Party seize the Communist Party oblast headquarters in Namangan in the Fergana Valley, demanding the establishment of an Islamic state.
December 12	Representatives of the five Asian republics (Kazakstan, Kyrgyzstan, Tojikiston, Turkmenistan, and Uzbekiston) meet in Ashgabat, Turkmenistan, and agree to support the concept of a wider Commonwealth.
December 16	The Kazakstan Supreme Soviet declares the political independence of Kazakstan.
December 17	U.S. Secretary of State James Baker III meets with Askar Akaev of Kyrgyzstan.

December 18	Baker meets with Nursultan Nazarbaev in Alma-Ata.
December 21	Leaders of eleven former Soviet republics gather in Alma-Ata to sign a series of agreements establishing a broader Commonwealth of Independent States. The USSR ceases to exist. Signatories include Azerbaijan, Armenia, Belarus, Kazakstan, Kyrgyzstan, Moldova, the Russian Federation, Tojikiston, Turkmenistan, Uzbekiston, and Ukraine—all of the former Soviet republics except Georgia and the three Baltic states.
December 25	Gorbachev resigns as president of the USSR.
December 29	Presidential election and a referendum on independence are held in Uzbekiston. Islam Karimov receives 86 percent of vote; the referendum on political independence receives 98 percent in favor.
December 30	Four successor states possessing nuclear weapons (Belarus, Kazakstan, Russia, Ukraine) sign an agreement in Minsk on nuclear nonproliferation.

1992

January 8	Uzbekiston changes regional administration, adopting hakim (governor) as the head of local political subdivisions; the post of vice president is abolished in Uzbekiston.
January 11	The Karakalpak Autonomous Socialist Republic becomes the Republic of Karakalpakistan.
January 16–19	Students riot at Tashkent State University; six are killed.
January 30	Tojikiston begins closing borders and establishes a national customs service.
January 30	Ten Soviet successor states—including Kazakstan, Kyrgyzstan, Tojikiston, Turkmenistan, and Uzbekiston—become full members of the Conference on Security and Cooperation in Europe.
February 3	U.S. Embassy opens in Almaty as the first foreign embassy in the new states of Central Asia.
February 6	Newmont Mining Corporation announces plans to undertake a joint venture with Uzbekiston's government at the Muruntau mine in Uzbekiston.
February 11	Kyrgyzstan's President Akaev issues a decree eliminating half of the Kyrgyzstan government ministries and transferring their functions to other government units.
February 13	U.S. Secretary of State James Baker visits Tojikiston, Turkmenistan, and Uzbekiston.
February 14	CIS heads of state meet in Minsk and sign twenty documents on military and economic matters.
February 17	The Economic Cooperation Organization (ECO) concludes meeting in Tehran with an agreement to introduce preferential tariffs among members, establish a regional bank, and cooperate in transportation, communications, and agriculture.

	ECO admits Azerbaijan, Turkmenistan, Uzbekiston, Tojikiston, and Kyrgyzstan as members. Kazakstan assumes observer status.
February 20	Ukraine's Prime Minister Vitalii Fokin flies to Ashgabat to discuss the recent tenfold increase in the price Russia must pay for Turkmenistan's natural gas.
February 26	Central Asian Muslim Religious Board appoints Muhamad Sadyk Muhamad Yusuf the mufti of the Muslim Religious Board for Central Asia.
February 27	Kazakstan's Nazarbaev issues a decree permitting Kazak citizens to engage in foreign trade without having to seek prior government permission.
March 4	Presidents of the Academies of Science of Azerbaijan, Kazakstan, Kyrgyzstan, Tojikiston, Turkmenistan, and Uzbekiston, meeting in Tashkent, sign an agreement to preserve a "single scientific space" in Central Asia.
March 5	Uzbekiston's President Karimov announces the discovery of large petroleum deposits at Ming-Bulak in the Namangan area of Uzbekiston's Fergana Valley.
March 6	Maksud Ikramov, mayor of Dushanbe and a deputy of Tojikiston's Supreme Soviet, is arrested on charges of accepting bribes.
March 16	U.S. Embassy opens in Tashkent, Uzbekiston.
March 20	Turkmenistan's President Niyazov exonerates twenty high officials convicted of economic crimes stemming from the Central Asian "cotton scandal."
March 20	CIS Military and Security Summit in Kiev results in agreement on defense matters. Turkmenistan alone among the Central Asian states elects not to sign.
March 25	Uzbekiston's President Karimov signs decree authorizing the formation of border-guard units, subordinated to the Uzbekiston National Security Service.
March 25	Intelligence services of the CIS member countries reportedly reach a cooperation agreement.
March 26	Major political demonstrations begin outside the presidential palace in Dushanbe, Tojikiston.
March 31	The Russian Treaty of Federation is signed.
April 6	Ukrainian presidential decree asserts that strategic forces on Ukrainian territory are subordinate to the Ukrainian Ministry of Defense.
April 10	The Russian Parliament formally adopts the Russian Treaty of Federation.
April 11	The Oblast Soviet of the Gorno-Badakhshan Autonomous Oblast in Tojikiston proclaims new status as the Gorno-Badakhshan Autonomous Republic.
April 15	A new Land Law goes into effect in Tojikiston.

April 17	The Tojikiston Parliament accedes to demands to adopt a new constitution and schedule general elections in exchange for a three-week ban on opposition political demonstrations.
April 23	The presidents of Kazakstan, Kyrgyzstan, and Turkmenistan meet in Bishkek to coordinate regional security policy.
April 27	The board of directors of the IMF votes in favor of admitting thirteen states of the former USSR as member states of the IMF. The board of directors of the IBRD votes in favor of admitting thirteen states of the former USSR as member states of the IBRD.
April 28	Turkish president Suleyman Demirel, leading a 200-member delegation, begins tour of Central Asian countries.
April 29	Meeting in Chalus, Iran, the Association of Caspian Countries is formed. Members include Iran, Russia, Azerbaijan, Kazakstan, and Turkmenistan.
April 30	Tojikiston's President Nabiev is given authority by the parliament to institute direct presidential rule.
May 2	Tojikiston's President Nabiev orders the creation of a National Guard reporting directly to him.
May 5	Tojikiston's President Nabiev declares a state of emergency after armed groups attempt to occupy the presidential palace.
May 6	The Russian Foreign Ministry announces that all of the tactical nuclear weapons previously deployed on CIS territory have been returned to Russia.
May 7	Forces opposing Tojikiston's government gain control of Dushanbe. President Nabiev flees presidential palace under fire.
May 8	Representatives of National Banks of the former USSR, meeting in Bishkek, sign an agreement creating the Interbank Coordinating Council.
May 9	The United States and Kyrgyzstan sign trade agreement conferring Most Favored Nation trade status on Kyrgyzstan.
May 9–10	Heads of state of seven Central Asian countries including Iran, Kazakstan, Kyrgyzstan, Pakistan, Tojikiston, Turkmenistan, and Uzbekiston meet in Ashgabat to coordinate regional policies.
May 10	CIS troops fire on demonstrators in Dushanbe.
May 10	Agreement reached in Tojikiston to form a coalition government. Opposition figures win one-third of posts in the cabinet including the leadership of the Ministries of Defense and Internal Affairs.
May 12	By decree of Tojikiston's president, a National Assembly (*Milli Majlis*) is formed in Dushanbe to act as interim legislature until a new Assembly can be elected in December elections.
May 12	Kyrgyzstan's President Akaev visits China.

May 13	Defense Ministers from CIS meet in Tashkent and issue an appeal to preserve the Joint Armed Forces.
May 14	First meeting of Tojikiston's coalition government in Dushanbe. Shodmon Yusupov, chairman of the Democratic Party of Tojikiston, calls for an end to the two-month-long antigovernment demonstrations in Dushanbe.
May 15	CIS Heads of state meet in Tashkent. Six states—Russia, Kazakstan, Kyrgyzstan, Uzbekiston, Tojikiston, and Armenia—sign a collective security agreement.
May 18	Turkmenistan Supreme Soviet adopts a new constitution. Turkmenistan thus is the first Central Asian state to adopt a constitution in the postindependence era.
May 18	U.S.-based Chevron signs an agreement with Kazakstan that envisages an investment of $20 billion over forty years.
May 19	Kazakstan's President Nazarbaev, in a visit to the United States, announces that Kazakstan will sign the nuclear nonproliferation treaty.
May 20	Authorities in the Leninabod Province in northern Tojikiston threaten to ask Uzbekiston to annex the province unless the Dushanbe government accedes to demands of the opposition.
May 22	Kazakstan announces it is making plans to introduce its own currency, the *tenge*.
May 23	Kazakstan joins the United States, Russia, Ukraine, and Belarus in signing the Lisbon Protocol regarding nuclear weapons.
May 30	Uzbekiston's President Karimov and Russia's President Yeltsin sign a treaty of friendship and cooperation in Moscow.
May 31	Draft of a new Tojikiston Constitution is published, which exacerbates political tensions.
June 1	Kyrgyzstan government announces intention to assume control of military units stationed in its territory.
June 2	Kazakstan's Supreme Soviet adopts a new Kazakstan Constitution.
June 4	The Supreme Soviet of the Gorno-Badakhshan Autonomous Oblast in Tojikiston votes to change the name of the area to Pamiro-Badakhshan Autonomous Republic.
June 8	Russian Defense Minister Pavel Grachev and Turkmenistan's Department of Defense boss Danatar Kopekov reach agreement on Russia-Turkmenistan military cooperation.
June 9	A month-long coal miners' strike in the Karaganda Coal Basin ends when Kazakstan's government meets strikers' demands.
June 10	Kyrgyz and Russian officials sign a treaty of friendship between the two republics.
June 12	Uzbek and Russian officials sign a treaty of friendship between the two republics.

June 15	Customs officials from eight CIS countries including Kazakstan, Turkmenistan, and Uzbekiston conclude an agreement on a single customs inspection list for member countries.
June 21	Turkmenistan's President Niyazov elected for second term by popular vote in uncontested election.
June 21	Committee for National Salvation is formed in Dushanbe as opposition government.
June 22	Uzbekiston's President Karimov concludes Asian diplomatic tour that includes visits to South Korea, Malaysia, and Indonesia.
June 23	First international train arrives from Urumchi, capital of Xinjiang-Uigur Autonomous Region of China, to Almaty.
June 25	The presidents of Kazakstan and Uzbekiston sign a mutual-assistance treaty in the town of Turkestan, Kazakstan, and pledge cooperation on political, economic, cultural, and ecological issues, including joint initiatives with respect to a region bordering the Aral Sea.
June 30	Leader of the popular movement Birlik, Abdurakhim Pulatov, is severely beaten by four attackers after leaving Tashkent's city prosecutor's office.
June 30	The Turkestan Military District is abolished.
June 30	Presidents of Kyrgyzstan, Turkmenistan, and Uzbekiston meet with Turkish President Turgut Ozal in Turkey.
July 1	Prices for foodstuffs freed in Kazakstan.
July 1	Tojikiston's Nabiev completes two-day visit to Iran, where he meets with President Hashemi Rafsanjani.
July 2	First session of Uzbekiston's new parliament.
July 2	Kazakstan's President Nazarbaev signs decree prohibiting the sale of grain to other countries until special instructions have been issued by Council of Ministers.
July 2	Kazakstan's parliament ratifies the START-1 Treaty.
July 7	Kazakstan's parliament passes new law intended to speed privatization by establishing a privatization commission.
July 10	Meeting of CSCE member nations is held in Helsinki.
July 14	Turkmenistan's Cabinet of Ministers announces the establishment of armed forces.
July 16	Kazakstan joins the IMF.
July 19	Uzbekiston's President Karimov pays official visit to South Korea.
July 20	Deputy Prime Minister Aleksandr Shokhin of Russia begins a tour of Tojikiston, Uzbekiston, Kazakstan, and Turkmenistan.
July 20	Kyrgyz National Guard takes oath in Kyrgyzstan.
July 20	Uzbek National Guard takes oath in Uzbekiston.
July 21	The Treaty of Friendship between Russia and Tojikiston is signed in Dushanbe.

July 24	Kazakstan joins IBRD and the International Development Agency.
July 28	Members of the peace talks in Khorog, Tojikiston, sign a cease-fire agreement and sign a protocol calling for the resignation of President Nabiev.
July 31	Russia and Turkmenistan sign a friendship treaty specifying mutual cooperation in security, the economy, and culture.
August 4	Uzbek poet Usman Azimov is elected chairman of the Fatherland Party, which was officially registered.
August 9	Uzbek authorities begin to restrict entrance into Uzbekiston from Tojikiston unless authorized and remove people from trains at the borders.
August 14–15	Viktor Barranikov, Russian Security Minister, negotiates in Ashgabat with Turkmen officials over status of border troops.
August 18	Kazakstan decrees the formation of a national border guard.
August 27	Turkmenistan and Russia sign an agreement on mutual protection of Turkmenistan's border and on military assistance.
September 1	The Chief Command of the Unified Forces of CIS, a central command structure for joint military forces established by the July 6, 1992, military agreement signed in Moscow, assumes authority.
September 1	Uzbekiston becomes member of Non-Aligned Movement at the annual meeting of that organization in Jakarta.
September 8	Uzbekiston's President Karimov appeals to UN General Secretary Boutros Boutros-Ghali to act to quell violence in Tojikiston.
September 16	CIS Interparliamentary Assembly concludes meeting in Bishkek.
September 19	Kazakstan's President Nazarbaev and Russia's President Yeltsin meet in Moscow, affirming principles of the Tashkent Agreement of May 15, 1992, and the intention of both sides to adhere to the principle of the inviolability of the existing state borders.
September 19	Kyrgyzstan becomes a member of the IBRD.
September 22	Uzbekiston becomes a member of the IBRD.
September 22	Turkmenistan becomes a member of the IMF—the last Central Asian state to join this international organization.
September 22	Kazakstan and Germany sign an economic cooperation agreement.
September 25	Kazakstan's President Nazarbaev concludes official visit to Germany and France.
September 25	CIS leaders meet in Bishkek.
September 29	A Treaty of Friendship and Cooperation between Kyrgyzstan and Uzbekiston is signed.
September 29	The General Agreement on Tariffs and Trade extends observer status to Kazakstan.

October 1	IMF Managing Director Michel Camdessus begins official visit to Central Asian countries.
October 9	Summit of CIS leaders concludes in Bishkek.
October 10	Meeting in Kokchetav, Yeltsin and Nazarbaev sign an agreement on economic arrangements that includes customs and currency agreements and measures to coordinate foreign economic sales, to cooperate in security and disarmament, to coordinate control of strategic nuclear forces, to support scientific and technical facilities at Baykonur and Semipalatinsk, and to accept the principle of the inviolability of the existing borders.
October 10	Russian Central Bank Chairman Victor Gerashchenko announces the creation of common bank by six CIS countries—Russia, Kazakstan, Uzbekiston, Belarus, Kyrgyzstan, and Armenia.
October 19	Abdurakhim Pulatov, leader of the Birlik opposition movement in Uzbekiston, is attacked by two armed men; Pulatov's friends repulse the attack.
October 29	Presidents of Azerbaijan, Kyrgyzstan, Turkmenistan, Uzbekiston, and Kazakstan meet in Ankara for the first meeting of leaders of Turkophone countries.
November 4	Leaders of Kazakstan, Kyrgyzstan, Uzbekiston, and Tojikiston meet in Almaty to discuss measures to deal with civil war in Tojikiston.
November 6	Russia's Foreign Minister Andrei Kozyrev meets with President Niyazov in Turkmenistan.
December 4	Ninth summit of CIS leaders held in Minsk.
December 8	Uzbekiston Constitution adopted by the Uzbek Supreme Soviet.

1993

January 3–4	Central Asian presidents meet in Tashkent to discuss regional cooperation. Karimov at a press conference after the meeting says that steps had been taken for creating a Central Asian common market.
January 13	Uzbekiston's Minister of Energy announces that Uzbekiston will withdraw from the Central Asian power grid.
February 4	Russia's Defense Minister Pavel Grachev visits Tojikiston and announces Russian assistance for the establishment of a new Tojik border guard.
February 27	Nazarbaev and Yeltsin meet to discuss Russo-Kazak bilateral relations in the context of CIS agreements on security and economics.
March 11	The Turkic Orthographical Conference, meeting in Istanbul, announces a communiqué calling for the transition to Latin alphabet for all the Turkic languages of Central Asia.

March 29	Sangak Safarov and Faisuli Saidov, former military commanders of the Tojik People's Front, are killed under mysterious circumstances in the city of Kurgan-Tiube in Tojikiston.
April 7	Final agreement is reached between Kazakstan and Chevron regarding the Tengiz oil field deal.
April 11	Rakhman Nabiev, deposed Tojik president, is found dead under mysterious circumstances.
April 16	Extraordinary CIS summit meets in Minsk.
April 21	Kyrgyzstan's President Akaev, in Tokyo on diplomatic mission, is told that Kyrgyzstan will receive $60 million in low-interest loans from the World Bank with the assistance of the Japanese government.
April 27	Kyrgyzstan is accorded the status of a "developing nation" by the World Bank, allowing it to qualify for special assistance.
April 30	Muhamad Sadyk Muhamad Yusuf is removed as head of the Muslim Religious Board of Mavarannalr (Transoxania) and replaced by Mukhtarkhan Abdullaev.
May 5	Kyrgyzstan's parliament adopts a new constitution.
May 14	Kyrgyzstan introduces its own currency, the *som*.
May 25	Russo-Tojik Mutual Assistance Treaty signed by Yeltsin and Rakhmonov in Moscow.
June 10	The Asian Development Bank agrees to admit the Central Asian states as members.
June 15	Defense Ministers of six CIS countries, meeting in Moscow, vote to disband the Supreme Command of the Commonwealth Joint Forces.
June 18	Uzbek and Kyrgyz presidents sign economic agreement in wake of disputes over Kyrgyz introduction of a national currency; Kyrgyzstan acknowledges outstanding debts to Uzbekiston.
June 21	Tojikiston's Supreme Court finds the leading four opposition parties (Democratic Party, Islamic Renaissance Party, Lale Badzakhson, and Rastokhez) to be illegal.
June 23–26	Tojikiston's Supreme Soviet meets and declares all decrees of Akbarsho Iskandarov, former president, illegal and thus null and void.
July 5	Russo-Kyrgyz Military Assistance Agreement signed in Bishkek.
July 8	The ECO meets in Istanbul.
July 20	Tojikiston's Prime Minister Abdullajanov signs agreement with Russia's Deputy Prime Minister Aleksandr Shokhin to reschedule Tojikiston's debt to Russia.
July 31	Evgenii Primakov meets with Burhaniddin Rabani, president of Afghanistan, and Ahmed Shah Masood, Afghanistan's former Minister of Defense, to discuss the Afghan-Tojik border issue.

August 6	Six Uzbek opposition figures are sentenced in Tashkent for attempting to organize a *Milli Majlis* (National Assembly); they are immediately granted amnesty by a presidential decree of Uzbekiston's President Karimov.
August 7	Heads of state of Kazakstan, Kyrgyzstan, Russia, and Uzbekiston meet in Moscow to adopt extraordinary measures to secure the Afghan-Tojik border.
August 15	Ministers of Foreign Affairs from Afghanistan and Tojikiston issue a communiqué calling for an end to all cross-border attacks.
August 22	Dinmukhamed A. Kunaev, former Communist Party first secretary for Kazakstan, dies.
September 2	Uzbekiston's parliament passes a new language law, officially switching Uzbekiston to Latin alphabet from Cyrillic by the year 2000.
September 2	Russo-Turkmen Mutual Cooperation Security Agreement signed in Ashgabat.
September 21	Turkmenistan's President Niyazov announces that on November 1, 1993, Turkmenistan will introduce its own currency, the *manat*, valued at 1:1 against the U.S. dollar.
September 21	Russia's President Yeltsin issues a decree abolishing the Russian Congress of People's Deputies, and a power struggle ensues. The Central Asian states remain technically neutral in the struggle but continue to cooperate with the Yeltsin government.
September 24	Meeting in Moscow, nine CIS prime ministers reach agreement on the creation of an economic union. Signatories include Armenia, Azerbaijan, Belarus, Moldova, Russia, and the Central Asian states of Kazakstan, Kyrgyzstan, Tojikiston, and Uzbekiston. Turkmenistan elects not to participate in the revised economic union.
September 24	Karimov, in France on a state visit, signs Paris Charter drafted by CSCE, which sets guidelines for democracy, human rights, and peace.
November 1	Turkmenistan introduces a national currency, the *manat*.
November 1	Kazakstan officials announce that Kazakstan may introduce a national currency, the *tenge*, on January 1, 1994.
November 10	Presidents of Kazakstan and Uzbekiston sign agreement to coordinate regional monetary policies and new national currencies.
November 20	Muhammad Babur Malikov, Uzbekiston's ambassador to the United States, relinquishes post and seeks political asylum in the United States.
December 1	Kazakstan's Minister of Science Galym Abilsiitov announces that Kazakstan seeks to lease the space center in Baykonur to Russia.

December 3	Forty-three deputies of Kazakstan's Supreme Soviet precipitate a crisis by resigning their mandates and calling on other deputies to follow their example. Self-dissolution of the soviets had begun in Kazakstan at the local and regional levels, with the Almaty city soviet having dissolved itself in November.
December 5	Tojikiston's Ministry of Press and Information formally revokes the registration of newspapers and journals that had been published by opposition democratic, nationalist, and Islamic parties and movements, which had been banned by the Supreme Court earlier in 1993. The publications of the Tojik opposition were closed down in December 1992 when the current government came to power.
December 8	Kazakstan's Supreme Soviet dissolves itself after designating March 7 as the date to elect a full-time legislature to replace the Soviet-style parliament. Nearly 200 of the Supreme Soviet's 350 deputies gave up their mandates before the session opened. In a special session two days later President Nazarbaev addressed the parliament, approving the Supreme Soviet's decision to dissolve itself and warning that the unresolved issues of dual citizenship and state language are worrying the country's Russian population. The Supreme Soviet had also adopted a new election code under which 135 of the deputies to the new parliament were to be elected in single-member constituencies and forty-two from a list compiled by the president.
December 8	Human rights activists from all Central Asian countries gather in Bishkek to establish the Congress of Non-Governmental Human Rights Organizations. The chairman of Kyrgyzstan's Human Rights Defense Committee, Tursunbai Akhunov, was chosen to head the new organization. Shukhrat Ismatullaev and Vasila Inoyatova, leading figures in the Uzbek opposition movement Birlik, were warned by Tashkent police not to attend the meeting.
December 13	Kazakhstan's parliament votes 283 to 1 to accede to the Nuclear Nonproliferation Treaty, fulfilling Nazarbaev's promise to the United States.
December 13	Kyrgyzstan's Supreme Soviet fails to obtain a two-thirds majority for a vote of no confidence in Prime Minister Tursunbek Chyngyshev; President Askar Akaev dismisses the country's government anyway. Some parliamentarians accused the prime minister of illegal export of part of the country's gold reserves, and much of the current session of the legislature has been taken up with disputes between the deputies and the prime minister.
December 18	Tojikiston's Prime Minister Abdumalik Abdullajanov resigns.

December 23	Russia and Turkmenistan sign an agreement on dual citizenship. The agreement permits Turkmenistan's 400,000 ethnic Russians (about 10 percent of the total population) to hold dual citizenship.
December 24	The fourteenth CIS summit meets in Ashgabat to consider cooperative agreements on the implementation of an economic union. The members fail to sign an accord proposed by Russia on the rights of national minorities. After the meeting, Yeltsin and Niyazov sign an agreement formalizing the status of Russian troops in Turkmenistan.
December 25	A memorandum of understanding between Russia and Kazakstan is signed regarding the Baykonur missile base in Kazakstan.
December 28	Uzbekiston's Supreme Soviet approves the holding of elections next year for the 250-seat *Majlis* (Assembly), the new legislature that will replace the Soviet-era legislature.
December 30	Turkmenistan's President Niyazov announces the registration of a second political party, the Peasants' Party, in Turkmenistan.
December 30	Nine Russian Baptists and a Russian Orthodox priest are murdered in Dushanbe.

1994

January 4	Tojikiston announces that the Russian ruble will be the only legal currency in Tojikiston.
January 5	Price liberalization begins in Kazakstan.
January 10	The presidents of Kazakstan and Uzbekiston agree to abolish trade tariffs and to establish a common market.
January 11	Presidents of the five Central Asian countries meet in Nukus, capital of Karakalpakistan, to sign an agreement on the creation of a fund to save the Aral Sea and on a three- to five-year program designed to improve the environmental situation in the Aral Basin.
January 12	Political dissidents announce the founding of a new political party, Istiqlal Yoli (Path of Independence) under Shodi Karimov, a history professor who sought to take over the leadership of Erk from founder Muhamad Solih at the party's congress in 1993.
February 13	Kazakstan's President Nazarbaev begins a five-day official visit to the United States.
February 24	Kyrgyzstan's President Akaev issues a decree entitling individuals to lease and cultivate plots of land for forty-nine years. During this period the leases of the plots may be sold, exchanged, inherited, or subleased.
March 2	Russia and Uzbekiston sign an agreement on economic integration. The agreement provides for Uzbekiston and Russia to coordinate economic reforms and fiscal policies, encourages

ties between enterprises in the two countries, and ensures the mutual convertibility of the two currencies.

March 7   Parliamentary elections take place in Kazakstan. A CSCE observer mission observes that the election procedures do not meet internationally accepted standards.

March 29   Kazakstan's President Nazarbaev calls on CIS states to form an organization much like the twelve-member European Union. He advocates establishing a sole currency and freedom of movement across national borders. Nazarbaev also advocates modifying the CIS to form a smaller grouping—proposing the name "Euro-Asiatic Union"—that would serve as a "belt of stability and security," and from which countries engaged in military conflicts would be excluded.

June 9   In a speech to Kazakstan's new Supreme Soviet, President Nazarbaev asks the parliament to move the country's capital from Almaty to Akmola (formerly Tselinograd).

June 11   NATO delegation visits Kyrgyzstan.

July 10   Mercedes-Benz announces plans to establish a truck factory in Uzbekiston.

September 28–30   CSCE holds a seminar in Tashkent focusing on conflict management and security in Central Asia.

November 6   Presidential election and a referendum on a new constitution are held in Tojikiston.

November 17   Hamid Hakimov, editor of the Uzbek-language weekly *Haq Suzi* and a prominent member of Tojikiston's Uzbek community, is shot at his apartment building in Dushanbe.

November 23   A total of 600 kilograms of highly enriched uranium are purchased from Kazakstan by the United States.

1995

January 6   Boris Shikhmuradov is appointed prime minister of Turkmenistan.

January 13   More than 100,000 coal miners in northern Kazakstan go on strike protesting the failure of the government mining trust to pay back wages.

February 10   Kazakstan, Kyrgyzstan, Tojikiston, and Uzbekiston agree to join a unified CIS air-defense system.

February 26   Parliamentary elections in Tojikiston are postponed due to low registration.

March 2   Central Asian presidents met in Dashkouz, Turkmenistan, to agree on measures to save the Aral Sea.

March 11   Kazakstan's President Nazarbaev upholds a Constitutional Court decision that found the March 1994 parliamentary elections invalid. The Kazakstan parliament is dissolved.

March 12   Tojikiston's parliamentary elections are held; sixty of the 181 seats go to the Communist Party.

March 26	Uzbekiston's voters cast ballots, 99.6 percent in favor of extending Karimov's mandate through 2000.
July 1	Kazakstan adopts new tax code.
August 28	Heads of state of Azerbaijan, Kazakstan, Kyrgyzstan, Turkey, Turkmenistan, and Uzbekiston meet in Bishkek and sign the Bishkek Declaration, which calls for unity of purpose of the Turkic states.
September 22	At a meeting of the presidium of the CIS Interstate Economic Committee, Kyrgyz, Uzbek, and Tojik officials express their desire to join the customs union that includes Russia, Belarus, and Kazakstan.
October 13	Uzbekiston's Defense Minister Rustam Akhmedov and U.S. Defense Secretary William Perry sign a bilateral cooperative defense agreement pursuant to NATO's Partnership for Peace program.
October 16	Kazakstan's Minister of Agriculture announces that the 1995 grain harvest ranks as the worst in thirty years.
October 17	Turkmenistan's President Niyazov issues new law permitting foreign ownership of land.
October 27	Uzbekiston's President Karimov publicly criticizes Turkmenistan President Niyazov for his reliance upon Russian border troops and his "efforts to restore" the former Soviet Union.
November 2	Defense ministers from CIS states meet to discuss military-technical cooperation, peacekeeper training, and the situation in Tojikiston. Russia agrees to assist Kyrgyzstan, Tojikiston, Kazakstan, and Uzbekiston in upgrading air-defense systems.
November 3	CIS prime ministers sign ten economic cooperation documents including agreements on scientific and technical cooperation, the transport of natural gas, and civil aviation at a meeting in Moscow. Kyrgyzstan, Uzbekiston, and Tojikiston join the Russia-Belarus-Kazakstan customs union.
November 17	The head of the Semirechie Cossacks in Kazakstan, Nikolai Gunkin, is convicted on charges of taking part in an illegal demonstration.
December 5	Elections are held in Kazakstan for the Kazakstan parliament's upper house. Each of the nineteen regional parliaments, the *maslihats*, elect two deputies.
December 9	Popular elections in Kazakstan are held for the Kazakstan parliament's lower house, the *Majilis*.
December 24	Presidential election and referendum on Russian language held in Kyrgyzstan.
December 30	Askar Akaev is inaugurated as president of Kyrgyzstan.

Sources on Central Asian Politics, Economics, ▪ and Society ▪

During the period of Soviet control of Central Asia most sources of information were filtered through official party and government information agencies. These organizations were dominated by the political agendas of Moscow officials. Since the breakup of the USSR the availability of information has increased significantly, although censorship is practiced in some of the Central Asian countries with more effectiveness than during the Soviet period. In addition to the governmental and nongovernmental media in these countries, a new source of information is the rapidly expanding electronic network in the region. Although e-mail connections in Central Asia are expensive and particularly subject to the vagaries of seriously outdated local phone systems, subscribership is substantial and growing. As the phone system is improved with fiber-optic cable and satellite uplinks, general access to the Internet is growing as well. Tojikiston, for instance, established its own webpage on the World Wide Web in the summer of 1995. Individuals seeking to gain direct access should consult online site and user directories.

Reliable information in the Western world about Central Asia can be found in the specialist journals devoted to Central Asian affairs, particularly *Central Asian Survey* and *Central Asian Monitor*. A professional organization, the Association for the Advancement of Central Asian Research, with offices at Kennesaw State College, Pennsylvania, publishes a regular newsletter entitled *AACAR Bulletin*. A few major U.S. universities have advanced research programs devoted to Central Asian affairs. Notable among these is the Forum for Central Asian Studies at Harvard's Russian Research Center, the Uralic-Altaic Studies Center of Indiana University, the Central Asian Studies Program of the University of Wisconsin, the Central Asian Studies Program of the University of Washington, and the Kazakh-American Studies Center of the University of Kentucky.

Encyclopedias, Reference Books, and Statistical Handbooks

Akiner, Shirin. *Islamic Peoples of the Soviet Union.* 2d edition. London: KPI, 1986.
Allworth, Edward. *Soviet Asia: Bibliographies.* New York: Praeger, 1975.
Entsiklopediiai Sovetii Tocik. Dushanbe: Arredaktsiiai ilmii Entsiklopediiai Sovetii Tocik, 1983.

Horak, Stephen M. *Guide to the Study of the Soviet Nationalities*. Littleton, Colo.: Libraries Unlimited, 1982.

Kazakhstan: A World Bank Country Study. Washington, D.C.: The World Bank, 1994.

Kozybaev, Orazaly Abilovich, gen.ed. *Kazakhskaia Sovetskaia Entsiklopediia*. Alma-Ata: Glavnaia redaktsiia Kazakhskoi Sovietskoi Inetsiklopedii, 1981.

Kyrgyz Sovet Entsiklopediiasy (1976–). Six volumes. Frunze: Kyrgyz Sovet Entsiklopediiasynyn Bashky Redaktsiiasy, 1976.

Kyrgyzskaia Sovetskaia Sotsialisticheskaia Respublika. Frunze: Ilim, 1982.

Kyrgyzstan: A World Bank Country Study. Washington, D.C.: The World Bank, 1994.

Narodnoe khoziaistvo Kazakhskoi SSR: statisticheskii ezhegodnik (1957–). Alma-Ata: Tsentral'noe statisticheskoe upravlenie, annually until 1991.

Narodnoe khoziaistvo Kyrgyzskoi SSR: statisticheskii ezhegodnik (1957–). Frunze: Tsentral'noe statisticheskoe upravlenie, annually until 1991.

Narodnoe khoziaistvo Srednei Azii: statisticheskii sbornik. Tashkent: Uzbekistan, 1968.

Narodnoe khoziaistvo SSSR, 1917–1987. Moscow: Tsentral'noe Statisticheskoe Upravlenie, 1988.

Narodnoe khoziaistvo Tadzhikskoi SSR: kratkii statisticheskii sbornik. Dushanbe: Gos. statisticheskoe izd-vo, annually until 1991.

Narodnoe khoziaistvo Tadzhikskoi SSR: statisticheskii ezhegodnik (1957–). Dushanbe: Tsentral'noe statisticheskoe upravlenie, annually until 1991.

Narodnoe khoziaistvo Turkmenskoi SSR: statisticheskii ezhegodnik (1957–). Ashkhabad: Tsentral'noe statisticheskoe upravlenie, annually until 1991.

Narodnoe khoziaistvo Uzbekskoi SSR: statisticheskii ezhegodnik (1957–). Tashkent: Tsentral'noe statisticheskoe upravlenie, annually until 1991.

Tadzhikskaia sovetskaia sotsialisticheskaia respublika. Dushanbe: Glavnaia nauchnaia redaktsiia tadzhikskoi sovetskoi entsiklopedii, 1984.

Tojikistan: A World Bank Country Study. Washington, D.C.: The World Bank, 1994.

Turkmen Sovet Entsiklopediiasy. Turkmen Sovet Entsiklopediiasynyn bash redaktsiiasy, 1974.

Turkmenistan: A World Bank Country Study. Washington, D.C.: The World Bank, 1994.

Uzbekskaia Sovetskaia Sotsialisticheskaia Respublika. Tashkent: Glavnaia redaktsiia Uzbekskoi Entsiklopedii, 1981.

Uzbekistan: A World Bank Country Study. Washington, D.C.: The World Bank, 1994.

Monographs and Edited Volumes (English Language)

Allworth, Edward, ed. *Central Asia: A Century of Russian Rule*. New York: Columbia University Press, 1967.

Allworth, Edward. *The Nationality Question in Soviet Central Asia*. New York: Praeger, 1973.

_____. *The Modern Uzbeks*. Stanford: Hoover Institution Press, 1990.

Bacon, Elizabeth E. *Central Asians Under Russian Rule: A Study in Culture Change*. Ithaca: Cornell University Press, 1966.

Bahry, Donna. *Outside Moscow*. New York: Columbia University Press, 1987.

Bandera, V.N., and A.L. Melnyk. *The Soviet Economy in Regional Perspective*. New York: Praeger, 1973.

Banuazizi, Ali, and Myron Weiner, eds. *The New Geopolitics of Central Asia and Its Borderlands.* Bloomington: Indiana University Press, 1994.

Bennigsen, Alexandre, and Chantal Lemercier-Quelquejay. *Islam in the Soviet Union.* New York: Praeger, 1967.

Bennigsen, Alexandre, and Marie Broxup. *The Islamic Threat to the Soviet State.* London: Croom Helm, 1983.

Bennigsen, Alexandre, and S. Enders Wimbush. *Muslim National Communism in the Soviet Union: A Revolutionary Strategy for the Colonial World.* Chicago: University of Chicago Press, 1979.

_____. *Muslims of the Soviet Empire.* Bloomington: Indiana University Press, 1986.

Caroe, Olaf. *Soviet Empire: The Turks of Central Asia and Stalinism.* London: Frank Cass, 1953.

Carrere d'Encausse, Helene. *Decline of an Empire: The Soviet Socialist Republics in Revolt.* New York: Newsweek, 1979.

_____. *The Great Challenge: Nationalities and the Bolshevik State, 1917–1930.* New York: Holmes and Meier, 1992.

Connor, Walker. *The National Question in Marxist-Leninist Theory and Strategy.* Princeton: Princeton University Press, 1984.

Conolly, Violet. *Beyond the Urals: Economic Developments in Soviet Asia.* London: Oxford University Press, 1967.

Critchlow, James. *Nationalism in Uzbekistan: A Soviet Republic's Road to Sovereignty.* Boulder: Westview, 1991.

Dawisha, Karen, and Bruce Parrott. *Russian and the New States of Eurasia: The Politics of Upheaval.* Cambridge: Cambridge University Press, 1994.

Ecker, Frank A. *Transition in Asia.* Ph.D. diss., University of Michigan, 1952.

Fierman, William, ed. *Soviet Central Asia: The Failed Transformation.* Boulder: Westview, 1991.

Fuller, Graham E. "Central Asia: The New Geopolitics." *Rand Report* R-4219-USDP (1992).

Furtado, Charles F. Jr., and Andrea M. Chandler. *Perestroika in the Soviet Republics: Documents on the National Question.* Boulder: Westview, 1991.

Gleason, Gregory. *Federalism and Nationalism: The Struggle for Republican Rights in the USSR.* Boulder: Westview Press, 1990.

Haghayeghi, Mehrdad. *The Politics of Islam in Central Asia.* New York: St. Martin's Press, 1994.

Hajda, Lubomyr, and Mark Beissinger. *The Nationalities Factor in Soviet Politics and Society.* Boulder: Westview Press, 1990.

Hambly, Gavin, ed. *Central Asia.* New York: Delacorte Press, 1969.

Hayit, Baymirza. *Turkestan im Zwanzigsten Jahrhundert.* Garmstadt, 1956.

Hopkirk, Peter. *The Great Game: The Struggle for Empire in Central Asia.* New York: Kodansha International, 1992.

Inoiatov, Khamid Sharapovich. *Central Asia and Kazakhstan Before and After the October Revolution.* Moscow: Progress Publishers, 1966.

Kaiser, Robert J. *The Geography of Nationalism in Russia and the USSR.* Princeton: Princeton University Press, 1994.

Kangas, Roger. *Uzbekistan in the Twentieth Century.* New York: St. Martin's Press, 1995.

Kaushik, Devendra. *Central Asia in Modern Times.* Moscow: Progress Publishers, 1970.

Kisch, Egon Erwin. *Changing Asia.* Trans. Rita Reil. New York: A.A. Knopf, 1935.

Kornai, Janos. *The Socialist System: The Political Economy of Communism.* Princeton: Princeton University Press, 1992.

Krader, Lawrence. *Peoples of Central Asia.* Bloomington: Indiana University Press, 1963.

Lubin, Nancy. *Labor and Nationality in Soviet Central Asia.* Princeton: Princeton University Press, 1984.

Malik, Hafeez, ed. *Central Asia: Its Strategic Importance and Future Prospects.* New York: St. Martin's Press, 1994.

Mandelbaum, Michael. *Central Asia and the World.* Washington, D.C.: Council on Foreign Relations Press, 1994.

Marx, Karl, and Friedrich Engels. *Ausgewählte Werke.* Berlin: Dietz Verlag, 1981.

Massell, Gregory J. *The Surrogate Proletariat: Moslem Women and Revolutionary Strategies in Soviet Central Asia.* Princeton: Princeton University Press, 1974.

Micklin, Philip P. *The Water Management Crisis in Soviet Central Asia.* The Carl Beck Papers in Russian and East European Studies, no. 905. University of Pittsburgh Center for Russian and East European Studies, 1991.

Motyl, Alexander J. *Sovietology, Rationality, and Nationality: Coming to Grips with Nationalism in the USSR.* New York: Columbia University Press, 1990.

Motyl, Alexander J., ed. *Thinking Theoretically About Soviet Nationalities.* New York: Columbia University Press, 1992.

Nove, Alec, and J.A. Newth. *The Soviet Middle East: A Communist Model for Development.* New York: Allen and Unwin, 1967.

Paksoy, H.B., ed. *Central Asian Monuments.* Instanbul: Isis Press, 1992.

Park, A. *Bolshevism in Turkestan, 1917–1927.* New York: Columbia University Press, 1957.

Pomfret, Richard. *The Economies of Central Asia.* Princeton: Princeton University Press, 1995.

Odling-Smee, John, ed. *Economic Review: Kazakhstan.* Washington, D.C.: International Monetary Fund, 1992.

_____. *Economic Review: Kyrgyzstan.* Washington, D.C.: International Monetary Fund, 1992.

_____. *Economic Review: Tajikistan.* Washington, D.C.: International Monetary Fund, 1992.

_____. *Economic Review: Turkmenistan.* Washington, D.C.: International Monetary Fund, 1992.

_____. *Economic Review: Uzbekistan.* Washington, D.C.: International Monetary Fund, 1992.

Olcott, Martha Brill. *The Kazakhs.* Stanford: Hoover Institution Press, 1991.

Olcott, Martha Brill, ed. *The Soviet Multinational State: Readings and Documents.* Armonk, N.Y.: M.E. Sharpe, 1990.

Pipes, Richard. *The Formation of the Soviet Union: Communism and Nationalism, 1917–1923.* Rev. ed. Cambridge: Harvard University Press, 1964.

Rakowska-Harmstone, Teresa. *Russia and Nationalism in Central Asia: The Case of Tadzhikistan.* Baltimore: Johns Hopkins University Press, 1970.

Roi, Yaacov, ed. *Muslim Eurasia: Conflicting Legacies.* London: Frank Cass, 1995.
Rumer, Boris. *Soviet Central Asia: "A Tragic Experiment."* London: Unwin Hyman, 1990.
Rywkin, Michael. *Moscow's Muslim Challenge.* 2d ed. Armonk, N.Y.: M.E. Sharpe, 1990.
Schuyler, Eugene. *Turkistan: Notes of a Journey in Russian Turkistan, Khodand, Bukhara, and Kuldja.* New York: Scribner, Armstrong, 1876.
Strong, Anna Louise. *Red Star in Samarkand.* New York: Coward-McCann, 1929.
Vaidyanath, R. *The Formation of the Soviet Central Asian Republics.* New Delhi: Peoples Publishing House, 1967.
Vambery, A.H. *Travels in Central Asia.* London: 1865.
Wheeler, Geoffrey. *The Modern History of Central Asia.* New York: Praeger, 1964.
_____. *The Peoples of Soviet Central Asia: A Background Study.* London: Bodley Head, 1966.

Monographs and Edited Volumes (Foreign Language)

Ikramov, Akmal. *Izbrannye trudy.* Three volumes. Tashkent: Uzbekistan, 1974.
Khodzhaev, Faizulla. *Izbrannye trudy.* Three volumes. Tashkent: Fan, 1970.
Kunaev, Dinumkhamed Akhmedovich. *O moem vremeni.* Alma-Ata: RGZhI Deuir, 1992.
Kuvanishev, A.K., ed. *Problemy Aral'skogo moria.* Alma-Ata: Nauka, 1984.
Muminova, I.M. *Istoriia Uzbekskoi SSR s drevneishikh vremen do nashikh dnei.* Tashkent: Fan, 1974.
Nusupbekov, A.N. ed. *Istoriia Kazakhskoi SSR.* Five volumes. Alma-Ata: Nauka Kazakhskoi SSR, 1981.
Rakhimov, E.D. *Sotsial'no-ekonomicheskie problemy arala i priaral'ia.* Tashkent: Fan, 1990.
Ubaidullaeva, R.A. *Trudovye resursy i effektivnost: ikh ispol'zovaniia.* Tashkent: Fan, 1979.
Zimanov, Salyk Z., and I.K. Reitor. *Sovetskaia natsional'naia gosudarstvennost' i sblizhenie natsii.* Alma-Ata: Nauka, 1983.

▪ About the Book and Author ▪

The lands of Central Asia are united by a common history and historical identity as well as by common traditions. A heritage of tribal mountain and steppe confederations and oasis emirates gave way in the Soviet period to the creation of artificial "nation-states" in the heart of Asia. With the collapse of the Soviet Union, these nations—Kazakstan, Kyrgyzstan, Tojikiston, Turkmenistan, and Uzbekiston—were thrust back into the international community as separate countries. Independence came as had bondage to Soviet power seven decades earlier—it was imposed from without. These new states are now struggling with the cultural, economic, and political transformations of decolonization and independence.

Exploring the forces of change in the new Central Asian states, Gregory Gleason analyzes their culture, their economic evolution, and their political institutions. He carefully traces the incorporation of Central Asia into the Soviet system, the region's path of development under socialism, and the vicissitudes of the economic and political collapse of socialism, before considering the trajectories of the new states as they chart their independent futures.

Gregory Gleason has lived and worked in Central Asia as a fellow of the USSR Academy of Sciences and, after independence, of the Academies of Sciences of Kazakstan, Turkmenistan, Uzbekiston, and the Russian Federation. As the first director of the "rule of law" program for Central Asia, he managed a broad-gauged U.S. government–funded effort to promote democracy and market economic institutions in the countries of Central Asia. He teaches international relations at the University of New Mexico.

Index